MW01134159

Excel and R Companion to the Second Edition of "Quantifying the User Experience: Practical Statistics for User Research"

Rapid Answers to over 100 Examples and Exercises

James R. Lewis & Jeff Sauro

Chapter 1: About this Book

This is a companion book to the second edition of *Quantifying the User Experience: Practical Statistics for User Research* (Sauro & Lewis, 2016). In that book, we provide a statistical resource for those who measure the behavior and attitudes of people as they interact with interfaces, with a focus on methods applicable to practical user research based on our experience, investigations, and reviews of the latest statistical literature.

In *Quantifying the User Experience: Practical Statistics for User Research* (2nd ed.), we provided over 100 examples and exercises, showing their step-by-step solutions in detail. To achieve a deep understanding of statistical methods, it's important to be able to work them out by hand. In your day-to-day work, however, it's also important to have resources that enable you to solve these types of problems accurately and efficiently.

In this companion book, we document how to solve the examples and exercises from *Quantifying the User Experience: Practical Statistics for User Research* (2nd ed.) using two different custom tools, one based on Microsoft Excel and the other on R, an open source programming language for statistics. Many of those methods are not available in standard statistics packages. Some are new; others are older methods for which new research supports their application to the kinds of data that user researchers encounter. It is our hope that it will be a valuable companion for practitioners who need to use the methods taught in *Quantifying the User Experience: Practical Statistics for User Research* (2nd ed.).

Chapter 2 documents how to get and use these custom tools. Chapters 3 through 10 correspond to the same chapters in *Quantifying the User Experience: Practical Statistics for User Research* (2nd ed.), with a summary description of each example or exercise, the answer(s), and how to solve the problem using the custom Excel and R tools. We also show how to solve some of the problems (when possible) using the Web tools available at www.measuringu.com. We wrap up the book in Chapter 11, and provide an appendix that documents all of our custom R functions.

In short, *Quantifying the User Experience: Practical Statistics for User Research* (2nd ed.) provides the **why** for the methods we recommend – the rationale and step-by-step computations; this companion book provides the **how**, using Excel and R.

Note: There may be some small discrepancies between the solutions that appear in *Quantifying the User Experience: Practical Statistics for User Research* (2nd ed.) and this companion book. In *Quantifying the User Experience: Practical Statistics for User Research* (2nd ed.), we showed how to work out many of the examples and exercises by hand, and in so doing rounded off values during intermediate steps (especially when logarithms were involved). In this companion book, we used our computers, so there was no rounding off until the final answer. The point is, don't worry about these small differences – it's just round-off error.

Chapter 2: How to Get What You Need

Getting and using the custom Excel tool

The Usability Statistics Package Expanded Edition Excel calculator is available for purchase on the MeasuringUsability.com website:
http://www.measuringu.com/products/expandedStats

The calculator is an Excel file which has been tested and used on the PC and Mac. You will need to enable macros for some of the functionality to work.

Getting and using the custom R functions

Getting R

The first step is to get and install R. R is a free software environment for statistical computing and graphics, available at http://www.r-project.org/. To install R:

1. Go to http://www.r-project.org/.

2. Find the Getting Started panel, then click "download R" – this takes you to a list of CRAN mirrors. CRAN is an acronym for Comprehensive R Archive Network. Each "mirror" is a website from which you can get R. Go down the list to find your country (e.g., USA) and select one of the sites (e.g., http://cran.case.edu/).

3. Depending on the type of computer you have, select the appropriate version of R to download (Linux, Mac OS, or Windows).

4. Select "base." This takes you to the download page for first-time installers.

5. Click the "Download R" link, which downloads an executable (.exe) file that you can double-click to complete the installation (following the on-screen instructions).

Getting the custom R functions

The custom R functions are at Jim's website in a file named PracStats_v20160801.R. To get this file:

1. Open your web browser and enter the **case-sensitive** url (note that there is an underscore before the version number, not a blank space):
   http://drjim.0catch.com/PracStatPackV2/PracStats_v20160801.R

2. Your browser will display a dialog box for you to open or save the file. Save it. Windows users – you can put this file in any folder, but if you put it in your My Documents folder, then it will be easy to select when you start R, which has default focus on My Documents. If you prefer to put it in a different folder, that's fine. You can point to that folder to open the custom functions file using the R menus: "File > Source R code…"

Starting R and loading the custom functions

For these instructions, we're assuming that you've put the custom functions file in the default directory ("My Documents" for Windows users). If you put them anywhere else, we're assuming that you know enough to be able to navigate to the file's location to select it.

1. After you install R, there will be an icon on your desktop, something like:

2. Double-click that icon to start R (as you can see from the icon, we used Version 2.8.0 for this book). You should see something like:

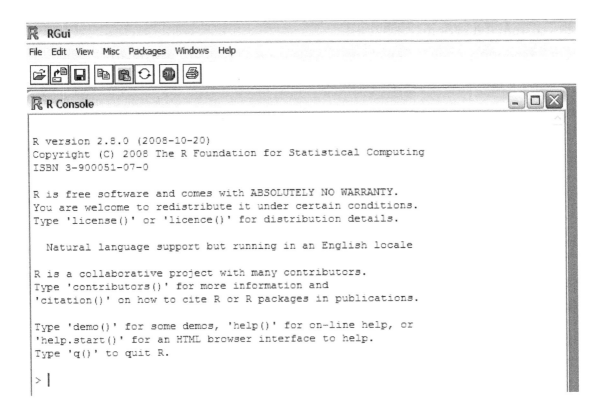

3. From the Main Menu, click "File > Source R code…"

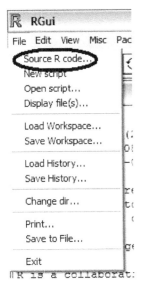

4. Then open PracStats_v20160801.R :

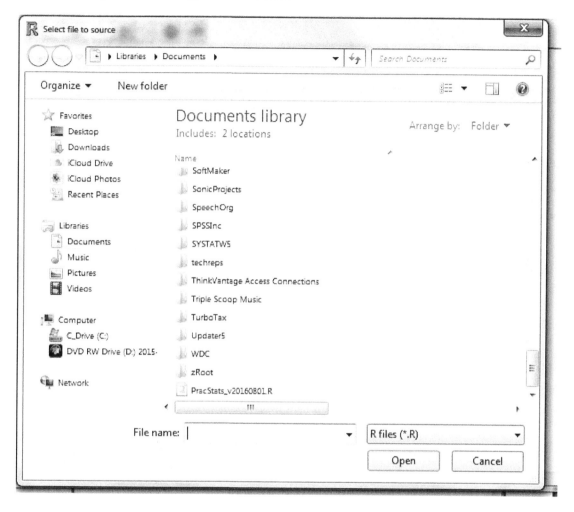

5. In the R console, you'll see something like:

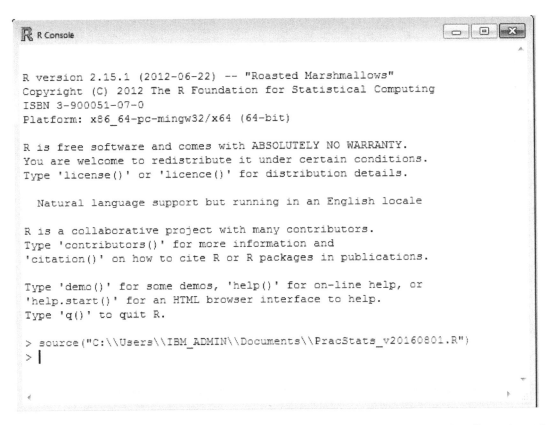

```
R R Console

R version 2.15.1 (2012-06-22) -- "Roasted Marshmallows"
Copyright (C) 2012 The R Foundation for Statistical Computing
ISBN 3-900051-07-0
Platform: x86_64-pc-mingw32/x64 (64-bit)

R is free software and comes with ABSOLUTELY NO WARRANTY.
You are welcome to redistribute it under certain conditions.
Type 'license()' or 'licence()' for distribution details.

  Natural language support but running in an English locale

R is a collaborative project with many contributors.
Type 'contributors()' for more information and
'citation()' on how to cite R or R packages in publications.

Type 'demo()' for some demos, 'help()' for on-line help, or
'help.start()' for an HTML browser interface to help.
Type 'q()' to quit R.

> source("C:\\Users\\IBM_ADMIN\\Documents\\PracStats_v20160801.R")
> |
```

6. To view a list of the custom R functions you've just loaded and will work with throughout this book, use the R command ls():

```
[1]  "analyze.01matrix.fromfile"              "analyze.01matrix.fromweb"
[3]  "analyze.pssuq.fromfile"                 "analyze.pssuq.fromweb"
[5]  "analyze.regression"                     "analyze.sus.fromfile"
[7]  "analyze.sus.fromweb"                    "bench.rate.largesample"
[9]  "bench.rate.smallsample"                 "bench.t.fromarray"
[11] "bench.t.fromarray.withlogconversion"    "bench.t.fromsummary"
[13] "ci.adjwald.fromarray"                   "ci.adjwald.fromsummary"
[15] "ci.independentproportions.difference"   "ci.matchedproportions.difference"
[17] "ci.median.fromarray"                    "ci.percentile.fromarray"
[19] "ci.t.fromarray"                         "ci.t.fromarray.withlogconversion"
[21] "ci.t.fromsummary"                       "compute.equivalentconfidence"
[23] "compute.logcritdiff"                    "compute.logsummary.fromarray"
[25] "compute.mcadjustments"                  "compute.nps.fromarray"
[27] "compute.padjfromp"                      "getdata.fromfile"
[29] "getdata.fromweb"                        "n.atleastonce"
[31] "n.bench.rate"                           "n.binomial.largesample"
[33] "n.binomial.smallsample"                 "n.correlation"
[35] "n.mcnemar"                              "n.nminusonechisquared"
[37] "n.prediction"                           "n.slope"
[39] "n.t.onesample.givensd"                  "n.t.onesample.givenvar"
[41] "n.t.twosample.givenequalsd"             "n.t.twosample.givenequalvar"
[43] "p.atleastonce"                          "p.xormore"
[45] "se.fromarray"                           "test.correlation"
[47] "test.nminusonetwoproportion.givenpandn" "test.nminusonetwoproportion.givenxandn"
[49] "test.phi"                               "test.t.independent.fromarrays"
[51] "test.t.independent.fromsummary"         "test.t.paired.fromarray.ofdifferences"
[53] "test.t.paired.fromarrays"               "test.t.paired.fromsummary"
[55] "test.twobytwo.dependent"                "test.twobytwo.independent"
> |
```

Once you've loaded the custom R functions, you're ready to use them to solve the examples and exercises. Note how the names of the functions categorize them into groups:

- **analyze**: comprehensive functions for analyzing sets of problem discovery, SUS, and PSSUQ scores

- **bench**: functions for assessing data against benchmarks

- **ci**: functions that produce confidence intervals

- **compute**: functions that do various special computations

- **n**: functions that estimate sample sizes

- **p**: functions that estimate various special probabilities

- **test**: functions that perform inferential statistical tests

19

Chapter 3: How Precise Are Our Estimates? Confidence Intervals

Chapter 3: How Precise Are Our Estimates?

Confidence Intervals

Abstract

To assess the precision of an estimate, you need to compute its confidence interval. Using confidence intervals around point estimates enhances your understanding of the most likely (plausible) range of the unknown population mean or proportion. Computing a confidence interval requires four things: an estimate of the mean, an estimate of the variability (derived from the sample standard deviation), the desired confidence level and the sample size. We recommend using the adjusted-Wald binomial confidence interval for binomial metrics such as completion rates. For satisfaction data using rating scales use the confidence intervals based on the *t*-distribution (which takes the sample size into account). For usability data, we've found that the geometric mean is the best estimate of the middle task time from small sample sizes (less than 25). Because task time data is positively skewed, you should use a log transformation before computing confidence intervals based on the *t*-distribution. For larger samples of task time data (>25), the median is the best point estimate of the middle task time, so we recommend computing the confidence interval around the median using the binomial distribution method.

Example 1: Binomial confidence interval around success rate

From page(s): 23

Summary: You've observed 7/10 successes and want to compute a 95% adjusted-Wald confidence interval to assess the precision of the estimated success rate.

Answer: The observed (maximum likelihood estimate) of *p* is .70 (70%), with an adjusted-Wald binomial confidence interval ranging from .392 to .897. Given these data, any success rate between 39.2% and 89.7% (roughly between 39 and 90%) is plausible, with 95% confidence. This is a wide interval, but indicates that it is unlikely that the population success rate is below 39.2% or above 89.7%.

Excel solution

1. Click on Completion Rate link under the Confidence Intervals section on the calculator's Home tab.

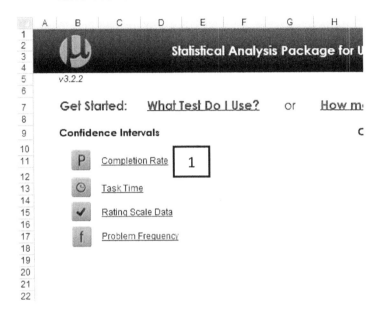

2. Enter 7 Successes and 10 Total.

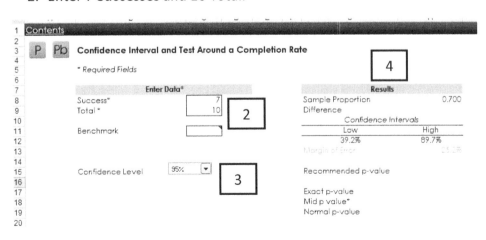

3. Set the confidence level drop down to 95%.

Chapter 3: How Precise Are Our Estimates? Confidence Intervals

4. The 95% confidence interval ranges from 39.2% to 89.7%.

R solution

Enter the following command (for 7 successes, 10 attempts, and a 95% confidence interval):

    ci.adjwald.fromsummary(7,10,.95)

The result is:

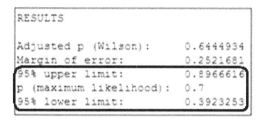

```
RESULTS

Adjusted p (Wilson):        0.6444934
Margin of error:            0.2521681
95% upper limit:            0.8966616
p (maximum likelihood):     0.7
95% lower limit:            0.3923253
```

Web solution

You can also solve this problem with the confidence interval calculator for a completion rate at http://www.measuringu.com/wald.htm. Putting in the values for 7 successes out of 10 attempts with 95% confidence, you get:

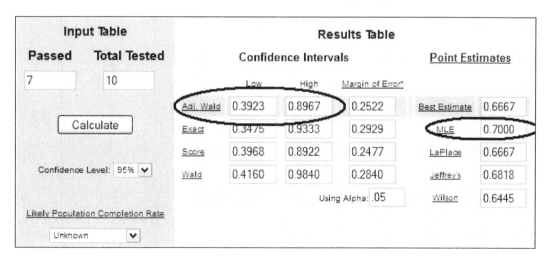

Chapter 3: How Precise Are Our Estimates? Confidence Intervals

Example 2: Binomial confidence interval around success rate

From page(s): 26

Summary: You've observed 3/5 successes and want to compute a 95% adjusted-Wald confidence interval to assess the precision of the estimated success rate.

Answer: The observed (maximum likelihood estimate) of *p* is .60 (60%), with an adjusted-Wald binomial confidence interval ranging from .23 to .88. Given these data, any success rate between 23% and 88% is plausible, with 95% confidence.

Excel solution

1. On the "CompRate CI and Test" tab, enter 3 successes and 5 total.

2. Set the confidence level drop down to 95%.

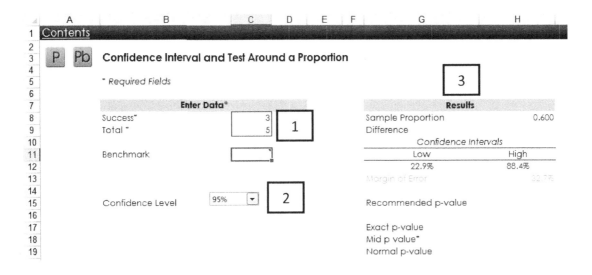

3. The 95% confidence interval ranges from about 23% to 88%.

R solution

Enter the following command (for 3 successes, 5 attempts, and a 95% confidence interval):

```
ci.adjwald.fromsummary(3,5,.95)
```

James R. Lewis & Jeff Sauro

23

Chapter 3: How Precise Are Our Estimates? Confidence Intervals

The result is:

```
Adjusted p (Wilson):     0.5565518
Margin of error:         0.3274616
95% upper limit:         0.8840134
p (maximum likelihood):  0.6
95% lower limit:         0.2290902
```

Web solution

You can also solve this problem with the confidence interval calculator for a completion rate at http://www.measuringu.com/wald.htm. Putting in the values for 3 successes out of 5 attempts with 95% confidence, you get:

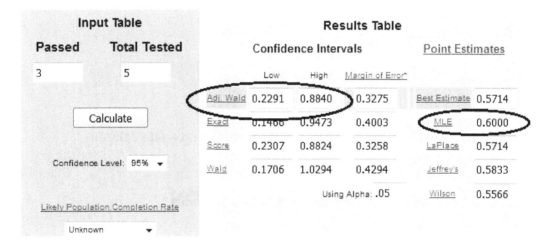

	Input Table			Results Table			
Passed	Total Tested		Confidence Intervals			Point Estimates	
3	5		Low	High	Margin of Error*		
		Adj. Wald	0.2291	0.8840	0.3275	Best Estimate	0.5714
Calculate		Exact	0.1466	0.9473	0.4003	MLE	0.6000
		Score	0.2307	0.8824	0.3258	LaPlace	0.5714
Confidence Level: 95%		Wald	0.1706	1.0294	0.4294	Jeffrey's	0.5833
					Using Alpha: .05	Wilson	0.5566
Likely Population Completion Rate							
Unknown							

Example 3: Confidence interval for a set of SUS scores

From page(s): 27-29

Summary: Compute a 95% confidence interval for the following SUS scores: 90, 77.5, 72.5, 95, 62.5, 57.5, 100, 95, 95, 80, 82.5, 87.5

Answer: The mean SUS score is 82.9, with a 95% confidence interval ranging from 74.3 to 91.5.

Excel solution

1. Click on the Rating Scale Data link under the Confidence Intervals section on the Home Tab.

2. Click the "Clear Values" button to delete values from the raw data column (macros must be enabled).

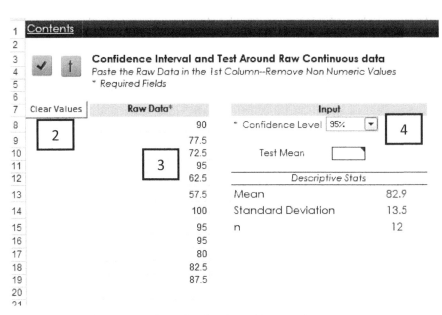

3. Enter the raw values in the Raw Data column.

Chapter 3: How Precise Are Our Estimates? Confidence Intervals

4. Set the confidence level to 95%.

5. The confidence interval appears in the Results section: 74.3 to 91.5.

6. The calculator generates a graph of the mean and confidence interval.

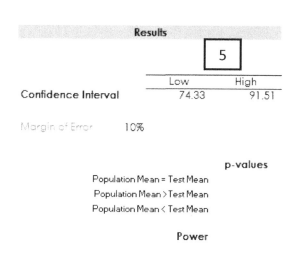

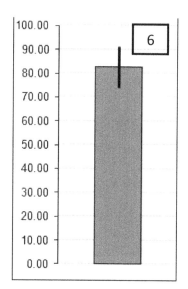

R solution

Enter the following commands:

```
sus <- c(90,77.5,72.5,95,62.5,57.5,100,95,95,80,82.5,87.5)

ci.t.fromarray(sus,.95)
```

The first command uses the R function "c" to assign the array of scores to an R variable named "sus". The second uses a custom function that requires as input the name of the variable and the confidence level (.95 for 95%). The result is:

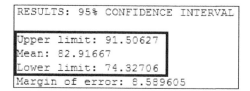

```
RESULTS: 95% CONFIDENCE INTERVAL

Upper limit: 91.50627
Mean: 82.91667
Lower limit: 74.32706
Margin of error: 8.589605
```

26

Chapter 3: How Precise Are Our Estimates? Confidence Intervals

Example 4: Confidence interval for a summary of SUS scores

From page(s): 27-29

Summary: You have the following information computed from a set of SUS scores: mean: 82.9; standard deviation: 13.5; sample size: 12. You want to know the precision of the estimated mean with 95% confidence.

Answer: The 95% confidence interval ranges from 74.3 to 91.5.

Excel solution

1. Click on the Rating Scale Scores against a Criterion (Summary) link under the Test a Mean or Proportion to Criterion section on the Home Tab.

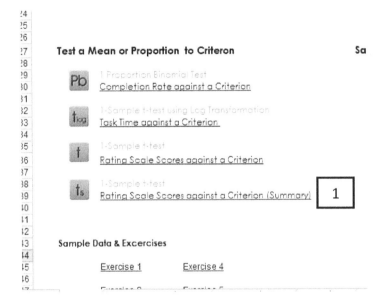

2. Enter the mean, standard deviation and sample size data into the Input fields.

3. Select the 95% level of confidence.

Chapter 3: How Precise Are Our Estimates? Confidence Intervals

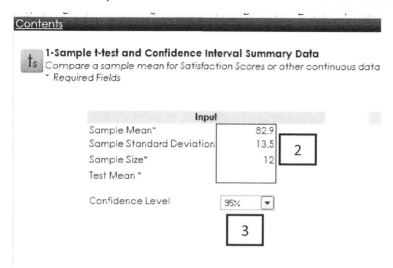

4. The confidence interval is in the Results section: 74.323 to 91.477.

5. The calculator also generates a graph of the mean and confidence interval.

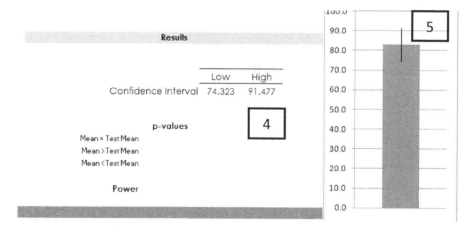

R solution

Enter the following command:

```
ci.t.fromsummary(82.9,13.5,12,.95)
```

This command needs the mean (82.9), the standard deviation (13.5), the sample size (12) and the desired confidence (.95). The result is:

28

Chapter 3: How Precise Are Our Estimates? Confidence Intervals

```
RESULTS: 95% CONFIDENCE INTERVAL

Upper limit: 91.47749
Mean: 82.9
Lower limit: 74.32251
Margin of error: 8.57749
Standard error: 3.897114
Critical value of t: 2.200985
```

Example 5: Compute the standard error for a set of SUS scores

From page(s): 27

Summary: The standard error for a set of scores is the standard deviation divided by the square root of the sample size. This is an important intermediate calculation for many inferential statistics. Here, you want to know the standard error for the set of SUS scores from Example 3.

Answer: The standard error is about 3.9.

Excel solution

1. Enter the values from Example 3 into the 1 Sample t tab.

2. Look in the Calculations Section to see the Standard Error (SE) of 3.9.

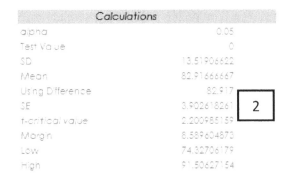

Calculations	
alpha	0.05
Test Value	0
SD	13.51906622
Mean	82.91666667
Using Difference	82.917
SE	3.902618261
t-critical value	2.200985159
Margin	8.589604873
Low	74.32706179
High	91.50627154

R solution

Enter the following command:

se.fromarray(sus)

The result is:

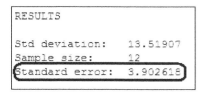

```
RESULTS

Std deviation:    13.51907
Sample size:      12
Standard error:   3.902618
```

Example 6: Confidence interval from set of Likert responses

From page(s): 29

Summary: Fifteen users rated the ease of finding information about a mutual fund on a financial services company website using a 7-point scale for which 1 was "very difficult" and 7 was "very easy," producing the following scores: 3, 5, 3, 7, 1, 6, 2, 5, 1, 1, 3, 2, 6, 2, 2. What is the mean and 95% confidence interval?

Answer: The mean is about 3.27, with a 95% confidence interval ranging from 2.15 to 4.38.

Excel solution

1. Click on the Rating Scale Data link under the Confidence Intervals section on the Home Tab.

Chapter 3: How Precise Are Our Estimates? Confidence Intervals

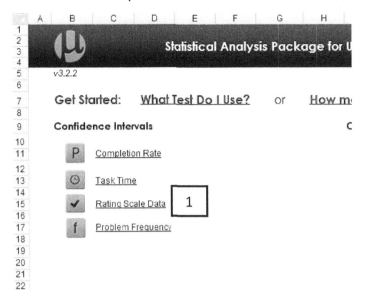

2. Click the "Clear Values" button to delete values from the raw data column (macros must be enabled).

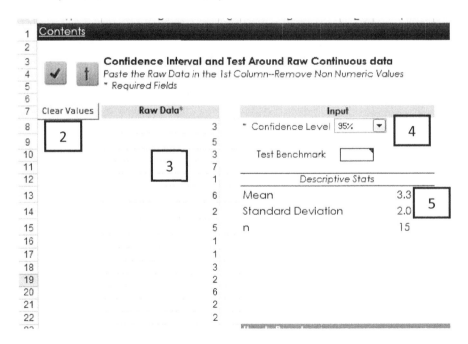

3. Enter the raw values in the Raw Data column.

4. Set the confidence level to 95%.

31

Chapter 3: How Precise Are Our Estimates? Confidence Intervals

5. The mean (rounded to the tenths) is 3.3.

6. The 95 confidence interval appears in the Results section: 2.15 to 4.38.

7. The calculator generates a graph of the mean and confidence interval.

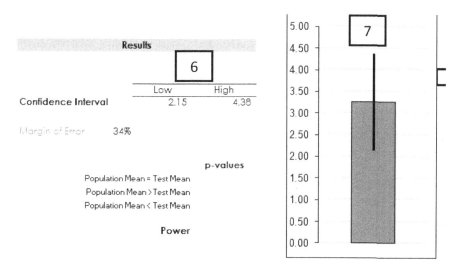

R solution

Enter the following commands:

responses <- c(3, 5, 3, 7, 1, 6, 2, 5, 1, 1, 3, 2, 6, 2, 2)

ci.t.fromarray(responses,.95)

The first command assigns the array of scores to a variable named "responses." The second command takes as input the name of that variable and the desired level of confidence (.95 for 95%). The result is:

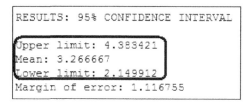

```
RESULTS: 95% CONFIDENCE INTERVAL

Upper limit: 4.383421
Mean: 3.266667
Lower limit: 2.149912
Margin of error: 1.116755
```

32

Chapter 3: How Precise Are Our Estimates? Confidence Intervals

Example 7: Confidence interval from summary of Likert responses

From page(s): 29

Summary: Suppose instead of having a full set of scores, you only know the mean (3.27), standard deviation (2.01), and sample size (15). This is all the information you need to compute a 95% confidence interval.

Answer: This is the same as the previous example. The 95% confidence interval ranges from about 2.15 to 4.38.

Excel solution

1. From the 1 Sample t (Summary) tab (used in previous examples) enter the summary data:

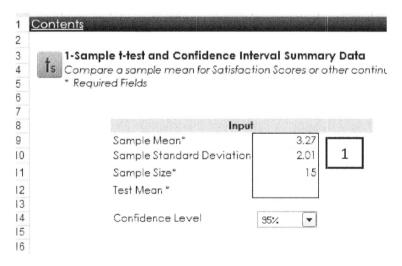

Chapter 3: How Precise Are Our Estimates? Confidence Intervals

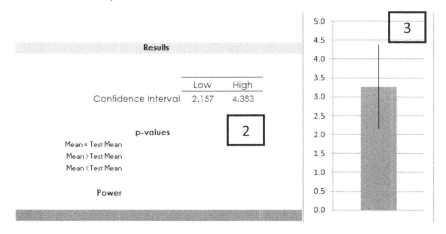

2. The 95 confidence interval appears in the Results section: 2.15 to 4.38 (Note the difference from Example 6 is due to round-off differences using summary data rather than the raw values).

3. The calculator generates a graph of the mean and confidence interval.

R solution

Enter the following command:

ci.t.fromsummary(3.27,2.01,15,.95)

The result is:

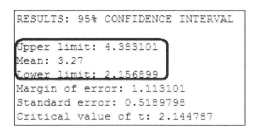

Example 8: Mean and median of a set of times

From page(s): 30

Summary: What are the mean and median of 100, 101, 102, 103, and 104?

34

Chapter 3: How Precise Are Our Estimates? Confidence Intervals

Answer: Unlike many distributions of completion times, this hypothetical one is symmetrical (not skewed). The mean and median are the same – 102.

Excel solution

1. Click on the Task Time link under the Confidence Intervals section on the Home Tab.

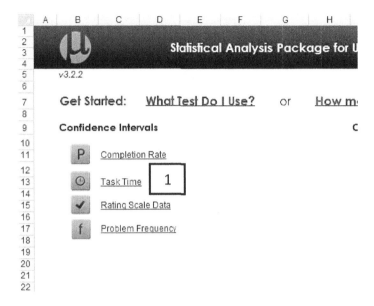

2. Clear out any previous values using the Clear Values button (macros must be enabled) and enter values in the "Raw Time Data" column.

3. The median appears along with the Arithmetic mean and Geometric means.

35

Chapter 3: How Precise Are Our Estimates? Confidence Intervals

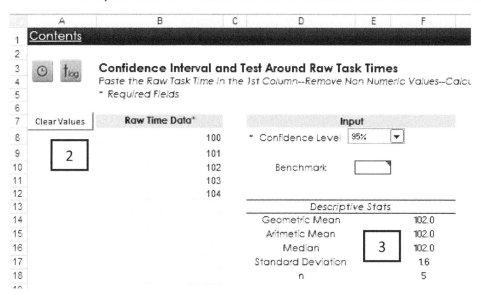

R solution

Enter the following standard R commands:

```
times <- c(100,101,102,103,104)

mean(times)

median(times)
```

The result is:

```
> times <- c(100,101,102,103,104)
> mean(times)
[1] 102
> median(times)
[1] 102
```

Example 9: Mean and median of a set of times

From page(s): 30

Summary: What are the mean and median of 100, 101, 102, 103, 104, and 200?

36

Chapter 3: How Precise Are Our Estimates? Confidence Intervals

Answer: With the addition of 200 to the hypothetical set of times the distribution is no longer symmetrical, so the mean and median are no longer equal. The median increases slightly to 102.5. The additional time has a greater effect on the mean, increasing it to 118.3.

Excel solution

1. From the "Time CI and Test" tab used in the previous example, clear out any values using the Clear Values button (macros must be enabled) and enter values in the "Raw Time Data" column.

2. The mean and median appear in the Descriptive Stats section.

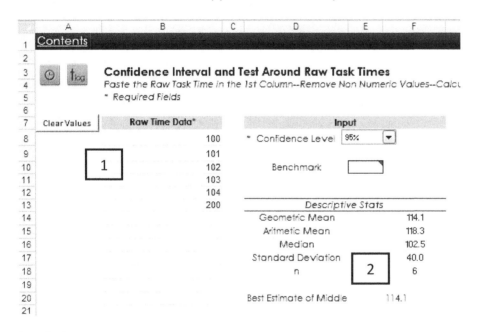

R solution

Enter the following standard R commands:

    times <- c(100,101,102,103,104,200)

    mean(times)

    median(times)

The result is:

37

Chapter 3: How Precise Are Our Estimates? Confidence Intervals

```
> times <- c(100,101,102,103,104,200)
> mean(times)
[1] 118.3333
> median(times)
[1] 102.5
```

Example 10: Computing log times and the geometric mean

From page(s): 31

Summary: Convert the following set of completion times (in seconds) to log-times and compute their geometric mean: 94, 95, 96, 113, 121, 132, 190, 193, 255, and 298.

Answer: The natural logs of the times (rounded to two decimal places) are 4.54, 4.55, 4.56, 4.73, 4.80, 4.88, 5.25, 5.26, 5.54, and 5.70. The mean of the log-times is 4.98. Exponentiating that value provides the geometric mean, about 146 seconds. Recent research (Sauro & Lewis, 2010) has shown that for smaller sample sizes ($n < 25$), the geometric mean is the best measure of central tendency for completion times, providing a better estimate of the population median than the sample median itself.

Excel solution

1. From the "Time CI and Test" tab used in the previous example, clear out any values using the Clear Values button (macros must be enabled) and enter values in the "Raw Time Data" column.

2. The Geometric mean appears in the Descriptive Stats section.

Chapter 3: How Precise Are Our Estimates? Confidence Intervals

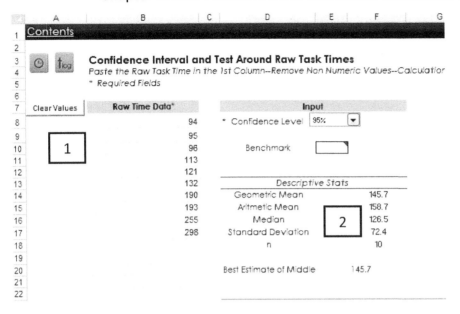

R solution

Enter the following standard R commands:

```
raw <- c(94,95,96,113,121,132,190,193,255,298)

lograw <- log(raw)

lograw

logmean <- mean(lograw)

logmean

geomean <- exp(logmean)

geomean
```

For this exercise we use a series of standard R functions. The first command assigns the array of time scores into a variable named "raw." The second uses the standard R function "log" to assign the log-times to a variable named "lograw." Typing "lograw" displays the new array of log-times. The next command assigns the mean of the "lograw" array to a variable named "logmean." The sixth command assigns

39

Chapter 3: How Precise Are Our Estimates? Confidence Intervals

the exponentiation of "logmean" to a variable named "geomean." Finally, typing "geomean" displays its value. The results are:

```
> raw <- c(94,95,96,113,121,132,190,193,255,298)
> lograw <- log(raw)
> lograw
 [1] 4.543295 4.553877 4.564348 4.727388 4.795791 4.882802 5.247024 5.262690
 [9] 5.541264 5.697093
> logmean <- mean(lograw)
> logmean
[1] 4.981557
> geomean <- exp(logmean)
> geomean
[1] 145.7011
```

Example 11: Computing the mean and median of a set of raw times

From page(s): 31

Summary: Compute the mean and median of the completion times from Example 10.

Answer: The mean is about 159 seconds; the median is about 127.

Excel solution

1. Using the same values from Exercise 10, the mean and median are in the Descriptive Stats section along with the geometric mean.

Chapter 3: How Precise Are Our Estimates? Confidence Intervals

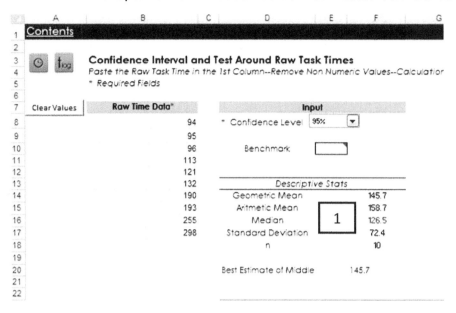

R solution

Enter the following standard R commands (assuming you've already done Exercise 10):

mean(raw)

median(raw)

The result is:

```
> mean(raw)
[1] 158.7
> median(raw)
[1] 126.5
```

41

Chapter 3: How Precise Are Our Estimates? Confidence Intervals

Example 12: Computing log-time mean and standard deviation

From page(s): 32

Summary: Continuing to work with the data from Example 10, what are the mean, standard deviation, and sample size of the log times?

Answer: The mean of the log-times is 4.98. The standard deviation is .426. The sample size is 10.

Excel solution

1. Using the data from Exercise 10, the mean and standard deviation of the log-times are in the calculations section as "Transformed Mean" and "Transformed SD."

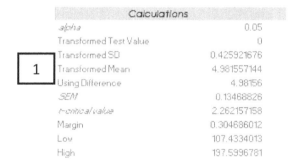

2. The sample size is in the Descriptive statistics section.

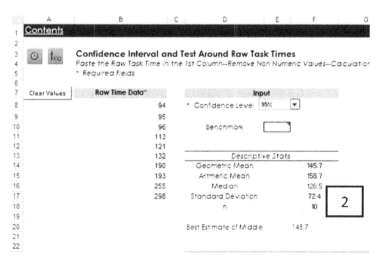

42

Chapter 3: How Precise Are Our Estimates? Confidence Intervals

R solution

Enter the following command:

    compute.logsummary.fromarray(raw,0)

This custom R function needs two inputs: the name of the array of raw times ("raw" – from Example 10) and a value to use for the log critical difference – not needed for this exercise, so the value is 0. Don't worry about that second value for now, but it will be important in later exercises, and you have to put something there for the function to work. The result is:

```
RESULTS

Arithmetic mean: 158.7
Median: 126.5
Geometric Mean: 145.7011
Mean of log data: 4.981557
Standard deviation of log data: 0.4259217
Variance of log data: 0.1814093
Standard error of the mean of the log data: 0.1346883
Sample size: 10
Value to use for log critical difference: 0
```

Example 13: Confidence interval of log times from summary

From page(s): 32

Summary: You can compute a 95% confidence interval for the times provided in Exercise 10 using the summary data from Example 12.

Answer: The 95% confidence interval for the log-times ranges from about 4.68 to 5.29.

Chapter 3: How Precise Are Our Estimates? Confidence Intervals

Excel solution

1. Click on the "Rating Scale Scores against a Criterion (Summary) link under the Test a Mean or Proportion to Criterion heading.

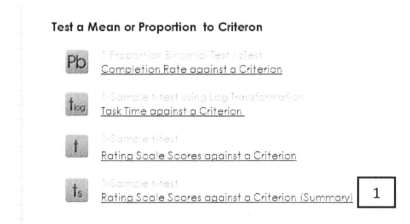

2. Enter the Mean (4.98), standard deviation (.426) and sample size (10) in the input section.

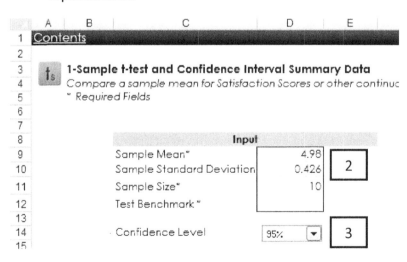

3. Set the confidence level to 95%.

Results

	Low	High
Confidence Interval	4.675	5.285

4. The confidence interval is in the Results section (4.675 to 5.285).

R solution

Enter the following command:

    ci.t.fromsummary(4.98,.426,10,.95)

The first value is the mean, the second is the standard deviation, the third is the sample size, and the fourth is the desired level of confidence (.95 for 95%). The result is:

```
RESULTS: 95% CONFIDENCE INTERVAL

Upper limit: 5.284742
Mean: 4.98
Lower limit: 4.675258
Margin of error: 0.3047420
Standard error: 0.1347130
Critical value of t: 2.262157
```

Example 14: Confidence interval of times after log conversion

From page(s): 32

Summary: Continuing from Example 13, it isn't very useful to know the confidence interval of the log-times – you really need to convert those log-times back to times.

Answer: Using exponentiation, the upper and lower bounds of the 95% confidence interval of log-times from Example 13 are, respectively, about 108 and 198 seconds.

Chapter 3: How Precise Are Our Estimates? Confidence Intervals

Excel solution

1. Note: The calculator does not provide summary log intervals. You can get around this by entering the raw data from Exercise 10.

2. The confidence intervals along with a graph are in the Results section.

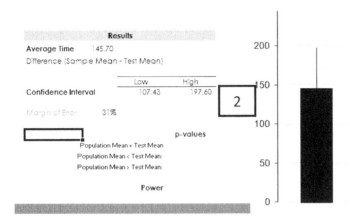

R solution

Enter the following command (note that we are still using the variable "raw" created in Exercise 10 and using .95 to specify 95% confidence):

```
ci.t.fromarray.withlogconversion(raw,.95)
```

The result is:

```
RESULTS: 95% CONFIDENCE INTERVAL

Arithmetic mean: 158.7
Median: 126.5
Upper limit: 197.5997
Geometric Mean: 145.7011
Lower limit: 107.4334
Critical value of t: 2.262157
```

Example 15: Converting raw times to log times

From page(s): 32

Summary: This is another example of converting raw times to log times, using the following raw times (in seconds): 40, 36, 53, 56, 110, 48, 34, 44, 30, 40, and 80.

Answer: The log-times (rounded to three decimal places) are 3.689, 3.584, 3.970, 4.025, 4.700, 3.871, 3.526, 3.784, 3.401, 3.689, and 4.382.

Excel solution

1. From the "Time CI and Test" tab as used in the previous examples, clear out any values using the Clear Values button (macros must be enabled) and enter values in the "Raw Time Data" column.

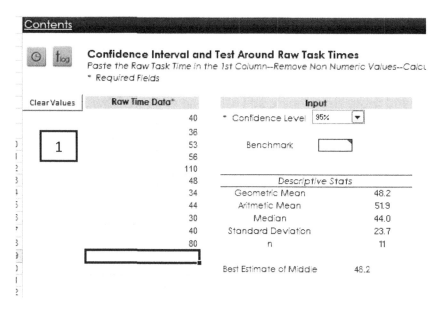

2. The log values are in column N which is normally hidden to prevent accidental overwrites. By un-hiding the column you can see the log values.

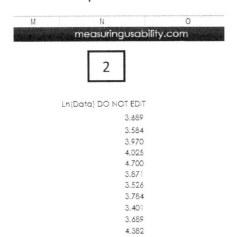

M	N	O

measuringusability.com

2

Ln(Data) DO NOT EDIT
3.689
3.584
3.970
4.025
4.700
3.871
3.526
3.784
3.401
3.689
4.382

R solution

Enter the following standard R commands:

```
raw2 <- c(40,36,53,56,110,48,34,44,30,40,80)

lograw2 <- log(raw2)

lograw2
```

See Example 10 for an explanation of the commands. The result is:

```
> raw2 <- c(40,36,53,56,110,48,34,44,30,40,80)
> lograw2 <- log(raw2)
> lograw2
 [1] 3.688879 3.583519 3.970292 4.025352 4.700480 3.871201 3.526361 3.784190
 [9] 3.401197 3.688879 4.382027
```

Example 16: Computing log time mean and standard deviation

From page(s): 32

Summary: What are the mean, standard deviation, and sample size of the log-times from Example 15?

Answer: The mean is about 3.87. The standard deviation is about .384. The sample size is 11.

Excel solution

1. Assuming the values from Example 15 are still in the "Time CI and Test" tab, the mean and standard deviation of the log values are in the Calculations section as the "Transformed Mean" and "Transformed SD" respectively.

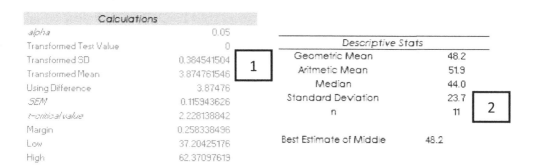

Calculations	
alpha	0.05
Transformed Test Value	0
Transformed SD	0.384541504
Transformed Mean	3.874761546
Using Difference	3.87476
SEM	0.115943626
t-critical value	2.228138842
Margin	0.258338496
Low	37.20425176
High	62.37097613

Descriptive Stats	
Geometric Mean	48.2
Aritmetic Mean	51.9
Median	44.0
Standard Deviation	23.7
n	11
Best Estimate of Middle	48.2

2. The sample size is in the Descriptive Stats section.

R solution

Enter the following command:

```
compute.logsummary.fromarray(raw2,0)
```

We're continuing to use the variable "raw2" from Exercise 15 and using 0 as a placeholder for the second value (not needed for this problem – see Example 12). The result is:

```
RESULTS

Arithmetic mean: 51.90909
Median: 44
Geometric Mean: 48.17121
Mean of log data: 3.874762
Standard deviation of log data: 0.3845415
Variance of log data: 0.1478722
Standard error of the mean of the log data: 0.1159436
Sample size: 11
Value to use for log critical difference: 0
```

49

Chapter 3: How Precise Are Our Estimates? Confidence Intervals

Example 17: Confidence interval of log times from summary

From page(s): 33

Summary: Compute a 95% confidence interval for the completion times from Example 15.

Answer: The confidence interval of the log-times ranges from about 3.62 to 4.13. Converted back to times, the confidence interval ranges from about 37 to 62 seconds.

Excel solution

1. Assuming the values from Example 15 are still in the "Time CI and Test" tab, the confidence intervals and graph appear in the Results section.

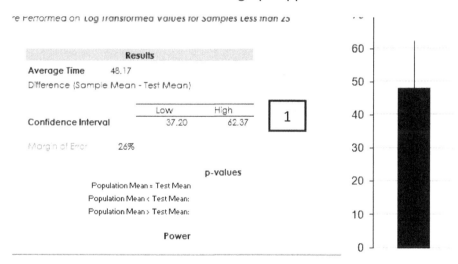

R solution

First enter the following command to get the confidence interval of log-times:

```
ci.t.fromsummary(3.87,.384,11,.95)
```

With the result:

```
RESULTS: 95% CONFIDENCE INTERVAL

Upper limit:(4.127975)
Mean: 3.87
Lower limit:(3.612025)
Margin of error: 0.2579747
Standard error: 0.1157804
Critical value of t: 2.228139
```

Then enter the following command to get the confidence interval of times (still using the variable "raw2" from Exercise 15):

ci.t.fromarray.withlogconversion(raw2,.95)

With the result:

```
RESULTS: 95% CONFIDENCE INTERVAL

Arithmetic mean: 51.90909
Median: 44
Upper limit:(62.37098)
Geometric Mean: 48.17121
Lower limit:(37.20425)
Critical value of t: 2.228139
```

Example 18: Confidence interval around median task time

From page(s): 34

Summary: When sample sizes are larger (*n* > 25), the median time becomes a better measure of central tendency than the geometric mean (Sauro & Lewis, 2010). What is the 95% confidence interval around the median for the following times (in seconds): 167, 124, 85, 136, 110, 330, 76, 57, 173, 76, 158, 77, 65, 80, 95, 96, 100, 122, 115, 152, 136, 317, 120, 186, 109, 116 ,248, 96, 137, and 149?

Answer: The median is 118 seconds with a 95% confidence interval ranging from 96-137 seconds.

Chapter 3: How Precise Are Our Estimates? Confidence Intervals

Excel solution

1. From the "Time CI and Test" tab used in the previous examples, clear out any values using the Clear Values button (macros must be enabled) and enter values in the "Raw Time Data" column.

2. Set the confidence level drop down to 95%.

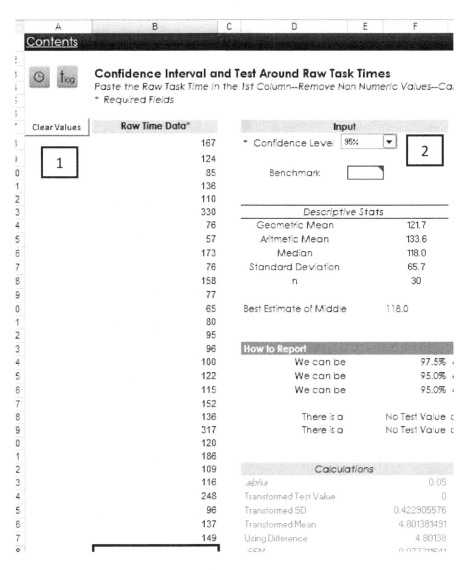

3. The 95% confidence interval around the median is in the Results section (both numeric and graphical forms).

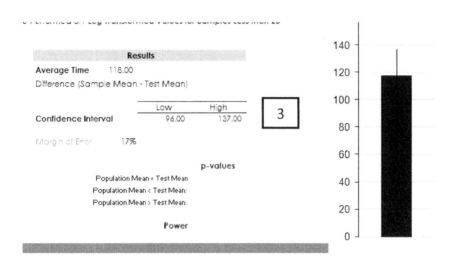

R solution

Enter the following commands:

```
raw3 <- c(167, 124, 85, 136, 110, 330, 76, 57, 173, 76, 158, 77, 65, 80, 95, 96, 100, 122, 115, 152, 136, 317, 120, 186, 109, 116, 248, 96, 137, 149)

ci.median.fromarray(raw3,.95)
```

The first standard R command puts the times in a variable named "raw3." The second custom command takes as input the variable name for the array of times and the desired level of confidence (.95 for 95%). The result is:

```
RESULTS: 95% CONFIDENCE INTERVAL

Upper limit: 137
Median: 118
Lower limit: 96
```

Example 19: Confidence interval around median task time

From page(s): 35

Summary: This is another example of computing a confidence interval around a median of a set of completion times with $n > 25$. What is the 95% confidence interval around the median for the following times (in seconds): 82, 96, 100, 104, 105, 110, 111, 117, 118, 118, 118, 127, 132, 133, 134, 134, 139, 141, 141, 150, 161, 178, 201, 201, 211, 223, and 256?

Answer: The median is 133 seconds with a 95% confidence interval ranging from 118-141 seconds.

Excel solution

1. From the "Time CI and Test" tab used in the previous examples, clear out any values using the Clear Values button (macros must be enabled) and enter the 26 values in the "Raw Time Data" column.

2. Set the confidence level drop down to 95%.

Chapter 3: How Precise Are Our Estimates? Confidence Intervals

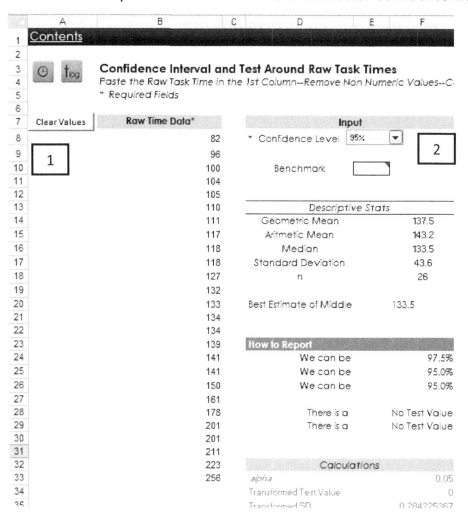

3. The 95% confidence interval around the median is in the Results section (both numeric and graphical forms).

Chapter 3: How Precise Are Our Estimates? Confidence Intervals

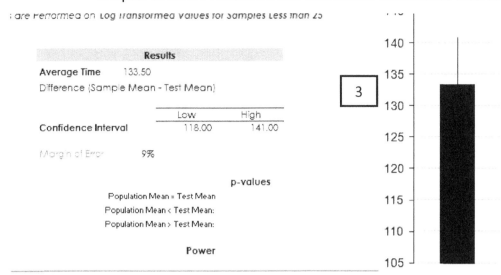

; are Performed on Log Transformed Values for Samples Less than 25

Results		
Average Time	133.50	
Difference (Sample Mean - Test Mean)		

	Low	High
Confidence Interval	118.00	141.00

Margin of Error   9%

p-values

Population Mean = Test Mean

Population Mean < Test Mean:

Population Mean > Test Mean:

Power

R solution

Enter the following commands:

```
raw4 <- c(82, 96, 100, 104, 105, 110, 111, 117, 118, 118, 118, 127, 132, 133, 134, 134, 139, 141, 141, 150, 161, 178, 201, 201, 211, 223, 256)

ci.median.fromarray(raw4,.95)
```

The first standard R command puts the times in a variable named "raw4." The second custom command takes as input the variable name for the array of times and the desired level of confidence (.95 for 95%). The result is:

```
RESULTS: 95% CONFIDENCE INTERVAL

Upper limit: 141
Median: 133
Lower limit: 118
```

Exercise 1: Confidence interval for completion rate

From page(s): 37

Problem: Find the 95% confidence interval around the completion rate from a sample of 12 users where 10 completed the task successfully.

Answer: The 95% adjusted-Wald confidence interval ranges from about 54.0 to 96.5%.

Excel solution

1. Click on the Completion Rate link under the Confidence Intervals section on the Home Tab.

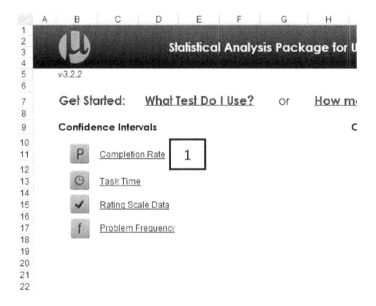

2. Enter 10 Success and 12 Total in the Enter Data section.

3. Set the confidence level to 95%.

Chapter 3: How Precise Are Our Estimates? Confidence Intervals

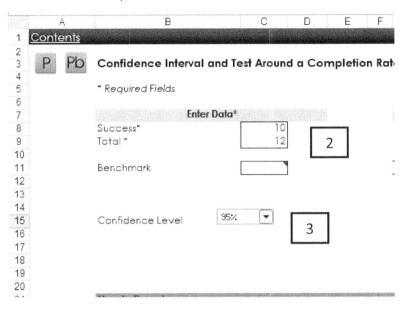

4. The 95% confidence interval (along with a graph) is in the Results section.

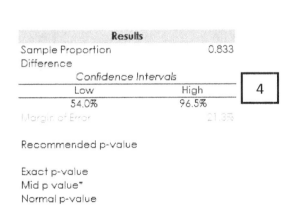

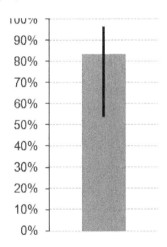

R solution

Enter the following command:

```
ci.adjwald.fromsummary(10,12,.95)
```

The result is:

```
RESULTS

Adjusted p (Wilson):        0.752502
Margin of error:            0.2125153
95% upper limit:            0.9650173
p (maximum likelihood):     0.8333333
95% lower limit:            0.5399867
```

Web solution

You can also solve this problem with the confidence interval calculator for a completion rate at http://www.measuringu.com/wald.htm. Putting in the values for 10 successes out of 12 attempts with 95% confidence, you get:

Input Table			Results Table				Point Estimates	
Passed	**Total Tested**		Confidence Intervals					
10	12		Low	High	Margin of Error*			
		Adj. Wald	0.5400	0.9650	0.2125		Best Estimate	0.7857
Calculate		Exact	0.5159	0.9791	0.2316		MLE	0.8333
		Score	0.5520	0.9530	0.2005		LaPlace	0.7857
Confidence Level: 95%		Wald	0.6225	1.0442	0.2109		Jeffrey's	0.8077
				Using Alpha: .05			Wilson	0.7525
Likely Population Completion Rate								
Unknown								

Exercise 2: Confidence interval for median task time (small sample)

From page(s): 37

Problem: What is the 95% confidence interval around the median for the following 12 task times: 198, 220, 136, 162, 143, 130, 199, 99, 136, 188, and 199?

Answer: The log-times are 5.288, 5.394, 4.913, 5.088, 4.963, 4.868, 5.293, 4.595, 4.913, 5.236, and 5.293. Because the sample size is less than 25, use the geometric mean as a proxy for the median. The geometric mean is 160.24 seconds. The 95% confidence interval around the geometric mean ranges from 136 to 189 seconds.

Chapter 3: How Precise Are Our Estimates? Confidence Intervals

Excel solution

1. Click on the Task Time link under the Confidence Intervals section on the Home Tab.

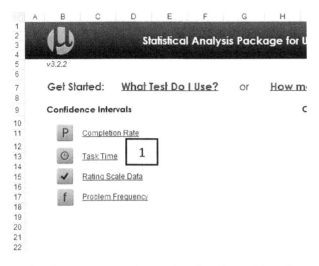

2. Clear out any values using the Clear Values button (macros must be enabled) and enter values in the "Raw Time Data" column.

3. Set the confidence level drop down to 95%.

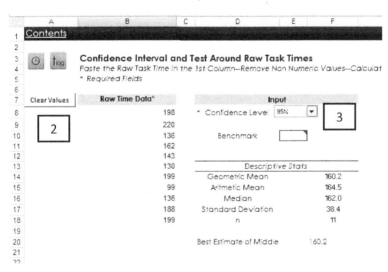

James R. Lewis & Jeff Sauro

60

Chapter 3: How Precise Are Our Estimates? Confidence Intervals

4. The confidence interval appears along with a graph in the Results section.

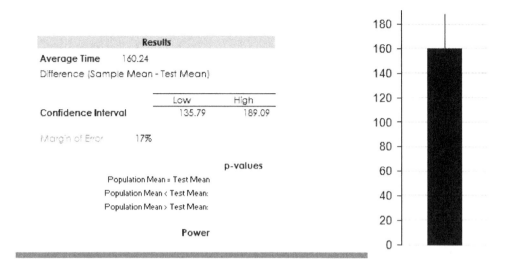

Results		
Average Time	160.24	
Difference (Sample Mean - Test Mean)		

	Low	High
Confidence Interval	135.79	189.09

Margin of Error   17%

p-values

Population Mean = Test Mean
Population Mean < Test Mean:
Population Mean > Test Mean:

Power

R solution

Enter the following commands:

```
raw5 <- c(198,220,136,162,143,130,199,99,136,188,199)

lograw5 <- log(raw5)

lograw5

compute.logsummary.fromarray(raw5,0)

ci.t.fromsummary(5.08,.246,11,.95)

ci.t.fromarray.withlogconversion(raw5,.95)
```

In addition to showing the answer to the problem, these commands show many of the intermediate computational steps, with the answers circled. The result is:

61

Chapter 3: How Precise Are Our Estimates? Confidence Intervals

```
> raw5 <- c(198,220,136,162,143,130,199,99,136,188,199)
> lograw5 <- log(raw5)
> lograw5
 [1] 5.288267 5.393628 4.912655 5.087596 4.962845 4.867534 5.293305 4.595120
 [9] 4.912655 5.236442 5.293305
> compute.logsummary.fromarray(raw5,0)

RESULTS

Arithmetic mean: 164.5455
Median: 162
Geometric Mean: 160.2393
Mean of log data: 5.076668
Standard deviation of log data: 0.2464
Variance of log data: 0.06071295
Standard error of the mean of the log data: 0.07429239
Sample size: 11
Value to use for log critical difference: 0

> ci.t.fromsummary(5.08,.246,11,.95)

RESULTS: 95% CONFIDENCE INTERVAL

Upper limit: 5.245265
Mean: 5.08
Lower limit: 4.914735
Margin of error: 0.1652650
Standard error: 0.07417179
Critical value of t: 2.228139

> ci.t.fromarray.withlogconversion(raw5,.95)

RESULTS: 95% CONFIDENCE INTERVAL

Arithmetic mean: 164.5455
Median: 162
Upper limit: 189.0860
Geometric Mean: 160.2393
Lower limit: 135.7934
Critical value of t: 2.228139
```

Exercise 3: Confidence interval for median task time (large sample)

From page(s): 37

Problem: What is the 90% confidence interval around the median time for the following 32 task times:

251	21	60
108	43	34
27	47	48
18	15	219
195	37	338
82	46	78
222	107	117
38	19	62
81	178	40
181	95	52
140	130	

Answer: Because the sample size is greater than 25, compute a confidence interval around the actual median. The sample median is 70 seconds, with a 90% confidence interval ranging from 47 to 107 seconds.

Excel solution

1. From the "Time CI and Test" tab, clear out any values using the Clear Values button (macros must be enabled) and enter values in the "Raw Time Data" column.

2. Set the confidence level drop down to **90%.**

Chapter 3: How Precise Are Our Estimates? Confidence Intervals

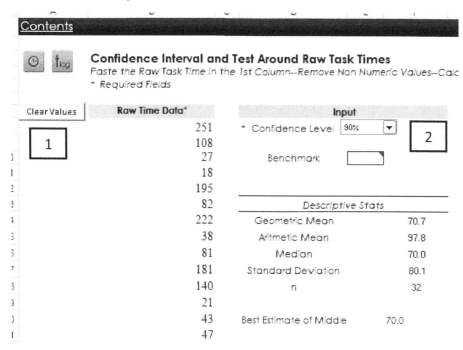

Contents

Confidence Interval and Test Around Raw Task Times
Paste the Raw Task Time in the 1st Column--Remove Non Numeric Values--Calc
* Required Fields

Clear Values	Raw Time Data*		Input	
1	251	* Confidence Level	90% ▼	2
	108			
	27	Benchmark		
	18			
	195			
	82		Descriptive Stats	
	222	Geometric Mean	70.7	
	38	Aritmetic Mean	97.8	
	81	Median	70.0	
	181	Standard Deviation	80.1	
	140	n	32	
	21			
	43	Best Estimate of Middle	70.0	
	47			

3. The confidence interval and graph are in the Results section.

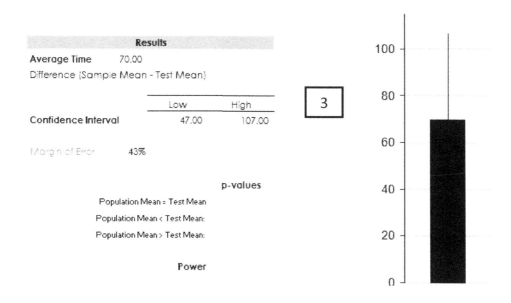

Results		
Average Time	70.00	
Difference (Sample Mean - Test Mean)		

	Low	High
Confidence Interval	47.00	107.00

Margin of Error   43%

p-values

Population Mean = Test Mean
Population Mean < Test Mean:
Population Mean > Test Mean:

Power

64

Chapter 3: How Precise Are Our Estimates? Confidence Intervals

R solution

Enter the following commands:

raw6 <- c(251, 108, 27, 18, 195, 82, 222, 38, 81, 181, 140, 21, 43, 47, 15, 37, 46, 107, 19, 178, 95, 130, 60, 34, 48, 219, 338, 78, 117, 62, 40, 52)

ci.median.fromarray(raw6,.9)

The first command gets the data into a variable named "raw6." The second command takes as input the variable name and the desired level of confidence (.9 for 90%). The result is:

```
RESULTS: 90% CONFIDENCE INTERVAL

Upper limit: 107
Median: 70
Lower limit: 47
```

Exercise 4: Confidence interval for SUS scores

From page(s): 37

Problem: Find the 95% confidence interval around the average SUS score for the following fifteen scores from a test of an automotive website: 70, 50, 67.5, 35, 27.5, 50, 30, 37.5, 65, 45, 82.5, 80, 47.5, 32.5, and 65.

Answer: The mean and standard deviation are, respectively, 52.3 and 18.2. The 95% confidence interval ranges from 42.2 to 62.4.

Excel solution

1. Click on the Rating Scale Data link under the Confidence Intervals section on the Home Tab.

Chapter 3: How Precise Are Our Estimates? Confidence Intervals

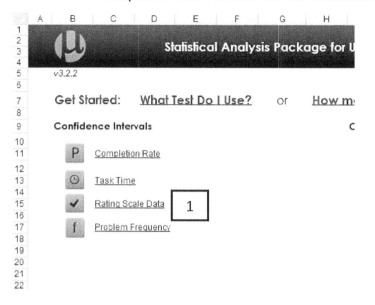

2. Clear out any values using the Clear Values button (macros must be enabled) and enter values in the "Raw Time Data" column.

3. Select a 95% confidence level.

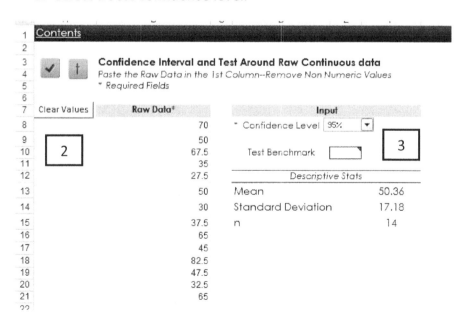

66

Chapter 3: How Precise Are Our Estimates? Confidence Intervals

4. The confidence interval and graph are in the Results section.

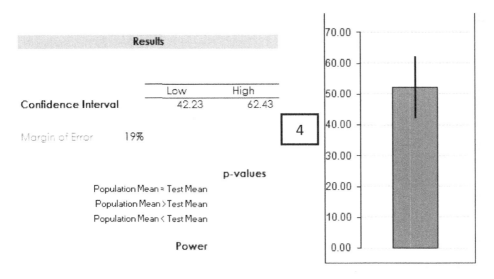

R solution

Enter the following commands:

```
sus2 <- c(70,50,67.5,35,27.5,50,30,37.5,65,45,82.5,80,47.5,32.5,65)

ci.t.fromarray(sus2,.95)
```

The result is:

```
RESULTS: 95% CONFIDENCE INTERVAL

Upper limit: 62.43221
Mean: 52.33333
Lower limit: 42.23445
Margin of error: 10.09888
```

67

Chapter 3: How Precise Are Our Estimates? Confidence Intervals

Exercise 5: Confidence interval for problem occurrence rate

From page(s): 37

Problem: With 90% confidence, if 2 out of 8 users experience a problem with a registration element in a web-form, what percent of all users could plausibly encounter the problem should it go uncorrected?

Answer: The 90% adjusted-Wald binary confidence interval ranges from 8.0 to 54.6%.

Excel solution

1. Click on the Problem Frequency link under the Confidence Intervals section on the Home Tab.

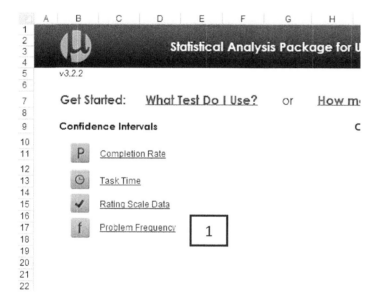

1. Clear out any values using the Clear Values button (macros must be enabled) and enter values in the "Raw Time Data" column.

2. Select a 90% Confidence Level.

3. Enter 2 users Encountering the Problem and 8 Total Users Tested.

68

Chapter 3: How Precise Are Our Estimates? Confidence Intervals

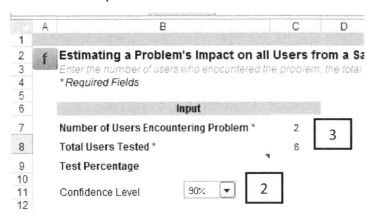

4. The confidence interval is in the Results section.

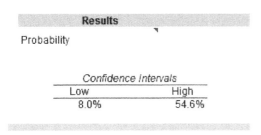

R solution

Enter the following command:

```
ci.adjwald.fromsummary(2,8,.9)
```

The result is:

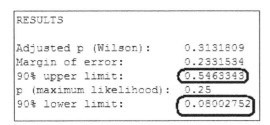

Web solution

You can also solve this problem with the confidence interval calculator for a completion rate at http://www.measuringu.com/wald.htm, using it to compute the problem occurrence rate rather than a success rate. Putting in the values for 2 users experiencing a particular problem (into the "Passed" field) out of 8 users attempting the task ("Total Tested") with 90% confidence, you get:

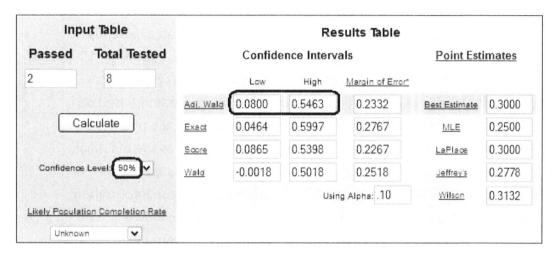

Chapter 4: Did We Meet or Exceed Our Goal?

Abstract

A common user research problem is determining whether a design has met or exceeded a specific goal. The statistical test you use for completion rates depends on the sample size. A sample size is considered small unless you have more than 15 successes and 15 failures. For determining whether a certain percentage of users can complete a task for small sample sizes use the mid-probability method based on the binomial distribution. For determining whether a certain percentage of users can complete a task for large sample sizes use the normal approximation to the binomial. You can always convert continuous rating scale data into discrete-binary data and test a percentage that agrees with a statement, but in so doing, you lose information. To compare a set of satisfaction scores from a survey or questionnaire with a benchmark, use the one-sample *t*-test for all sample sizes. When determining whether a task time falls below a benchmark, first log-transform the times then perform a one-sample *t*-test for all sample sizes. For most statistical testing we recommend two-tailed tests, but for testing against a benchmark, we recommend one-tailed testing.

Example 1: Confidence interval for completion rate

From page(s): 39

Summary: If 8 of 9 users complete a task successfully, what is the 95% confidence interval for the completion rate?

Answer: The observed percentage of completions (maximum likelihood estimate) is 88.9%, with a 95% adjusted-Wald binomial confidence interval ranging from 54.3 to 99.999%.

Excel solution

1. Click on the Completion Rate link under the Confidence Intervals section on the Home Tab.

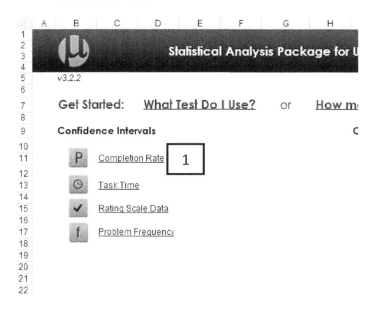

2. Select a 95% Confidence Level.

3. Enter 8 Success and 9 Total in the Enter Data Section.

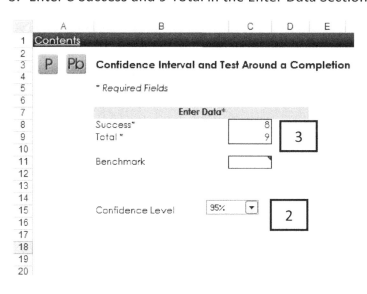

4. The confidence interval and graph are in the Results section.

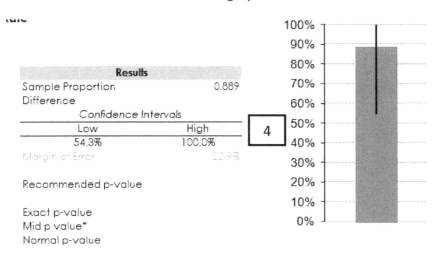

R solution

Enter the following command:

```
ci.adjwald.fromsummary(8,9,.95)
```

This command requires the number of successes, the number of attempts, and the desired confidence level (.95 for 95%). The result is:

```
RESULTS

Adjusted p (Wilson):       0.7725547
Margin of error:           0.2292683
95% upper limit:           >.999999
p (maximum likelihood):    0.8888889
95% lower limit:           0.5432864
```

Web solution

You can also solve this problem with the confidence interval calculator for a completion rate at http://www.measuringu.com/wald.htm. Putting in the values for 8 successes out of 9 attempts with 95% confidence, you get:

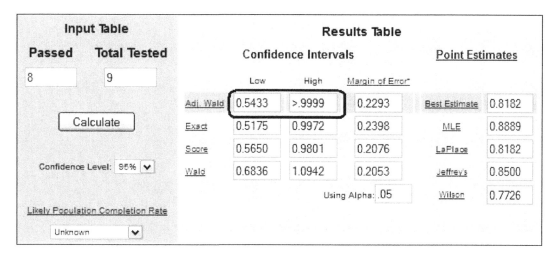

Example 2: Comparison of success rate with benchmark (small sample)

From page(s): 44-45

Summary: You've observed 8 successes out of 9 attempts. How likely is it that the population success rate is at least 70%?

Answer: For small-sample tests (fewer than 15 successes and fewer than 15 failures), we recommend using a mid-probability binomial test. Using this type of test, the probability of getting 8 successes out of 9 attempts if the true success rate is 70% is .1182. In other words, there is an 88.2% chance the completion rate exceeds 70%.

Excel solution

1. Click on the Completion Rate against a Criterion link under the Test a Mean or Proportion to Criterion section off the home tab (the Confidence Interval for a Completion Rate will take you to the same calculator).

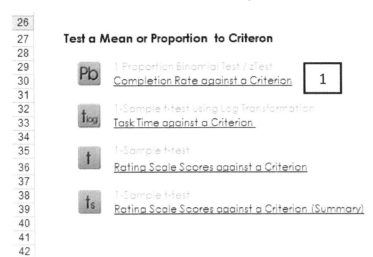

2. Enter 8 Successes and 9 Total in the Enter Data Section.

3. Enter .7 as the Benchmark.

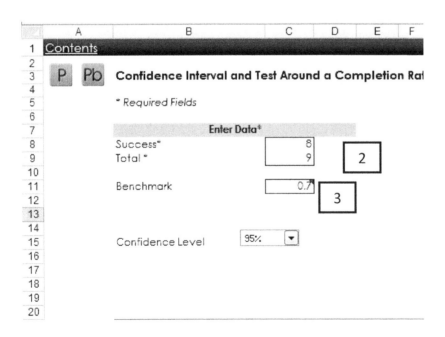

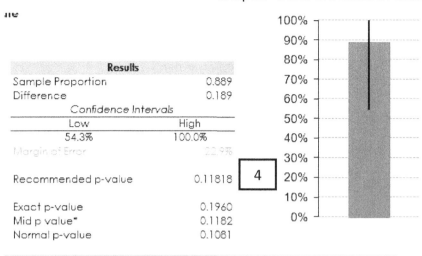

Results	
Sample Proportion	0.889
Difference	0.189

Confidence Intervals	
Low	High
54.3%	100.0%
Margin of Error	22.9%

Recommended p-value	0.11818
Exact p-value	0.1960
Mid p value*	0.1182
Normal p-value	0.1081

4. The recommended *p*-value (mid-*p* for this example) is in the Results section along with the confidence intervals.

R solution

Enter the following command:

```
bench.rate.smallsample(8,9,.7)
```

The result is:

```
RESULTS (mid-p recommended)

Observed proportion: 0.8888889
Exact probability of exceeding benchmark: 0.8039968 (p < 0.1960032 )
Mid probability of exceeding benchmark: 0.8818216 (p < 0.1181784 )
Exact probability of being below benchmark: 0.4035361 (p < 0.9596464 )
Mid probability of being below benchmark: 0.1181784 (p < 0.8818216 )
```

Web solution

You can also solve this problem with the confidence interval calculator for a completion rate at http://measuringu.com/onep.php. Putting in the values for 8 successes out of 9 attempts to assess the probability of the population success rate being greater than 70%, you get:

Use this calculator to generate both a one-sample confidence interval and to test against a critera or benchmark.

 # Passed   **Total Tested**   **Test Proportion**

8   9   Is Greater Than ▼   .70

Submit

Results

The probability the observed proportion 0.89 comes from a population greater than .70 is 88.18% .

Exact Binomial P-Value is 0.196

95% Adjusted Wald CI (54.31, 100)

Example 3: Comparison of success rate with benchmark (small sample)

From page(s): 46

Summary: Suppose there were 18 successes out of 20 attempts. How likely would that result be if the population success rate was 70%?

Answer: The mid-p value is .0216. This is less than the typical testing criterion of .05, which indicates that the observed success rate of 90% is significantly better than the benchmark of 70%.

Excel solution

1. From the "CompRate CI and Test" tab, enter 18 Successes and 20 Total in the Enter Data Section.

2. Enter .7 as the Benchmark.

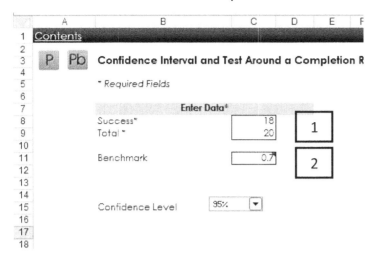

3. The recommended *p*-value (mid-*p* for this example) is in the Results section along with the confidence intervals.

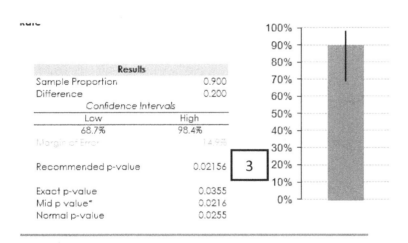

R solution

Enter the following command:

```
bench.rate.smallsample(18,20,.7)
```

The result is:

```
RESULTS (mid-p recommended)

Observed proportion: 0.9
Exact probability of exceeding benchmark: 0.9645169 (p < 0.03548313 )
Mid probability of exceeding benchmark: 0.9784398 (p < 0.02156020 )
Exact probability of being below benchmark: 0.00763726 (p < 0.9923627 )
Mid probability of being below benchmark: 0.02156020 (p < 0.9784398 )
```

Web solution

You can also solve this problem with the confidence interval calculator for a completion rate at http://measuringusability.com/onep.php. Putting in the values for 8 successes out of 9 attempts to assess the probability of the population success rate being greater than 70%, you get:

Use this calculator to generate both a one-sample confidence interval and to test against a critera or benchmark.

# Passed	Total Tested		Test Proportion
18	20	Is Greater Than ✔	.70

Submit

Results

The probability the observed proportion 0.9 comes from a population greater than .70 is **97.84%** .

Exact Binomial P-Value is 0.0355

95% Adjusted Wald CI (68.66, 98.44)

Example 4: Comparing success rate benchmark to confidence interval

From page(s): 46

Summary: An alternative way to determine if you've achieved a testing goal is to compute a confidence interval and see if the interval includes or excludes the benchmark value. If the interval excludes the benchmark, then you have statistically significant evidence of having achieved the goal. To make this equivalent to a one-tailed test (which we recommend for comparisons to benchmarks), you need to adjust the confidence level. For example, if you intend to conduct the test using the standard criterion of .05, then instead of setting the confidence to 95%, you should set it to 90%. In general, to determine the appropriate confidence level, decide on the test criterion, double that, and then subtract it from 100%. For this example, find out if the 90% confidence interval for 18 successes out of 20 attempts includes or excludes the benchmark of 70% successes?

Answer: The adjusted-Wald binomial confidence interval for 18 successes out of 20 attempts ranges from 73.0 to 97.5%. The benchmark of 70% lies outside of this interval, so the data indicate that the design has met the goal of exceeding a 70% success rate.

Excel solution

1. From the "CompRate CI and Test" tab, enter 18 Successes and 20 Total in the Enter Data Section.

2. Set the confidence level to 90%.

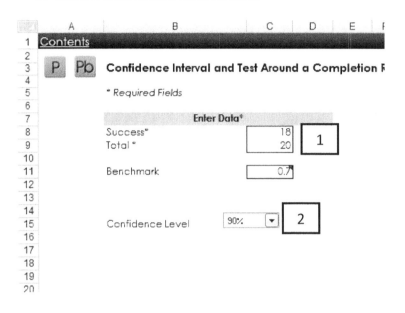

3. The confidence interval is in the Results section. The lower boundary of the interval is 73%, which is above the benchmark of 70%. Also note the mid-*p* value of .02156. Both approaches result in the same conclusion: the population completion rate likely exceeds 70%.

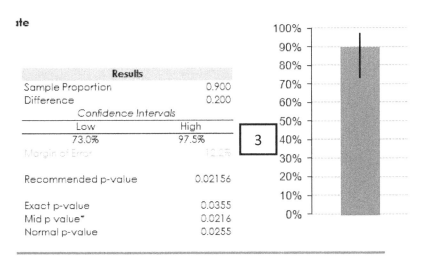

ıte

Results	
Sample Proportion	0.900
Difference	0.200

Confidence Intervals	
Low	High
73.0%	97.5%
Margin of Error	12.2%

Recommended p-value	0.02156
Exact p-value	0.0355
Mid p value*	0.0216
Normal p-value	0.0255

R solution

Enter the following command:

```
ci.adjwald.fromsummary(18,20,.9)
```

The result is:

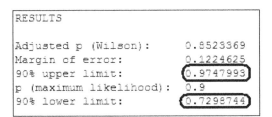

```
RESULTS

Adjusted p (Wilson):        0.8523369
Margin of error:            0.1224625
90% upper limit:            0.9747993
p (maximum likelihood):     0.9
90% lower limit:            0.7298744
```

Web solution

You can also solve this problem with the confidence interval calculator for a completion rate at http://www.measuringu.com/wald.htm. Putting in the values for 18 successes out of 20 attempts with 90% confidence, you get:

Input Table			Results Table				
Passed	**Total Tested**		**Confidence Intervals**			**Point Estimates**	
18	20		Low	High	Margin of Error*		
		Adj. Wald	0.7299	0.9748	0.1225	Best Estimate	0.8636
Calculate		Exact	0.7174	0.9819	0.1323	MLE	0.9000
		Score	0.7383	0.9663	0.1140	LaPlace	0.8636
Confidence Level: 90%		Wald	0.7897	1.0103	0.1103	Jeffrey's	0.8810
				Using Alpha: .10		Wilson	0.8523
Likely Population Completion Rate							
Unknown							

Example 5: Comparing success rate to benchmark (large sample)

From page(s): 47

Summary: The results from a remote-unmoderated test of a website task found that 85 out of 100 users were able to successfully locate a specific product and add it to their shopping cart. Is there enough evidence to conclude that at least 75% of all users can complete this task successfully? Note that this is a large sample because there are at least 15 successes and 15 failures.

Answer: The one-tailed probability of this result if the true population success rate is 75% is just .0105. Thus, there is around a 99% chance at least 75% of users can complete the task, so the data strongly support that the design has met this goal.

Excel solution

1. From the "CompRate CI and Test" tab, enter 85 Successes and 100 Total in the Enter Data Section.

2. Set the Benchmark to .75.

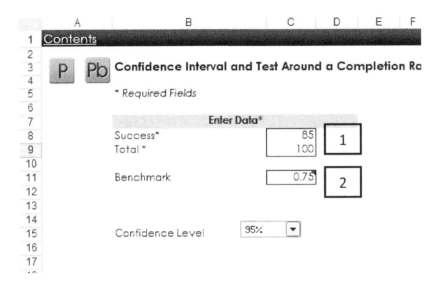

3. The recommended *p*-value (from the normal distribution in this example due to the size of the sample) is .01046, as shown in the Results section.

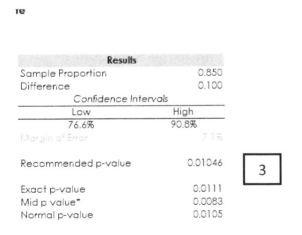

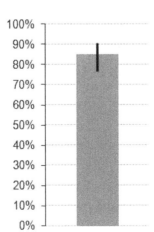

R solution

Enter the following command:

bench.rate.largesample(85,100,.75)

The result is:

```
RESULTS

Observed proportion: 0.85
z: 2.309401
Probability of exceeding benchmark: 0.9895393 (p < 0.01046067 )
Probability of being below benchmark: 0.01046067 (p < 0.9895393 )
```

Example 6: Comparing success rate benchmark to confidence interval

From page(s): 47

Summary: As in Example 4, an alternative way to assess having met a goal is to construct a confidence interval to see if the benchmark is inside or outside of the interval. Using the data from Example 5, it the benchmark of 75% success inside or outside of the 95% confidence interval (setting the test rejection criterion to .025)?

Answer: The 95% adjusted-Wald binomial confidence interval for 85 successes out of 100 attempts ranges from 76.6 to 90.8%. Because the lower limit of the interval is higher than the benchmark, there is compelling evidence that the design has met this goal.

Excel solution

1. From the "CompRate CI and Test" tab, enter 85 Successes and 100 Total in the Enter Data Section.

2. Set the confidence level to 95%.

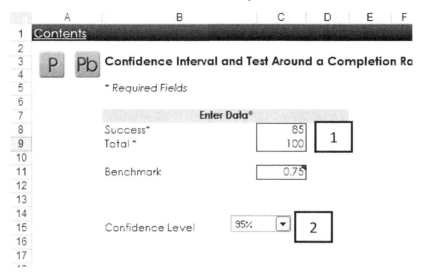

3. The confidence interval and graph are in the Results section. The lower boundary of the interval (76.6%) exceeds the benchmark of 75%.

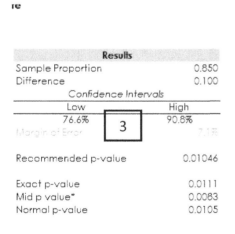

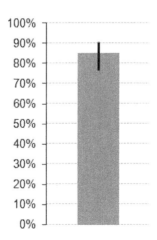

R solution

Enter the following command:

    ci.adjwald.fromsummary(85,100,.95)

The result is:

```
RESULTS

Adjusted p (Wilson):       0.8370523
Margin of error:           0.07103349
95% upper limit:          (0.9080858)
p (maximum likelihood):    0.85
95% lower limit:          (0.7660188)
```

Web solution

You can also solve this problem with the confidence interval calculator for a completion rate at http://www.measuringu.com/wald.htm. Putting in the values for 85 successes out of 100 attempts with 95% confidence, you get:

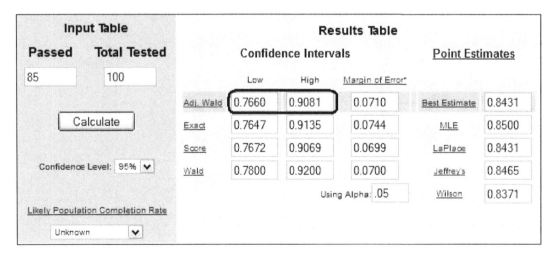

Example 7: Comparing success rate to benchmark (large sample)

From page(s): 48

Summary: If 233 out of 250 users were able to complete a task in an unmoderated usability test, is there enough evidence to conclude at least 90% of all users can complete the task?

Answer: The one-tailed *p*-value is .0459, which indicates a statistically significant result (less than the standard criterion of .05). We can be 95.4% sure at least 90% of users can complete the task given 233 successes out of 250 attempts.

Excel solution

1. From the "CompRate CI and Test" tab, enter 233 Successes and 250 Total in the Enter Data Section.

2. Set the benchmark to .90.

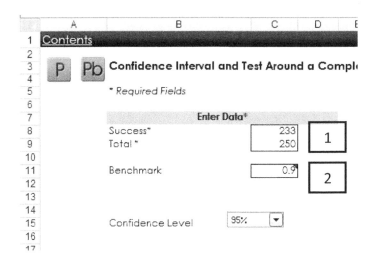

Results	
Sample Proportion	0.932
Difference	0.032

Confidence Intervals	
Low	High
89.3%	95.8%
Margin of Error	3.2%

Recommended p-value	0.04585	3

Exact p-value	0.0513
Mid p value*	0.0411
Normal p-value	0.0458

3. The recommended *p*-value (from the normal distribution in this example due to the large sample size) is .04585, shown in the Results section.

R solution

Enter the following command:

```
bench.rate.largesample(233,250,.9)
```

The result is:

```
RESULTS

Observed proportion: 0.932
z: 1.686548
Probability of exceeding benchmark: 0.9541549 (p < 0.04584514 )
Probability of being below benchmark: 0.04584514 (p < 0.9541549 )
```

Example 8: Comparing benchmark to confidence interval

From page(s): 48

Summary: For the data in Example 7 (233 successes out of 250 attempts), does a 90% confidence interval exclude the benchmark of 90% successes?

Answer: The adjusted-Wald binomial confidence interval ranges from about 90.1 to 95.4%. The lower limit is higher than the benchmark, indicating sufficient evidence to conclude that the design has met this goal.

Excel solution

1. From the "CompRate CI and Test" tab, enter 233 Successes and 250 Total in the Enter Data Section.

2. Set the confidence level to 90%.

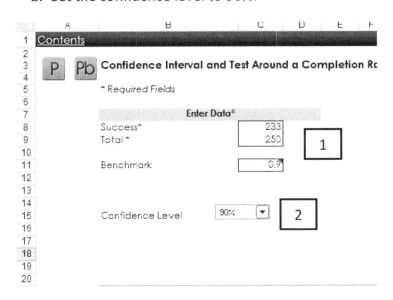

te

Results	
Sample Proportion	0.932
Difference	0.032

Confidence Intervals	
Low	High
90.1%	95.4%
Margin of Error 3	2.7%

Recommended p-value	0.04585
Exact p-value	0.0513
Mid p value*	0.0411
Normal p-value	0.0458

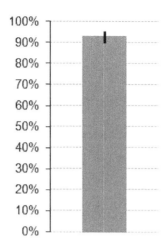

3. The confidence interval and graph are in the Results section. The lower boundary of the interval (90.1%) exceeds the benchmark of 90%.

R solution

Enter the following command:

```
ci.adjwald.fromsummary(233,250,.9)
```

The result is:

```
RESULTS

Adjusted p (Wilson):      0.9273749
Margin of error:          0.02685289
90% upper limit:          0.9542278
p (maximum likelihood):   0.932
90% lower limit:          0.900522
```

Web solution

You can also solve this problem with the confidence interval calculator for a completion rate at http://www.measuringu.com/wald.htm. Putting in the values for 233 successes out of 250 attempts with 90% confidence, you get:

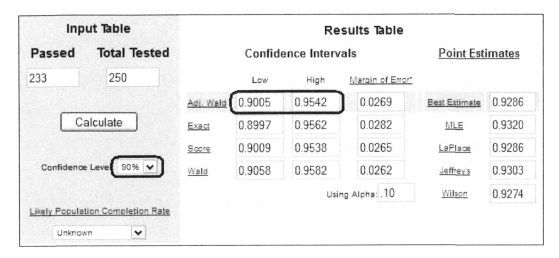

Example 9: Comparing mean SUS score to benchmark

From page(s): 48-49

Summary: Twenty users completed some common tasks (dialing, adding contacts and texting) on a new cell-phone design. At the end of the test they responded to the SUS questionnaire. The mean SUS score was 73 and the standard deviation was 19. Is there enough evidence to conclude that the perceived usability of this cell phone is better than the current industry average of 67?

Answer: This outcome has a probability of .0874, meaning we can be around 91% confident this cell-phone has an average score greater than the industry average of 67.

Excel solution

1. Click on the Rating Scale Scores against a Criterion (Summary) link under the Test a Mean or Proportion to Criterion section.

2. Enter the mean, standard deviation, sample size and the industry average (Test Benchmark) in the Input section.

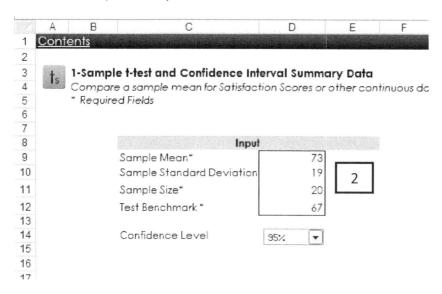

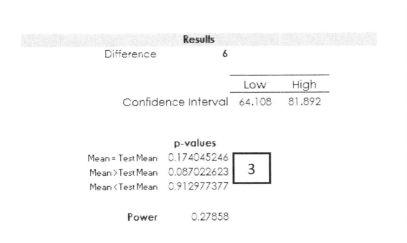

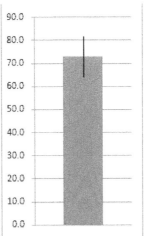

3. The one-tailed *p*-value (Mean > Test Mean) of .087 is in the Results section.

R solution

Enter the following command:

bench.t.fromsummary(73,67,19,20)

For this function, the information required is the observed mean, the benchmark, the standard deviation, and the sample size. The result is:

```
RESULTS

t: 1.412253
df: 19
Probability of exceeding benchmark: 0.9129774 (p < 0.08702262 )
Probability of being below benchmark: 0.08702262 (p < 0.9129774 )
```

Example 10: Comparing SUS benchmark to confidence interval

From page(s): 49

Summary: An alternative way to assess a benchmark is to compare it to a confidence interval. For this exercise, assume that the criterion for significance is a probability less than .10. In that case, as discussed previously, the appropriate level of confidence is 80% (1 - 2(.10)). For the data in Example 9, does an 80% confidence interval include or exclude the criterion of 67?

Answer: The 80% confidence interval ranges from 67.4 to 78.6. The lower bound of the confidence interval is slightly higher than the criterion, so the conclusion is that the design achieved this goal.

Excel solution

1. From the "1 Sample t (Summary)" tab, enter the mean, standard deviation and sample size data from Example 9 in the Input section.

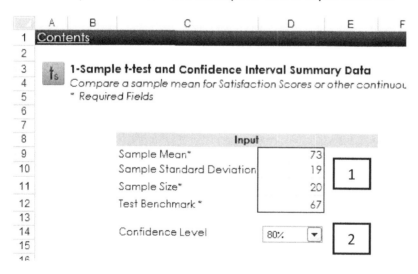

2. Set the confidence level to 80%.

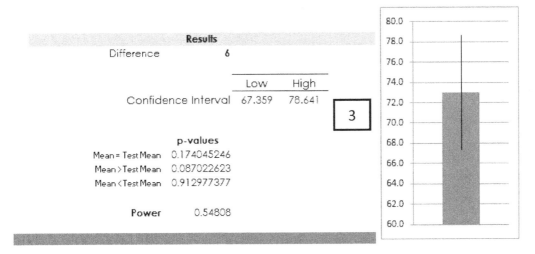

Results	
Difference	6

	Low	High
Confidence Interval	67.359	78.641

3

p-values	
Mean = Test Mean	0.174045246
Mean > Test Mean	0.087022623
Mean < Test Mean	0.912977377

Power	0.54808

3. The confidence interval and graph are in the Results section. The lower boundary of the interval (67.359) is above the Test Benchmark of 67.

R solution

Enter the following command:

```
ci.t.fromsummary(73,19,20,.8)
```

For this function, the inputs are the observed mean, the standard deviation, the sample size, and the desired level of confidence (.8 for 80%). The result is:

```
RESULTS: 80% CONFIDENCE INTERVAL

Upper limit: 78.64089
Mean: 73
Lower limit: 67.35911
Margin of error: 5.640892
Standard error: 4.248529
Critical value of t: 1.327728
```

Example 11: Comparing mean SUS score to benchmark

From page(s): 49-50

Summary: In a recent unmoderated usability test 172 users attempted tasks on a rental-car website then answered the SUS questionnaire. The mean response was 80 and the standard deviation was 23. Can we conclude the average SUS score for the population is greater than 75?

Answer: The probability of this result is .002. There is less than a 1% chance that a mean of 80 from a sample size of 172 would come from a population with a mean less than 75. In other words we can be more than 99% confident that the average score for all users of this website exceeds 75.

Excel solution

1. From the "1 Sample t (Summary)" tab, enter the mean, standard deviation and sample size data from Example 9 in the Input section.

2. Enter the Test Benchmark as 75.

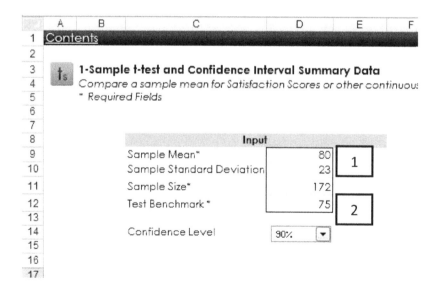

3. The one-tailed *p*-value (Mean > Test Mean) of .0024 is in the Results section, indicating strong evidence to support the hypothesis that the population SUS score exceeds 75.

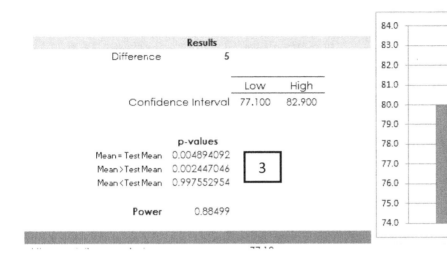

R solution

Enter the following command:

    bench.t.fromsummary(80,75,23,172)

The result is:

```
RESULTS

t: 2.85106
df: 171
Probability of exceeding benchmark: 0.997553 (p < 0.002447046 )
Probability of being below benchmark: 0.002447046 (p < 0.997553 )
```

Example 12: Comparing SUS benchmark to confidence interval

From page(s): 50

Summary: Does a 90% confidence interval using the data from Example 11 include or exclude the benchmark of 75?

Answer: The 90% confidence interval ranges from 77.1 to 82.9. The lower bound of the confidence interval exceeds the criterion, so there is reasonable evidence that the design has met this goal.

Excel solution

1. From the "1 Sample t (Summary)" tab, enter the mean, standard deviation and sample size data from Example 9 in the Input section.

2. Set the Confidence Level to 90%.

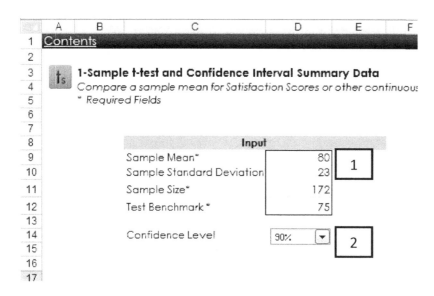

3. The confidence interval and graph are in the Results section. The lower boundary of the interval (77.1) is above the Test Benchmark of 75.

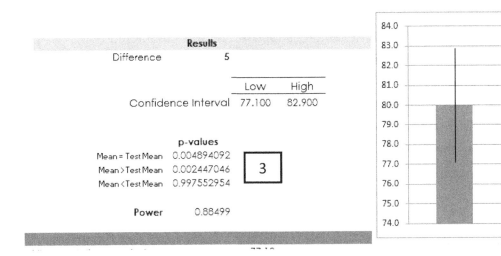

R solution

Enter the following command:

ci.t.fromsummary(80,23,172,.9)

The result is:

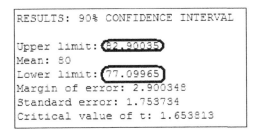

```
RESULTS: 90% CONFIDENCE INTERVAL

Upper limit: 82.90035
Mean: 80
Lower limit: 77.09965
Margin of error: 2.900348
Standard error: 1.753734
Critical value of t: 1.653813
```

Example 13: Comparing agreement rate to benchmark

From page(s): 50

Summary: A common (but not necessarily good) practice is to "degrade" multipoint rating scale scores into binary scores. For example, suppose 12 users completed two tasks on a website and responded to the item "I feel confident conducting business with this website" at the end of the test. A 1 is "Strongly Disagree" and a 5 is "Strongly Agree". Can we conclude at least 75% of users feel confident conducting business on Walmart.com (ratings of 4 or 5) if their ratings were 4, 4, 5, 5, 5, 5, 3, 5, 1, 5, 5, and 5? Converting these responses to binary we get 1, 1, 1, 1, 1, 1, 0, 1, 0, 1, 1, and 1, so we have 10 out of 12 users who agreed with the statement.

Answer: The probability of getting 10 agreements out of 12 users is .275, which indicates a 72.5% chance that 75% of all users agree with the statement. This would not inspire a high level of confidence that the design had achieved this goal.

Excel solution

1. Click on the Completion Rate against a Criterion link under the Test a Mean or Proportion to Criterion section.

26	
27	**Test a Mean or Proportion to Criteron**
28	
29	Pb 1 Proportion Binomial Test / zTest
30	Completion Rate against a Criterion [1]
31	
32	t_{log} 1-Sample t-test using Log Transformation
33	Task Time against a Criterion
34	
35	t 1-Sample t-test
36	Rating Scale Scores against a Criterion
37	
38	t_s 1-Sample t-test
39	Rating Scale Scores against a Criterion (Summary)
40	
41	

2. Enter 10 Successes and 12 Total tested in the Enter Data section.

3. Set the Benchmark to .75.

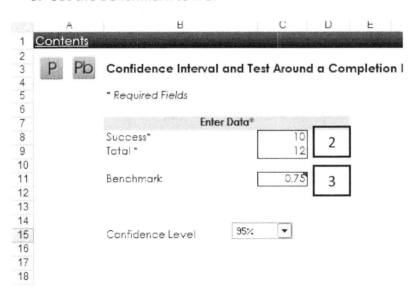

4. The recommended *p*-value (mid-*p*) of .275 is in the Results section.

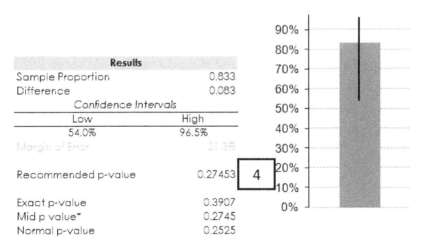

R solution

Enter the following command:

    bench.rate.smallsample(10,12,.75)

The result is:

```
RESULTS (mid-p recommended)

Observed proportion: 0.8333333
Exact probability of exceeding benchmark: 0.609325 (p < 0.390675 )
Mid probability of exceeding benchmark: 0.7254716 (p < 0.2745284 )
Exact probability of being below benchmark: 0.1583818 (p < 0.8416182 )
Mid probability of being below benchmark: 0.2745284 (p < 0.7254716 )
```

Example 14: Comparing agreement benchmark to confidence interval

From page(s): 50

Summary: Continuing with the alternative practice of comparing benchmarks to confidence intervals, determine if the confidence interval for the data in Example 13 would include or exclude the benchmark of 75%.

Answer: The 80% adjusted-Wald confidence interval around the percentage of users who agree is between 65.3% and 93.4%. The interval contains the benchmark of 75%, which isn't even near the lower limit of 65.3%, reinforcing the point that we don't have convincing evidence from this data that at least 75% of users agree.

Excel solution

1. On the "CompRate CI and Test" tab, enter 10 Successes and 12 Total tested in the Enter Data section.

2. Set the confidence level to 80%.

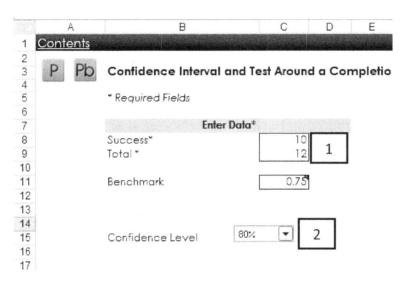

3. The confidence interval and graph are in the Results section. The lower boundary of the interval (65.3%) falls below the 75% benchmark.

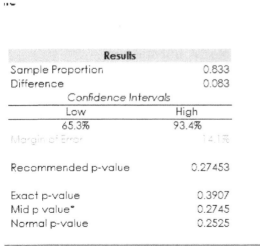

Results	
Sample Proportion	0.833
Difference	0.083

Confidence Intervals	
Low	High
65.3%	93.4%
Margin of Error	14.1%

Recommended p-value	0.27453
Exact p-value	0.3907
Mid p value*	0.2745
Normal p-value	0.2525

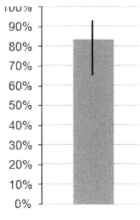

R solution

Enter the following command:

ci.adjwald.fromsummary(10,12,.8)

The result is:

```
RESULTS

Adjusted p (Wilson):        0.7932041
Margin of error:            0.1405253
80% upper limit:           (0.9337294)
p (maximum likelihood):     0.8333333
80% lower limit:           (0.6526788)
```

Example 15: Comparison of mean Likert score with benchmark

From page(s): 51

Summary: Rather than converting the data in Example 13 to binary data, you could see if the mean of the original rating data is significantly greater than 4. For that set of 12 ratings (4, 4, 5, 5, 5, 5, 3, 5, 1, 5, 5, and 5), the mean is 4.33 and the standard deviation is 1.23. What is the probability of this outcome if the population mean is 4?

Answer: The probability of this result is .186, so there is an 81.4% chance that the mean for all users exceeds 4 (a better result than in Example 14, but still not compelling).

Excel solution

1. Click on the Rating Scale Scores against a Criterion link under the Test a Mean or Proportion to Criterion section.

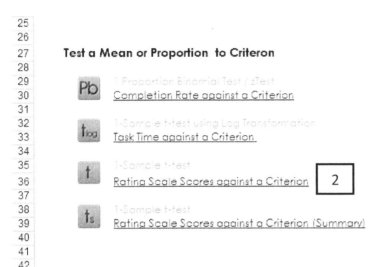

2. Clear out any previous values using the Clear Values button (macros must be enabled) and enter the scores in the Raw Data column.

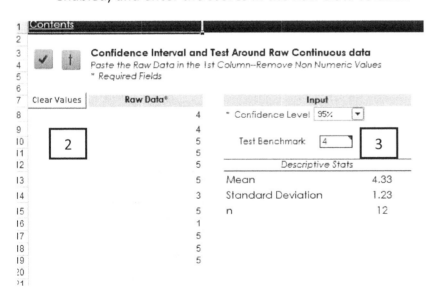

3. Set the Test Benchmark to 4.

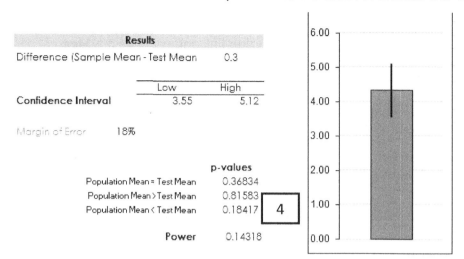

4. The *p*-value for the directional test (Population Mean < Test Mean) is .184, shown in the Results section. There is some, although not strong, evidence to support the claim that the average score exceeds 4.

R solution

Enter the following command:

bench.t.fromsummary(4.33,4,1.23,12)

The result is:

```
RESULTS

t: 0.9293931
df: 11
Probability of exceeding benchmark: 0.8136842 (p < 0.1863158 )
Probability of being below benchmark: 0.1863158 (p < 0.8136842 )
```

Example 16: Compute the Net Promoter Score®[1] from a set of Likelihood to Recommend ratings

From page(s): 51

Summary: The Net Promoter Score (NPS) is a measure of loyalty that uses only a single question "How likely are you to recommend this product to a friend?" and is measured on an 11 point scale (0 = Not at all Likely to 10= Extremely Likely). Promoters are those who rate a 9 or 10 (top-2-box), detractors are those who rate 0 to 6 and passive responders are those who respond 7 or 8. The "Net" in Net Promoter Score comes from the scoring process whereby you subtract the percent of detractors from the percent of promoters. In this example, suppose 15 users attempted to make online travel arrangements and at the end of the usability test they answered the Net Promoter question with the following responses: 10, 7, 6, 9, 10, 8, 10, 10, 9, 8, 7, 5, 8, 0, and 9. How many promoters, detractors, and passive responders were there? What is the resulting Net Promoter Score?

Answer: There were seven promoters, three detractors, and five passive responders, generating a Net Promoter Score of 4/15 =26.7%.

---

[1] Net Promoter, NPS, and Net Promoter Score are trademarks of Satmetrix Systems, Inc., Bain & Company, and Fred Reichheld.

Excel solution

1. Although there is not a dedicated Excel calculator for computing the Net Promoter Score, you can do this in Excel by stacking the data in a column.

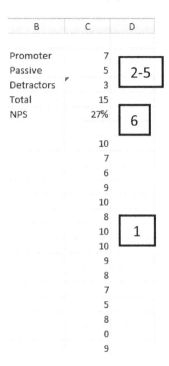

2. Assuming the data are in column C, count the number of promoters by using the formula: =COUNTIF(C8:C22,">8").

3. Count the number of passive responses using the formula:
   =SUM(COUNTIF(C8:C22,8), COUNTIF(C8:C22,7))

4. Count the number of detractors using the formula =COUNTIF(C10:C24,"<7")

5. Count the total number of responses =SUM(C2:C4)

6. Compute the Net Promoter Score by subtracting detractors from promoters and dividing by the total =(C2-C4)/C5.

R solution

Enter the following commands:

ltr <- c(10,7,6,9,10,8,10,10,9,8,7,5,8,0,9)

compute.nps.fromarray(ltr)

The first command assigns the array of Likelihood-to-Recommend scores to the variable "ltr." The second is a custom function that counts the numbers of promoters, passives, and detractors, and then computes the NPS. The result is:

```
RESULTS

Number of promoters: 7
Number of passives: 5
Number of detractors: 3
Net Promoter Score (NPS): 26.67%
```

Example 17: Comparison of completion times to benchmark
From page(s): 52-54

Summary: As mentioned in the previous chapter, distributions of completion times tend to be skewed. This is not a serious problem when comparing two sets of completion times (next chapter), but can be an issue for one-sample statistics such as confidence intervals (previous chapter) and comparisons with a benchmark (this chapter). As in the previous chapter, the solution to this is to work with log-times rather than their raw values. For this example, assume you've collected the following 12 task times from users renting a car online: 215, 131, 260, 171, 187, 147, 74, 170, 131, 165, 347, and 90. Do these times support the claim that the average user can rent a car in less than 60 seconds?

Answer: No, they clearly don't. The geometric mean is 160 seconds, which alone is reason to reject the claim. A 95% confidence interval around the geometric mean ranges from about 123 to 210 seconds, well above the benchmark of 60 seconds. The probability of this result is .9999965. In other words there's far less than a 1% chance of obtaining an average time of 160 seconds if the population average time is less than 60 seconds.

Excel solution

1. Click on the Task Time against a Criterion link under the Test a Mean or Proportion to Criterion section.

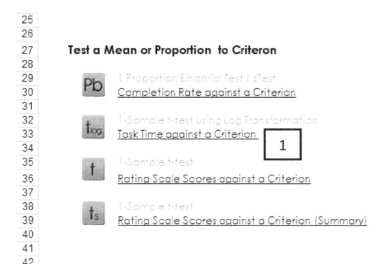

2. Clear out any previous values using the Clear Values button (macros must be enabled) and enter the scores in the Raw Data column.

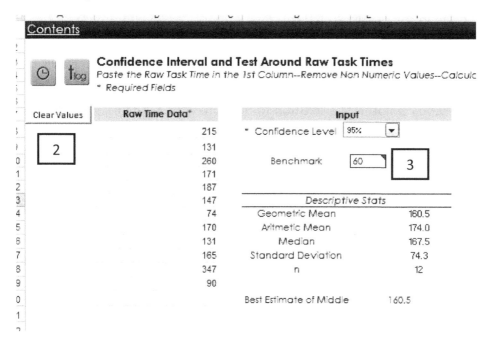

3. Set the Test Benchmark to 60.

4. The average time (Geometric Mean for this example) is in the Results section along with the confidence interval.

5. The one-sided *p*-value for this hypothesis is above .9999, meaning there is very little evidence that the average time is less than 60 sections.

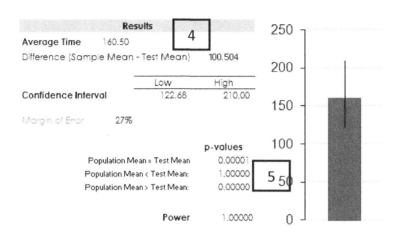

R solution

Enter the following commands:

```
ex41 <- c(215,131,260,171,187,147,74,170,131,165,347,90)

ex41logs <- log(ex41)

ex41logs

compute.logsummary.fromarray(ex41,0)

log(60)

bench.t.fromarray.withlogconversion(ex41,60)

ci.t.fromarray.withlogconversion(ex41,.95)
```

The result is:

```
> ex41 <- c(215,131,260,171,187,147,74,170,131,165,347,90)
> ex41logs <- log(ex41)
> ex41logs
 [1] 5.370638 4.875197 5.560682 5.141664 5.231109 4.990433 4.304065 5.135798
 [9] 4.875197 5.105945 5.849325 4.499810
> compute.logsummary.fromarray(ex41,0)

RESULTS

Arithmetic mean: 174
Median: 167.5
Geometric Mean: 160.5045
Mean of log data: 5.078322
Standard deviation of log data: 0.4230174
Variance of log data: 0.1789438
Standard error of the mean of the log data: 0.1221146
Sample size: 12
Value to use for log critical difference: 0

> log(60)
[1] 4.094345
> bench.t.fromarray.withlogconversion(ex41,60)

RESULTS

Arithmetic mean: 174
Median: 167.5
Geometric mean: 160.5045
t: 8.057818    df: 11
Probability of exceeding benchmark: 0.999997 (p < 3.049758e-06 )
Probability of being below benchmark: 3.049758e-06 (p < 0.999997 )

> ci.t.fromarray.withlogconversion(ex41,.95)

RESULTS: 95% CONFIDENCE INTERVAL

Arithmetic mean: 174
Median: 167.5
Upper limit: 209.9972
Geometric Mean: 160.5045
Lower limit: 122.6763
Critical value of t: 2.200985
```

The first three commands assign the data to a variable ("ex41"), do the log transform and put the results in a second variable ("ex41logs"), and print the log-times. The next four provide a summary of the data, show the log of the benchmark, conduct a *t*-test on the log-times, and construct a confidence interval around the geometric mean.

Example 18: Comparison of completion times to benchmark

From page(s): 54-55

Summary: This example is similar to Example 17. This time you need to determine if the following 11 completion times provide evidence that the average user can complete the given task in less than 100 seconds: 90, 59, 54, 55, 171, 86, 107, 53, 79, 72, and 157.

Answer: The probability of this result is .0739. The most commonly used criterion for statistical significance is for the probability of a result to be less than .05, but as discussed in *Quantifying the User Experience: Practical Statistics for User Research* (2nd ed.), this doesn't necessarily apply in all situations. Assuming that the criterion for this test was .10, the conclusion would be that the outcome is statistically significant. The appropriate 80% confidence interval (1 - 2(.10)) for this criterion ranges from 69-98 seconds, with the upper limit just below the benchmark, indicating that the design successfully met this goal.

Excel solution

1. From the "Time CI and Test" calculator, clear out any previous values using the Clear Values button (macros must be enabled) and enter the scores in the Raw Data column.

2. Enter 100 as the Benchmark Value.

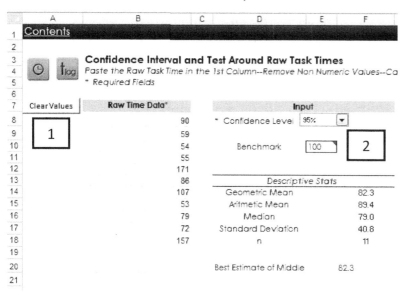

3. The average time of 82.31 seconds (Geometric Mean for this example) is in the Results section along with the confidence interval.

4. The one-sided *p*-value for this hypothesis is .0739, so there is good evidence that the average time is less than 100 seconds.

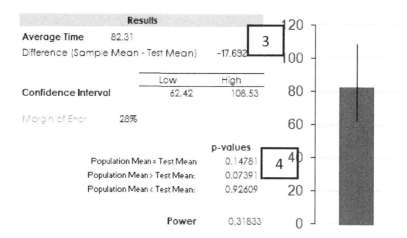

R solution

Enter the following commands:

```
ex42 <- c(90,59,54,55,171,86,107,53,79,72,157)

ex42logs <- log(ex42)

ex42logs

compute.logsummary.fromarray(ex42,0)

log(100)

bench.t.fromarray.withlogconversion(ex42,100)

ci.t.fromarray.withlogconversion(ex42,.80)
```

The result is:

```
> ex42 <- c(90,59,54,55,171,86,107,53,79,72,157)
> ex42logs <- log(ex42)
> ex42logs
 [1] 4.499810 4.077537 3.988984 4.007333 5.141664 4.454347 4.672829 3.970292
 [9] 4.369448 4.276666 5.056246
> compute.logsummary.fromarray(ex42,0)

RESULTS

Arithmetic mean: 89.36364
Median: 79
Geometric Mean: 82.30803
Mean of log data: 4.410469
Standard deviation of log data: 0.4116754
Variance of log data: 0.1694766
Standard error of the mean of the log data: 0.1241248
Sample size: 11
Value to use for log critical difference: 0

> log(100)
[1] 4.60517
> bench.t.fromarray.withlogconversion(ex42,100)

RESULTS

Arithmetic mean: 89.36364
Median: 79
Geometric mean: 82.30803
t: -1.568595    df: 10
Probability of exceeding benchmark: 0.07390691 (p < 0.926093 )
Probability of being below benchmark: 0.926093 (p < 0.07390691 )

> ci.t.fromarray.withlogconversion(ex42,.80)

RESULTS: 80% CONFIDENCE INTERVAL

Arithmetic mean: 89.36364
Median: 79
Upper limit: 97.59153
Geometric Mean: 82.30803
Lower limit: 69.41803
Critical value of t: 1.372184
```

Exercise 1: Comparison of completion rate to benchmark (small sample)

From page(s): 56-57

Problem: 25 out of 26 users were able to create an expense report in a financial application. Does the evidence support the claim that at least 90% of all users can complete the same task?

Answer: The mid-probability of this result is .158 – not terribly large, but not compelling evidence. With the rejection criterion set to .10, an 80% adjusted-Wald binomial confidence interval ranges from 87.4 to 99.5%. Because the adjusted-Wald interval contains the benchmark of .90, there is insufficient evidence to conclude that in the tested population at least 90% of users could successfully complete the task. An advantage of computing the confidence interval is that you get an idea about what benchmarks the data in hand would support. For example, because the lower limit of the interval is 87.4%, the data would support the claim that at least 85% of users could successfully complete the task.

Excel solution

1. Click on the Completion Rate against a Criterion link under the Test a Mean or Proportion to Criterion section.

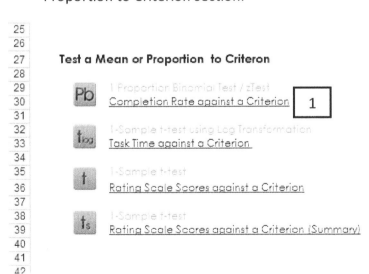

2. Enter 25 Successes and 26 Total tested in the Enter Data Section.

3. Enter .9 as the benchmark.

4. Set the confidence level to 80%.

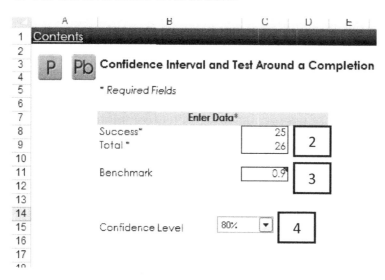

5. The confidence interval and recommended p-value of .15794 appear in the Results section.

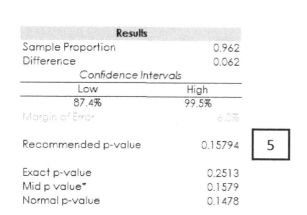

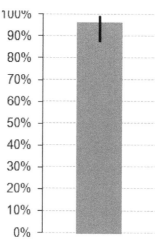

R solution

Enter the following commands:

bench.rate.smallsample(25,26,.9)

ci.adjwald.fromsummary(25,26,.80)

The result is:

```
> bench.rate.smallsample(25,26,.9)

RESULTS (mid-p recommended)

Observed proportion: 0.9615385
Exact probability of exceeding benchmark: 0.7487357 (p < 0.2512643 )
Mid probability of exceeding benchmark: 0.8420624 (p < 0.1579376 )
Exact probability of being below benchmark: 0.06461082 (p < 0.9353892 )
Mid probability of being below benchmark: 0.1579376 (p < 0.8420624 )

> ci.adjwald.fromsummary(25,26,.80)

RESULTS

Adjusted p (Wilson):        0.9341161
Margin of error:            0.06046979
80% upper limit:            0.9945859
p (maximum likelihood):     0.9615385
80% lower limit:            0.8736463
```

Web solution

You can also solve this problem with the confidence interval calculator for a completion rate at http://www.measuringu.com/wald.htm. Putting in the values for 25 successes out of 26 attempts with 80% confidence, you get:

Input Table		Results Table				
Passed	**Total Tested**	**Confidence Intervals**			**Point Estimates**	
25	26	Low	High	Margin of Error*		
		Adj. Wald **0.8736**	**0.9946**	0.0605	Best Estimate	0.9286
Calculate		Exact 0.8585	0.9960	0.0687	MLE	0.9615
		Score 0.8798	0.9884	0.0543	LaPlace	0.9286
Confidence Level: **80%** ∨		Wald 0.9132	1.0099	0.0483	Jeffrey's	0.9444
				Using Alpha: .20	Wilson	0.9341
Likely Population Completion Rate						
Unknown ∨						

The adjusted-Wald confidence interval includes the criterion of .90, so there is insufficient evidence to support the claim that the design has met this goal.

Exercise 2: Comparison of completion rate to benchmark (large sample)

From page(s): 57-58

Problem: In an unmoderated usability test of an automotive website, 150 out of 180 participants correctly answered a qualifying question at the end of a task to demonstrate they'd successfully completed the task. Can at least 75% of users complete the task?

Answer: For this test, 150 out of 180 participants completed the task successfully, and the question is whether this provides compelling evidence that at least 75% of users from the tested population would also successfully complete the task. Because there are more than 15 successes and more than 15 failures, it is OK to use the large sample method – the normal approximation to the binomial – to answer the question. The observed success rate is 150/180 = .833, the sample size is 180, and the benchmark is .75, so the probability of getting this result is a statistically significant .0049. If the rejection criterion for this test were a conservative .01, the corresponding 98% adjusted-Wald binomial confidence interval ranges from 75.9 to

88.9%. The lower limit of this confidence interval is higher than the criterion, so the evidence indicates that the design has met this goal.

Excel solution

1. From the "CompRate CI and Test" tab, enter 150 Successes and 180 Total tested.

2. Enter the Benchmark as .75.

3. Enter a confidence level of 98% for the confidence intervals.

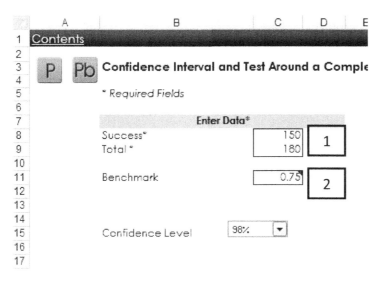

4. The *p*-value of .00491 (from the Normal distribution due to the large sample size) is in the Results section along with the 98% confidence interval.

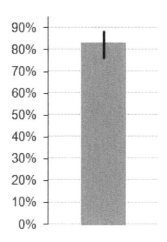

Results	
Sample Proportion	0.833
Difference	0.083
Confidence Intervals	
Low	High
75.8%	88.9%
Margin of Error	6.5%
Recommended p-value	0.00491
Exact p-value	0.0048
Mid p value*	0.0038
Normal p-value	0.0049

R solution

Enter the following commands:

bench.rate.largesample(150,180,.75)

ci.adjwald.fromsummary(150,180,.98)

The result is:

```
> bench.rate.largesample(150,180,.75)

RESULTS

Observed proportion: 0.8333333
z: 2.581989
Probability of exceeding benchmark: 0.9950884 (p < 0.004911637 )
Probability of being below benchmark: 0.004911637 (p < 0.9950884 )

> ci.adjwald.fromsummary(150,180,.98)

RESULTS

Adjusted p (Wilson):      0.8236038
Margin of error:          0.06511928
98% upper limit:          0.8887231
p (maximum likelihood):   0.8333333
98% lower limit:          0.7584846
```

Web solution

You can also solve this problem with the confidence interval calculator for a completion rate at http://www.measuringu.com/wald.htm. Putting in the values for 150 successes out of 180 attempts with 98% confidence, you get:

Input Table		Results Table				
Passed	Total Tested	Confidence Intervals			Point Estimates	
150	180	Low	High	Margin of Error*		
		Adj. Wald 0.7585	0.8887	0.0651	Best Estimate	0.8297
Calculate		Exact 0.7587	0.8927	0.0670	MLE	0.8333
		Score 0.7592	0.8880	0.0644	LaPlace	0.8297
Confidence Level 98%		Wald 0.7687	0.8980	0.0646	Jeffrey's	0.8315
				Using Alpha: .02	Wilson	0.8236
Likely Population Completion Rate						
Unknown						

Exercise 3: Comparison of mean SUS to benchmark

From page(s): 58

Problem: Assume an "average" score for websites using the System Usability Scale is 70. After completing two tasks on the Travelocity.com website, the average SUS score from 15 users was a 74.7 ($s = 12.9$). Is this website's usability significantly above average?

Answer: Using a one-tailed one-sample t-test, the likelihood of this result is .09, just achieving statistical significance if the rejection criterion were set to .10. Assuming that criterion, an 80% confidence interval ranges from 70.2 to 79.2. The lower limit of the interval is higher than the criterion, indicating that the design has met this goal.

Excel solution

1. Click on the Rating Scale Scores against a Criterion (Summary) link under the Test a Mean or Proportion to Criterion section.

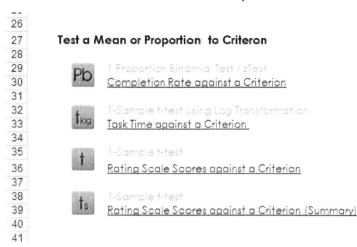

2. Enter the mean, standard deviation, sample size and Test Benchmark (70) in the Input section.

3. Set the confidence level to 80%.

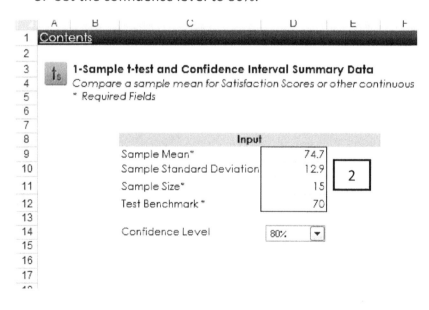

4. The one-tailed *p*-value of .09 appears in the Results section along with the 80% confidence interval.

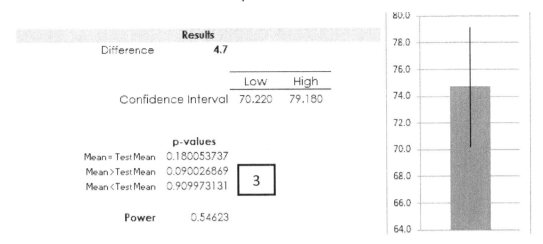

Results		
Difference	4.7	

	Low	High
Confidence Interval	70.220	79.180

p-values	
Mean = Test Mean	0.180053737
Mean > Test Mean	0.090026869
Mean < Test Mean	0.909973131

3

Power	0.54623

R solution

Enter the following commands:

bench.t.fromsummary(74.7,70,12.9,15)

ci.t.fromsummary(74.7,12.9,15,.8)

The result is:

```
> bench.t.fromsummary(74.7,70,12.9,15)

RESULTS

t: 1.411087
df: 14
Probability of exceeding benchmark: 0.9099731 (p < 0.09002687 )
Probability of being below benchmark: 0.09002687 (p < 0.9099731 )

> ci.t.fromsummary(74.7,12.9,15,.8)

RESULTS: 80% CONFIDENCE INTERVAL

Upper limit: 79.17998
Mean: 74.7
Lower limit: 70.22002
Margin of error: 4.479981
Standard error: 3.330766
Critical value of t: 1.345030
```

Exercise 4: Comparison of mean Likert score to benchmark

From page(s): 58-59

Problem: Twelve users attempted to locate a toy on the toysrus.com website and rated the difficulty of the task an average of 5.6 ($s = 1.4$) on a 7-point scale (where a 7 means very easy). Is there evidence that the average rating is greater than 5?

Answer: In this problem we need to determine if the observed mean of 5.6, given a sample size of 12 (so there are 11 degrees of freedom) and standard deviation of 1.4, is significantly greater than the benchmark of 5. Using a one-tailed one-sample *t*-test, the probability of this result is .08, just achieving statistical significance if the rejection criterion were set to .10. An 80% confidence interval ranges from 5.05 to 6.15. As in Exercise 3, the lower limit of the confidence interval just exceeds the benchmark, so there is reasonable, though not overwhelming, evidence of having met the goal.

Excel solution

1. Click on the Rating Scale Scores against a Criterion (Summary) link under the Test a Mean or Proportion to Criterion section.

2. Enter the mean, standard deviation, sample size and Test Benchmark (5) in the Input section.

3. Set the confidence level to 80%.

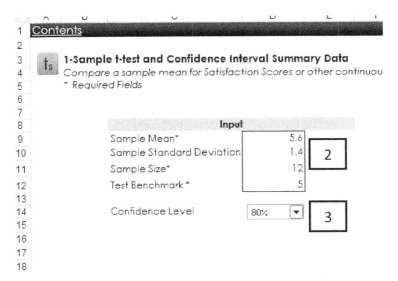

4. The one-tailed *p*-value of .083 is in the Results section along with the 80% confidence interval.

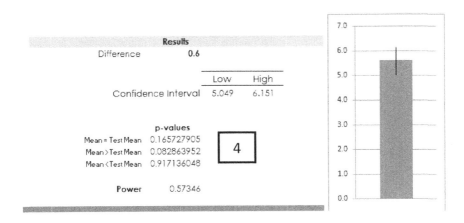

R solution

Enter the following commands:

    bench.t.fromsummary(5.6,5,1.4,12)

    ci.t.fromsummary(5.6,1.4,12,.8)

The result is:

```
> bench.t.fromsummary(5.6,5,1.4,12)

RESULTS

t: 1.484615
df: 11
Probability of exceeding benchmark: 0.917136 (p < 0.08286395 )
Probability of being below benchmark: 0.08286395 (p < 0.917136 )

> ci.t.fromsummary(5.6,1.4,12,.8)

RESULTS: 80% CONFIDENCE INTERVAL

Upper limit: 6.151024
Mean: 5.6
Lower limit: 5.048976
Margin of error: 0.5510238
Standard error: 0.4041452
Critical value of t: 1.363430
```

Exercise 5: Comparison of completion times to benchmark

From page(s): 59

Problem: Six participants called an interactive voice response system to find out the appropriate replacement head for an electric shaver and the nearest location to pick one up. All participants completed the task successfully, with the following task completion times (in minutes): 3.4, 3.5, 1.7, 2.9, 2.5, and 3.2. Do the data support the claim that callers, on average, can complete this task in less than three minutes?

Answer: After converting the times to log-times and conducting a one-tailed one-sample *t*-test against the benchmark of 3 minutes, the probability of this outcome is just .27. There is only about a 73% chance that the mean completion time for the population is as low as 3 minutes. An 80% confidence interval around the geometric mean ranges from 2.4 to 3.3 minutes. Because this interval contains the benchmark, there is insufficient evidence to conclude that the design has met this goal.

Excel solution

1. Click on the Task Times against a Criterion link under the Test a Mean or Proportion to Criterion section.

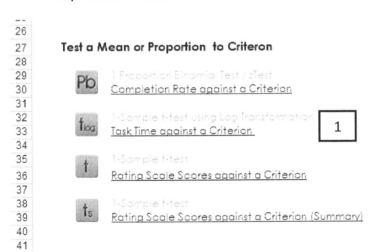

2. Click the "Clear Values" button to delete values from the raw data column (macros must be enabled) and enter in the raw times in the Raw Time Data column.

3. Set the confidence level to 80%.

4. Enter the Benchmark of 3 minutes.

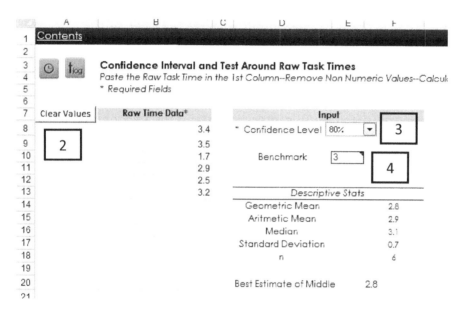

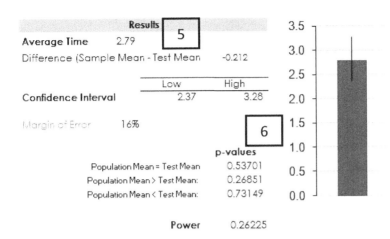

5. The average time (Geometric Mean in this example) is 2.79 minutes.

6. The one-tailed *p*-value of .26851 appears in the Results section along with the 80% confidence interval.

R solution

Enter the following commands (same pattern as used in Examples 17 and 18):

```
prob45 <- c(3.4,3.5,1.7,2.9,2.5,3.2)

prob45logs <- log(prob45)

prob45logs

compute.logsummary.fromarray(prob45,0)

log(3)

bench.t.fromarray.withlogconversion(prob45,3)

ci.t.fromarray.withlogconversion(prob45,.8)
```

The result is:

```
> prob45 <- c(3.4,3.5,1.7,2.9,2.5,3.2)
> prob45logs <- log(prob45)
> prob45logs
[1] 1.2237754 1.2527630 0.5306283 1.0647107 0.9162907 1.1631508
> compute.logsummary.fromarray(prob45,0)

RESULTS

Arithmetic mean: 2.866667
Median: 3.05
Geometric Mean: 2.787708
Mean of log data: 1.025220
Standard deviation of log data: 0.2713931
Variance of log data: 0.07365421
Standard error of the mean of the log data: 0.1107958
Sample size: 6
Value to use for log critical difference: 0

> log(3)
[1] 1.098612
> bench.t.fromarray.withlogconversion(prob45,3)

RESULTS

Arithmetic mean: 2.866667
Median: 3.05
Geometric mean: 2.787708
t: -0.6624122     df: 5
Probability of exceeding benchmark: 0.2685075 (p < 0.7314925 )
Probability of being below benchmark: 0.7314925 (p < 0.2685075 )

> ci.t.fromarray.withlogconversion(prob45,.8)

RESULTS: 80% CONFIDENCE INTERVAL

Arithmetic mean: 2.866667
Median: 3.05
Upper limit: 3.282947
Geometric Mean: 2.787708
Lower limit: 2.367177
Critical value of t: 1.475884
```

Chapter 5: Is There a Statistical Difference between Designs?

Abstract

This goal of this chapter is to cover methods for determining if a difference is statistically significant and how large or small of a difference likely exists in the untested population. It is important to account for chance differences when comparing two designs or products. To do this, you need to find a p-value from the appropriate statistical test. To understand the likely range of the difference between designs or products, you should compute a confidence interval around the difference. To determine which statistical test you need to use, you need to identify whether your outcome measure is binary or continuous and whether you have the same users in each group (within-subjects, assessed with a test for dependent data) or a different set of users (between-subjects, assessed with a test for independent data). When assessing differences between two designs, we recommend using two-tailed tests.

Example 1: Paired *t*-test of SUS questionnaire data (continuous, dependent)
From page(s): 62-64

Summary: In a test between two expense-reporting applications, 26 users worked (in random order) with two web-applications (A and B). They performed several tasks on both systems and then completed the 10-item System Usability Scale (SUS) questionnaire, with the results shown below. Is there a significant difference in the average ratings for the two applications?

User	A	B	Difference
1	77.5	60	17.5
2	90	62.5	27.5
3	80	45	35
4	77.5	20	57.5
5	100	80	20
6	95	42.5	52.5
7	82.5	32.5	50
8	97.5	80	17.5
9	80	52.5	27.5
10	87.5	60	27.5
11	77.5	42.5	35
12	87.5	87.5	0
13	82.5	52.5	30
14	50	10	40
15	77.5	67.5	10
16	82.5	40	42.5
17	80	57.5	22.5
18	65	32.5	32.5
19	72.5	67.5	5
20	85	47.5	37.5
21	80	45	35
22	100	62.5	37.5
23	80	40	40
24	57.5	45	12.5
25	97.5	65	32.5
26	95	72.5	22.5
Mean	82.2	52.7	29.5

Answer: Each participant used and rated each application, so this is a within-subjects experiment. Even though, strictly speaking, SUS scores are not continuous, they are continuous enough to use an independent groups *t*-test to assess the data. The mean difference is 29.5, with a standard deviation of 14.125. With 26 scores, the number of degrees of freedom for the test is 25 (n - 1). The result of the *t*-test is $t(25) = 10.656$, $p = .0000000001$. This *p*-value is well below the standard rejection criterion of .05, so the result is highly significant, especially given the relatively small sample size. A 95% confidence interval around the mean difference ranges from 23.8 to 35.2, so not only is a difference of 0 implausible, it is also implausible that the true difference is less than 23 or more than 35.

James R. Lewis & Jeff Sauro

Excel solution

1. Click the Task Times and Rating Scale Scores from the Same Users link under the Compare Two Means or Proportions heading.

Compare Two Means or Proportions

2p	2 Proportion Test 2 Completion Rates
2t	2 Sample t-test Task Times and Satisfaction Scores
2ts	2 Sample t-test Task Times and Rating Scale Scores (Summary)
tt	Paired t-test Task Times and Rating Scale Scores from the Same Users 1
pp	McNemar Chi-Square Exact Test 2 Completion Rates from the Same Users

2. Clear out any values in the calculator by clicking the "Clear Values" button (macros must be enabled).

3. Enter the raw values in columns labeled A and B. Do not enter or delete the values in the "Difference" column. These are the automatically computed difference scores for each participant (A minus B).

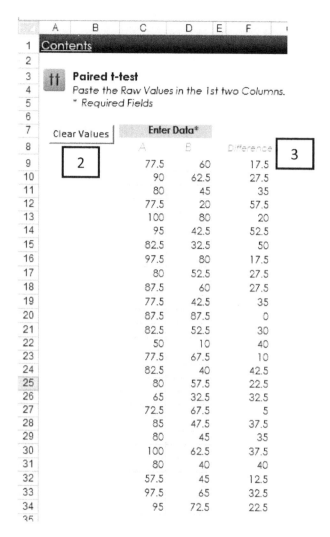

			A	B	Difference
			77.5	60	17.5
			90	62.5	27.5
			80	45	35
			77.5	20	57.5
			100	80	20
			95	42.5	52.5
			82.5	32.5	50
			97.5	80	17.5
			80	52.5	27.5
			87.5	60	27.5
			77.5	42.5	35
			87.5	87.5	0
			82.5	52.5	30
			50	10	40
			77.5	67.5	10
			82.5	40	42.5
			80	57.5	22.5
			65	32.5	32.5
			72.5	67.5	5
			85	47.5	37.5
			80	45	35
			100	62.5	37.5
			80	40	40
			57.5	45	12.5
			97.5	65	32.5
			95	72.5	22.5

4. Set the confidence level to 95%.

5. Set the difference to detect to 0.

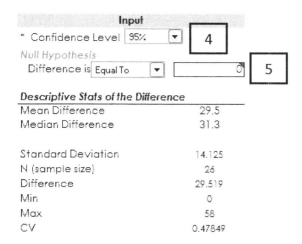

6. The *p*-value appears in the results section (*p* < .000001) along with the 95% confidence interval around the difference.

7. The results also include graphs of the difference between the means and the confidence interval around the difference.

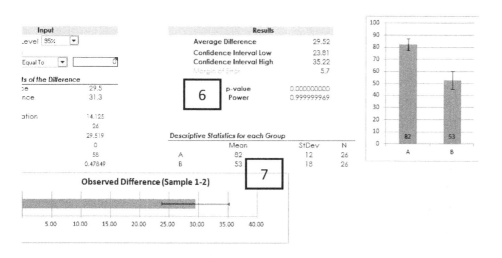

R solution

Enter the following commands:

getdata.fromweb("table501.txt")

test.t.paired.fromarrays(A,B,.95)

The first command gets the data in the table (which is Table 5.1 from the second edition of *Quantifying the User Experience: Practical Statistics for User Research*) from Jim's website (you need to be connected to the Web for this to work, but these days, who isn't). Getting this table creates the variables A and B. The second command uses that data from A and B and the designated confidence (.95 for 95%) to perform a *t*-test and compute the appropriate confidence interval. The result is:

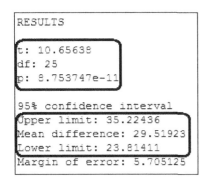

```
RESULTS

t: 10.65638
df: 25
p: 8.753747e-11

95% confidence interval
Upper limit: 35.22436
Mean difference: 29.51923
Lower limit: 23.81411
Margin of error: 5.705125
```

For a version of the first command that you can modify to input data from tables on your local computer, see "getdata.fromfile" in the Appendix.

Example 2: Paired *t*-test of completion time data (continuous, dependent)

From page(s): 65-66

Summary: In the same test of two accounting systems used in Example 1, task times were also collected. One task asked users to create an expense report. Of the 26 users who attempted the task, 21 completed it successfully on both products. These 21 task times and their difference scores appear in Table 5.2. Failed task attempts are indicated with NA and not included in the calculation. For the successful completions, is there a significant difference in completion times?

User	A	B	Difference
1	223	NA	NA
2	140	NA	NA
3	178	184	-6
4	145	195	-50
5	256	NA	NA
6	148	210	-62
7	222	299	-77
8	141	148	-7
9	149	184	-35
10	150	NA	NA
11	133	229	-96
12	160	NA	NA
13	117	200	-83
14	292	549	-257
15	127	235	-108
16	151	210	-59
17	127	218	-91
18	211	196	15
19	106	162	-56
20	121	176	-55
21	146	269	-123
22	135	336	-201
23	111	167	-56
24	116	203	-87
25	187	247	-60
26	120	174	-54
Mean	**158**	**228**	**-77**

Answer: On average, the completion time for A was 77 seconds faster than B, with a standard deviation of 61 seconds. With 21 times, the number of degrees of freedom for the paired t-test is 20 (n - 1). The result is $t(20) = -5.72$, $p = .00001$, so there is strong evidence that users take less time to complete an expense report on Product A. The 95% confidence interval for this difference ranges from about -49 to -104 seconds – a difference that users are likely to notice.

Excel solution

1. From the "Paired t-test" tab, clear out any values in the calculator by clicking the "Clear Values" button (macros must be enabled).

2. Enter the raw values in columns labeled A and B. For values that are NA leave the cell blank. Do not enter or delete the automatically computed values in the "Difference" column.

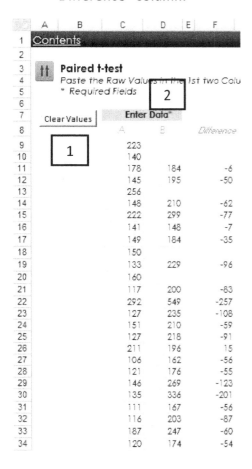

	A	B	C	D	E	F
1	Contents					
2						
3	††	**Paired t-test**				
4		Paste the Raw Values in the 1st two Colu				
5		* Required Fields		2		
6						
7		Clear Values	Enter Data*			
8			A	B		Difference
9		1	223			
10			140			
11			178	184		-6
12			145	195		-50
13			256			
14			148	210		-62
15			222	299		-77
16			141	148		-7
17			149	184		-35
18			150			
19			133	229		-96
20			160			
21			117	200		-83
22			292	549		-257
23			127	235		-108
24			151	210		-59
25			127	218		-91
26			211	196		15
27			106	162		-56
28			121	176		-55
29			146	269		-123
30			135	336		-201
31			111	167		-56
32			116	203		-87
33			187	247		-60
34			120	174		-54

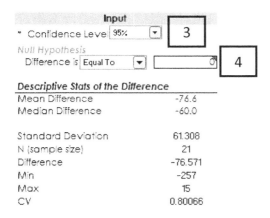

* Confidence Leve| 95%   ▼   3

Null Hypothesis
Difference is| Equal To | ▼ | Ò| 4

Descriptive Stats of the Difference

Mean Difference	-76.6
Median Difference	-60.0
Standard Deviation	61.308
N (sample size)	21
Difference	-76.571
Min	-257
Max	15
CV	0.80066

3. Set the confidence level to 95%.

4. Set the difference to detect to 0.

5. The *p*-value appears in the results section (*p* < .000001) along with the 95% confidence interval around the difference. Negative values are in parentheses.

6. The results include graphs of the difference between the means and the confidence interval around the difference. The interval for the observed difference does not cross 0.

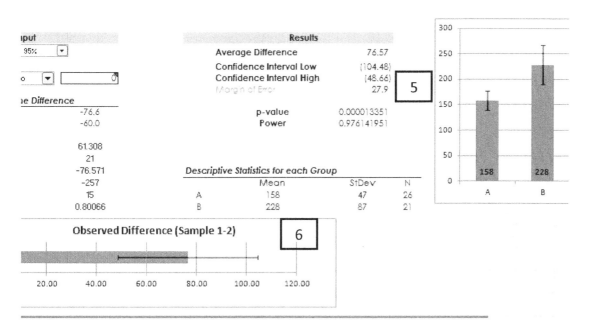

iput

95%   ▼

o ▼ | Ò|

ıe Difference

-76.6
-60.0

61.308
21
-76.571
-257
15
0.80066

Results

Average Difference	76.57
Confidence Interval Low	(104.48)
Confidence Interval High	(48.66)
Margin of Error	27.9

5

p-value	0.000013351
Power	0.976141951

Descriptive Statistics for each Group

	Mean	StDev	N
A	158	47	26
B	228	87	21

Observed Difference (Sample 1-2)   6

20.00   40.00   60.00   80.00   100.00   120.00

R solution

Enter the following commands:

getdata.fromweb("table502.txt")

test.t.paired.fromarrays(A,B,.95)

As in the previous example, the first command gets the data from a table stored on Jim's website, which puts the data for A and B into the variables of the same name. The second function uses those variables and the designated confidence level to compute the t-test and confidence interval. The result is:

```
RESULTS

t: -5.723478
df: 20
p: 1.335086e-05

95% confidence interval
Upper limit: -48.66441
Mean difference: -76.57143
Lower limit: -104.4784
Margin of error: 27.90702
```

Example 3: Independent groups *t*-test of SUS data (continuous, independent)

From page(s): 67-70

Summary: In a test between two CRM applications, the following SUS scores were obtained after 11 users attempted tasks on Product A and 12 different users attempted the same tasks on Product B (for a total of 23 different users). Is the difference in average SUS scores between the applications statistically significant?

A	B
50	50
45	52.5
57.5	52.5
47.5	50
52.5	52.5
57.5	47.5
52.5	50
50	50
52.5	50
55	40
47.5	42.5
	57.5
51.6	**49.6**

Answer: Product A had a mean SUS score of 51.6 (s = 4.07) and Product B had a mean SUS score of 49.6 (s = 4.6) – a difference of 2 points. For this test, there are 20 degrees of freedom, and the outcome is $t(20)$ = 1.1, p = .28. Because this value is rather large (well above .10), the difference is not significant (not appreciably greater than chance). The probability that this difference of 2 points is due to chance is 28.16%, so we can be only about 71.8% sure that products A and B have different SUS scores – a level of certainty that is better than 50-50 but that falls well below the usual criterion for claiming a significant difference. Product A's SUS score of 51.6, while higher, is not statistically distinguishable from Product B's score of 49.6 at this sample size and amount of score variance. The 95% confidence interval around this mean difference ranges from -1.8 to 5.8. Because the interval contains zero, we can't be 95% sure that a difference exists; we're only 71.8% sure. Although Product A appears to be a little better than Product B, the confidence interval tells us that there is still a modest chance that Product B has a higher SUS score (by as much as 1.8 points).

Excel solution

1. Click the Task Times and Rating Scale Scores link under the Compare Two Means or Proportions heading.

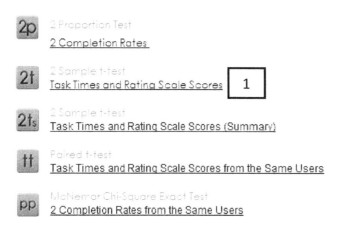

2. Clear out any values in the calculator by clicking the "Clear Values" button (macros must be enabled). Enter the values in the Enter Data section for both products.

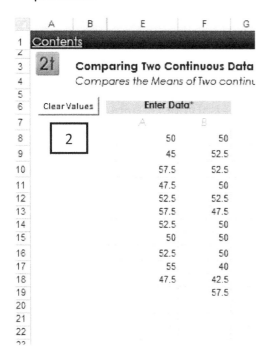

3. Set the confidence level to 95%.

4. The mean, standard deviation and sample size for both groups will be in the Results section.

5. The *p*-value (.2816) and the 95% confidence interval are in the Results section.

6. The graph of the difference between means shows that the confidence interval crosses 0, which means we cannot be 95% confident a difference exists between the means.

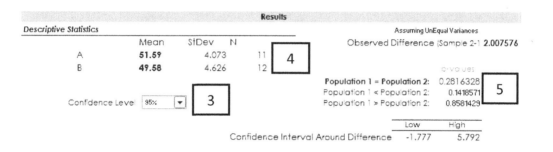

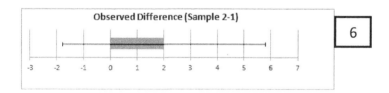

R solution

Enter the following commands:

```
A <- c(50,45,57.5,47.5,52.5,57.5,52.5,50,52.5,55,47.5)

B <- c(50,52.5,52.5,50,52.5,47.5,50,50,50,40,42.5,57.5)

test.t.independent.fromarrays(A,B,.95)
```

The first two commands put the data into the variables A and B. The third command uses A and B and the designated level of confidence (.95 for 95%) to compute the *t*-test and confidence interval. The result is:

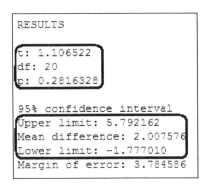

```
RESULTS

t: 1.106522
df: 20
p: 0.2816328

95% confidence interval
Upper limit: 5.792162
Mean difference: 2.007576
Lower limit: -1.777010
Margin of error: 3.784586
```

Example 4: Independent groups *t*-test of time data (continuous, independent)

From page(s): 70-71

Summary: Twenty users successfully added a contact to a CRM application. Eleven users completed the task on the existing version and nine different users completed the same task on the new enhanced version. Is there compelling evidence to conclude that there has been a reduction in the mean time to complete the task? The raw values (in seconds) appear below.

Old	New
18	12
44	35
35	21
78	9
38	2
18	10
16	5
22	38
40	30
77	
20	

Answer: The mean task time for the 11 users of the old version was 37 seconds with a standard deviation of 22.4 seconds. The mean task time for the 9 users of the new version was 18 seconds with a standard deviation of 13.4 seconds. With a 21-second difference in means and 16 degrees of freedom, this was a significant result ($t(16)$ = 2.33, p = .033). The 95% confidence interval for the difference in mean times ranges from 2 to 36 seconds.

Excel solution

1. From the "2 Sample t" tab, clear out any values using the "Clear Values" button (macros must be enabled) and enter the values in the Enter Data section for both products. Optionally, you can add the labels "Old" and "New."

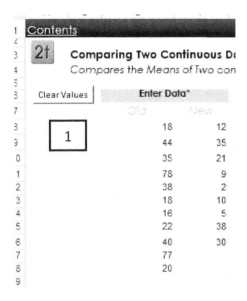

2. Set the confidence level to 95%.

3. The mean, standard deviation and sample size appears for both groups in the Results section.

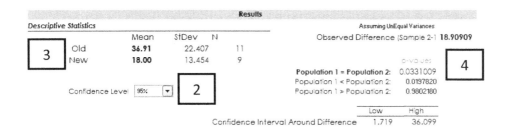

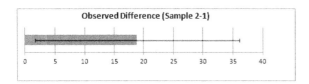

4. The *p*-value (.033) and the 95% confidence interval are in the Results section.

5. Corroborating the *p*-value, the graph of the difference between means shows that the confidence interval does not cross 0, so we can be at least 95% confident a difference exists between the means.

R solution

Enter the following commands:

Old <- c(18,44,35,78,38,18,16,22,40,77,20)

New <- c(12,35,21,9,2,10,5,38,30)

test.t.independent.fromarrays(Old,New,.95)

The first two commands put the data into the variables Old and New. The third command uses Old and New and the designated level of confidence (.95 for 95%) to compute the *t*-test and confidence interval. The result is:

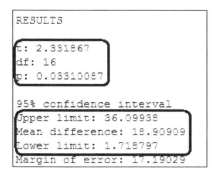

```
RESULTS

t: 2.331867
df: 16
p: 0.03310087

95% confidence interval
Upper limit: 36.09938
Mean difference: 18.90909
Lower limit: 1.718797
Margin of error: 17.19029
```

Example 5: Chi-squared test of 2x2 contingency table (binary, independent)

From page(s): 74

Summary: If 40 out of 60 (67%) users complete a task on Design A, can we conclude it is statistically different from Design B where 15 out of 35 (43%) different users passed? Setting this up in a contingency table we have:

	Pass	Fail	Total
Design A	40 (*a*)	20 (*b*)	60 (*m*)
Design B	15 (*c*)	20 (*d*)	35 (*n*)
Total	55 (*r*)	40 (*s*)	95 (*N*)

Answer: Assessing this with a standard chi-squared test, we get $\chi^2(1) = 5.14$, $p = .0234$ (the degrees of freedom for a 2x2 contingency table is always 1). This small p-value indicates a statistically significant outcome – the evidence supports the claim that the successful completion rate for Design A is higher than for Design B.

Excel solution

1. Click the "2+ Large Sample Completion Rates" link under the Compare 3 or More Means or Proportions heading.

Compare 3 or More Means or Proportions

2. Enter the number of users who passed and failed for each design in the Input section. The Row and Column labels are optional.

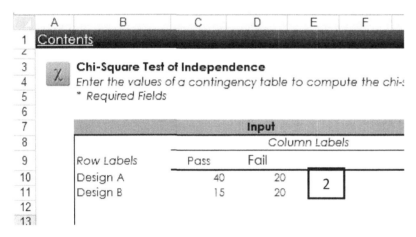

3. The p-value (.0234) appears in the Results section.

Results	
Chi-Square	5.141
Degrees of Freedom	1
p-value	0.0233713 3

How to Report

There is a   97.663%   chance at least 1 population proportion is different.

Calculations

R solution

Enter the following command:

test.twobytwo.independent(40,20,15,20,.95)

This command processes independent 2x2 contingency tables, taking as input the table values for *a*, *b*, *c*, and *d* in that order, followed by the desired level for the confidence interval (.95 for 95%). The result is:

```
RESULTS

Recommended test: N-1 Chi-Squared Test

N-1 chi-squared: 5.08658
df: 1
p: 0.02411170

N-1 two-proportion z: 2.255345
p: 0.02411170

95% confidence interval of difference between proportions
p1: 0.6666667
p2: 0.4285714
Adjusted value of p1: 0.6614968
Adjusted value of p2: 0.4322874
Adjusted difference: 0.2292094
Margin of error: 0.1985599
Upper limit: 0.4277693
Maximum likelihood estimate (observed difference): 0.2380952
Lower limit: 0.03064956

Fisher Exact Probability: 0.03145601

Standard chi-squared: 5.140693
df: 1
p: 0.02337132

Standard chi-squared with Yates correction: 4.210356
df: 1
p: 0.04017791
```

Note that for the data in this example, the standard chi-squared is not the preferred test. For more information, see Example 6.

Example 6: Various tests of 2x2 contingency table (binary, independent)

From page(s): 75-80

Summary: Recent research (Campbell, 2007) has shown that an alternative form of the standard chi-squared test – the *N*-1 chi-squared test – generally works better with small samples, as long as the expected number in each cell of the 2x2 table is greater than or equal to 1. When that condition isn't true, the Fisher exact test is better. In this example, assume 11 of 12 users (92%) completed a task on Design A; 5 out of 10 (50%) completed it on Design B. Does this outcome indicate a significantly better completion rate for Design A?

Answer: For this data, the appropriate test is the *N*-1 chi-squared test, which is $\chi^2(1)$ = 4.557, *p* = .0328. A 95% confidence interval around the difference of .338 between these independent proportions ranges from .022 to .697. That is, we can be 95% confident that the plausible range for the difference between design completion rates is between 2% and 70%, significantly favoring Design A.

Excel solution

1. Click the 2 Completion Rates link under the Compare Two Means or Proportions heading.

2. Enter the number that passed in the Success field and the total sample size in the Total field for both groups.

3. Set the confidence level (around the difference between means) to 95%.

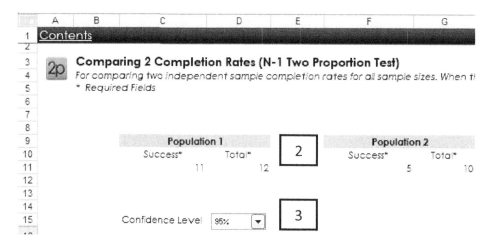

4. The *p*-value (.03278) and confidence interval around the difference are in the Results section. The upper boundary of the interval (-.022) does not cross 0.

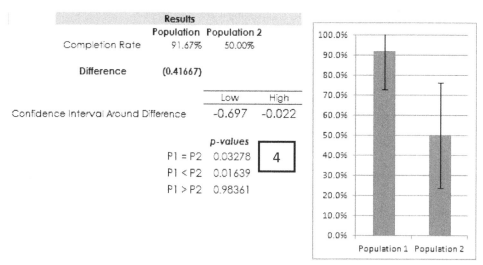

Note: The negative confidence interval values are from the calculator subtracting Population 1 from Population 2. Subtracting Population 2 from 1 would generate the same p-value and have the confidence interval equal to .022 to .697.

R solution

Enter the following command:

    test.twobytwo.independent(11,1,5,5,.95)

This command processes independent 2x2 contingency tables, taking as input the table values for *a*, *b*, *c*, and *d* in that order, followed by the desired level for the confidence interval (.95 for 95%). The result is:

```
RESULTS

Recommended test: N-1 Chi-Squared Test

N-1 chi-squared: 4.557292
df: 1
p: 0.03277887

N-1 two-proportion z: 2.134781
p: 0.03277887

95% confidence interval of difference between proportions
p1: 0.9166667
p2: 0.5
Adjusted value of p1: 0.8591766
Adjusted value of p2: 0.5
Adjusted difference: 0.3591766
Margin of error: 0.3375658
Upper limit: 0.6967424
Maximum likelihood estimate (observed difference): 0.4166667
Lower limit: 0.02161079

Fisher Exact Probability: 0.05572755

Standard chi-squared: 4.774306
df: 1
p: 0.02888750

Standard chi-squared with Yates correction: 2.904688
df: 1
p: 0.08832237
```

Example 7: Comparison of success rates (binary, independent)

From page(s): 80-81

Summary: A new version of a CRM software application was created to improve the process of adding contacts to a distribution list. Four out of nine users (44.4%) completed the task on the old version and eleven out of 12 (91.7%) completed it on the new version. Is there compelling evidence that the new design improves completion rates?

Answer: Given the data in this form, the appropriate test to use is the *N*-1 two-proportion test, which is mathematically equivalent to the *N*-1 chi-squared test. For this test, the result is $z = 2.313$, $p = .0207$. The 95% confidence interval around the observed difference of .473 ranges from .058 to .752, that is, we can be 95% confident the actual improvement in completion rates on the new task design is somewhere between 6% and 75%.

Excel solution

1. From the "2 Comp Rates" tab, enter the total successes and total number tested for both groups.

2. Set the confidence level (around the difference between proportions) to 95%.

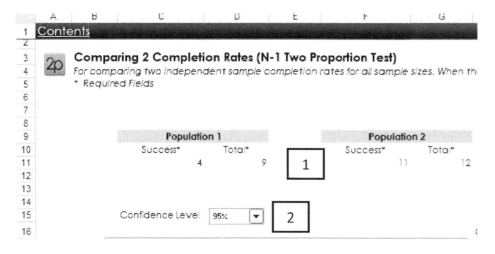

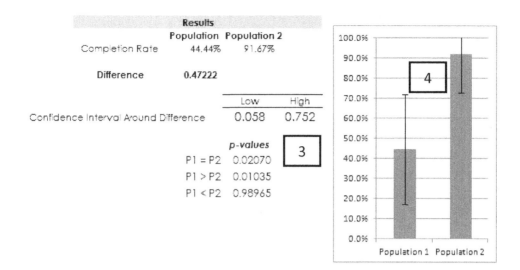

3. The *p*-value (.0207) and associated confidence intervals are in the Results section. The lower boundary of the interval (.058) does not cross 0.

4. Consistent with the *p*-value, the graph of the proportions shows the confidence intervals do not overlap.

R solution

Enter the following command:

    test.nminusonetwoproportion.givenxandn(4,9,11,12,.95)

This command takes as input the number of successes for the first condition, the sample size for the first condition, the number of successes for the second condition, and the sample size for the second condition, followed by the desired level for the confidence interval (.95 for 95%). The result is:

```
RESULTS

N-1 Two-Proportion z: -2.313407
p: 0.02070027

95% confidence interval of difference between proportions
p1: 0.4444444
p2: 0.9166667
P: 0.7142857
Adjusted value of p1: 0.4542155
Adjusted value of p2: 0.8591766
Adjusted difference: -0.4049611
Margin of error: 0.3472612
Upper limit: -0.05769988
Maximum likelihood estimate (observed difference): -0.4722222
Lower limit: -0.7522223
```

Example 8: Comparison of conversion rates (binary, independent)

From page(s): 82

Summary: An A/B test was conducted live on an e-commerce website for two weeks to determine which product page converted more users to purchase a product. 455 users experienced Concept A and 37 (8.13%) of those purchased the product. 438 different users experienced Concept B and of those 22 (5.02%) purchased the product. Is there compelling evidence that the conversion rate for one concept is better than the other?

Answer: Given the form of this data, the *N*-1 two-proportion test is appropriate (z = 1.87, p = .06) – a statistically significant outcome if setting the rejection criterion to .10; not significant if using the standard criterion of .05. In practice, it would probably be wise to consider this a significant result. There is about a 94% probability the completion rates are different.   A 90% confidence interval around the difference in conversion rates (3.1%) ranges from 0.4 to 5.8%. That is, if all users experienced Concept A, we would expect it to convert between 0.4% and 6% more users than Concept B. As with any confidence interval, the actual long term conversion rate is more likely to be closer to the middle value of 3.1% than to either of the extreme end-points. For many large-volume e-commerce websites, even the small lower limit estimated advantage of 0.4% for Concept A could translate into considerably greater revenue.

Excel solution

1. From the "2 Comp Rates" tab, enter the total successes and total number tested for both groups.

2. Set the confidence level (around the difference between proportions) to 95%.

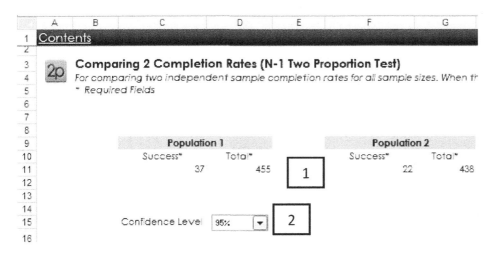

3. The *p*-value (.06166) and associated confidence intervals are in the Results section.

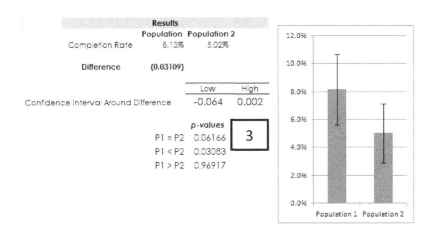

R solution

Enter the following command:

test.nminusonetwoproportion.givenxandn(37,455,22,438,.9)

This command takes as input the number of conversions for the first condition, the sample size for the first condition, the number of conversions for the second condition, and the sample size for the second condition, followed by the desired level for the confidence interval (.9 for 90%). The result is:

```
RESULTS

N-1 Two-Proportion z: 1.868711
p: 0.06166309

90% confidence interval of difference between proportions
p1: 0.08131868
p2: 0.05022831
P: 0.06606943
Adjusted value of p1: 0.08255978
Adjusted value of p2: 0.05161316
Adjusted difference: 0.03094662
Margin of error: 0.027395
Upper limit: 0.05834162
Maximum likelihood estimate (observed difference): 0.03109037
Lower limit: 0.00355162
```

Example 9: Comparison of success rates (binary, dependent)

From page(s): 84-89

Summary: Fifteen users attempted the same task on two different designs. The completion rate on Design A was 87% and on Design B was 53%. The following table shows how each user performed, with 0's representing failed task attempts and 1's for passing attempts. Do the data indicate a significant difference in successful completions between the two designs?

User	Design A	Design B
1	1	0
2	1	1
3	1	1
4	1	0
5	1	0
6	1	1
7	1	1
8	0	1
9	1	0
10	1	1
11	0	0
12	1	1
13	1	0
14	1	1
15	1	0
Comp	87%	53%

Answer: For these data, the appropriate test is the McNemar test using mid-probabilities. A McNemar test focuses on the discordant pairs – those users who succeeded with one design but failed with the other, as shown in the table below (see cells b and c).

	Design B Pass	Design B Fail	Total
Design A Pass	7 (*a*)	6 (*b*)	13 (*m*)
Design A Fail	1 (*c*)	1 (*d*)	2 (*n*)
Total	8 (*r*)	7 (*s*)	15 (*N*)

The two-tailed probability of this outcome is .0704, a significant difference if the rejection criterion is .10; not significant if the rejection criterion is the standard .05. Thus, the probability is .0704 that 1 out of 7 users will perform better on Design A than B if there really was no difference. Put another way, we can be about 93% sure Design A has a better completion rate than Design B. A 95% confidence interval around the observed difference of 34% ranges from 0.1 to 59.1%.

Excel solution

1. Click the 2 Completion Rates from the Same Users link under the Compare Two Means or Proportions heading.

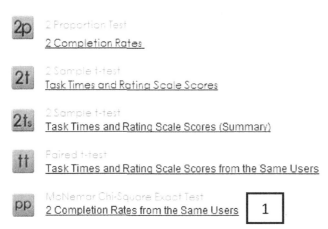

2. Clear out any previous values using the "Clear Values" button (macros must be enabled) and enter in the 1's or 0's for each user on both designs.

3. Set the confidence level (around the difference between proportions) to 95%.

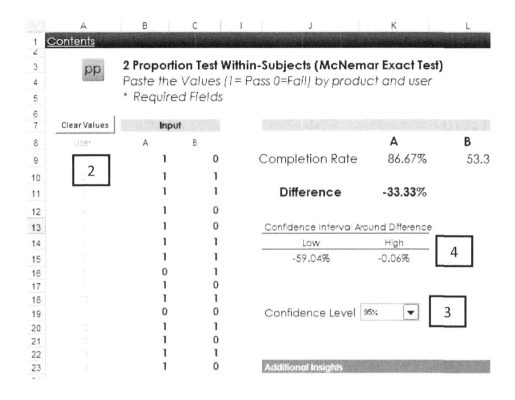

4. The confidence interval around the difference is in the Results section.

5. The *p*-value (.0703) is also in the Results section.

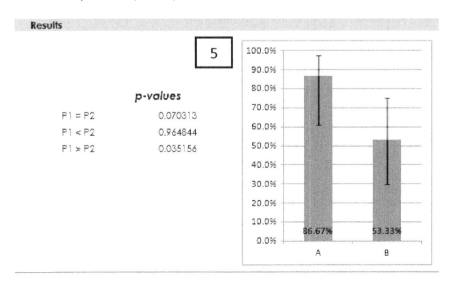

R solution

Enter the following command:

test.twobytwo.dependent(7,6,1,1,.95)

This command requires the dependent 2x2 table values of *a*, *b*, *c*, and *d* in that order, followed by the desired level for the confidence interval (.95 for 95%). The result is:

```
RESULTS

McNemar Mid Probability (recommended): (0.0703125)

Alternate analyses (not recommended)
McNemar Exact Probability: 0.125
McNemar Chi-Squared: 3.571429    df: 1    p: 0.05878172
McNemar z: -1.889822    p: 0.05878172
McNemar Chi-Squared with Yates Correction: 2.285714    df: 1    p: 0.1305700

95% CONFIDENCE INTERVAL

p1: 0.8666667
p2: 0.5333333
Adjusted value of p1: 0.8250451
Adjusted value of p2: 0.5295496
Adjusted difference in p: -0.2954955
Margin of error: 0.2949261
Upper limit: (-0.0005694156)
Observed difference: -0.3333333
Lower limit: (-0.5904217)
```

Example 10: Comparison of success rates (binary, dependent)

From page(s): 90-93

Summary: In a comparative usability test, 14 users attempted to rent the same type of car in the same city on two different websites (Avis.com and Enterprise.com). All 14 users completed the task on Avis.com but only 10 of 14 completed it on Enterprise.com. The users and their task results appear below. Is there sufficient evidence that more users could complete the task on Avis.com than on Enterprise.com (as designed at the time of this study)?

User	Avis.com	Enterprise.com
1	1	1
2	1	1
3	1	0
4	1	0
5	1	1
6	1	1
7	1	1
8	1	0
9	1	1
10	1	1
11	1	1
12	1	0
13	1	1
14	1	1
Comp	100%	71%

	Enterprise.com	Enterprise.com Fail	Total
Avis.com Pass	10 *(a)*	4 *(b)*	14 *(m)*
Avis.com Fail	0 *(c)*	0 *(d)*	0 *(n)*
Total	10*(r)*	4*(s)*	14 *(N)*

Answer: Again, the appropriate test is the McNemar test using mid-probabilities. The probability of this outcome if there is really no difference is .0625. A 95% confidence interval around the observed difference of 29% ranges from 0.5 to 49.5%. As in the previous example, the mid-*p* McNemar test fell just short of significance at the standard level of .05, but the 95% confidence interval excluded 0, indicating significance at the .05 level. With the outcome this close and significant according to the confidence interval, it seems wise to conclude that this is a significant difference.

Excel solution

1. From the "McNemar Exact Test" tab, clear out any previous values using the "Clear Values" button (macros must be enabled) and enter in the 1's or 0's for each user on both designs.

2. Set the confidence level (around the difference between means) to 95%.

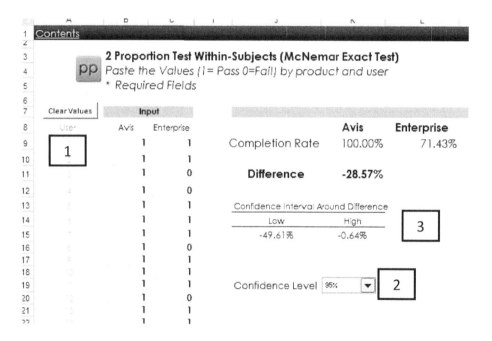

3. The confidence interval around the difference is in the Results section.

4. The *p*-value (.0625) is also in the Results section along with graphs of the 95% confidence intervals around each website.

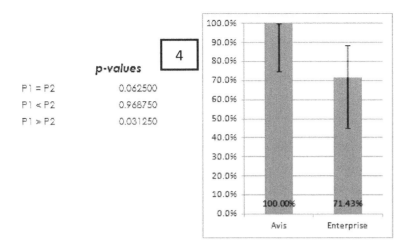

p-values	
P1 = P2	0.062500
P1 < P2	0.968750
P1 > P2	0.031250

R solution

Enter the following command:

```
test.twobytwo.dependent(10,4,0,0,.95)
```

This command requires the dependent 2x2 table values of *a*, *b*, *c*, and *d* in that order, followed by the desired level for the confidence interval (.95 for 95%). The result is:

```
RESULTS

McNemar Mid Probability (recommended): 0.0625

Alternate analyses (not recommended)
McNemar Exact Probability: 0.125
McNemar Chi-Squared: 4     df: 1     p: 0.04550026
McNemar z: -2     p: 0.04550026
McNemar Chi-Squared with Yates Correction: 2.25     df: 1     p: 0.1336144

95% CONFIDENCE INTERVAL

p1: 1
p2: 0.7142857
Adjusted value of p1: 0.9396783
Adjusted value of p2: 0.6884336
Adjusted difference in p: -0.2512448
Margin of error: 0.2448384
Upper limit: -0.006406363
Observed difference: -0.2857143
Lower limit: -0.4960832
```

Exercise 1: Comparison of SEQ ratings (continuous, independent)

From page(s): 97-98

Problem: Ten users completed the task to find the best priced non-stop roundtrip ticket on JetBlue.com. A different set of 14 users attempted the same task on AmericanAirlines.com. After each task attempt, the users answered the 7-point Single Ease Question (SEQ). Higher responses indicate an easier task. The mean response of JetBlue was 6.1 (s = .88) and the mean response on American Airlines was 4.86 (s = 1.61). Is there enough evidence from the sample to conclude that users think booking a flight on American Airlines is more difficult than on JetBlue? What is the likely range of the difference between mean ratings using a 90% level of confidence?

Answer: An independent groups *t*-test is appropriate for these data and indicates that users perceived that the task was easier on JetBlue. With a mean difference of 1.24 and 20 degrees of freedom, you get $t(20) = 2.42$, $p = .025$. The 90% confidence interval ranges from 0.36 to 2.12.

Excel solution

1. Click on the "Task Times and Rating Scale Scores (Summary)" link under the Compare Two Means or Proportions heading.

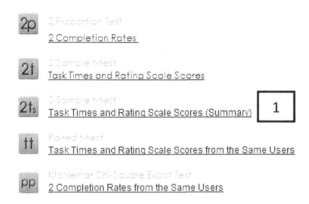

2. Enter the mean, standard deviation and sample size for both groups in the Input section.

3. Set the confidence level to 90%.

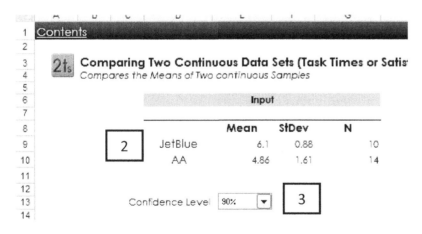

4. The *p*-value (.02517) appears in the Results section along with the 90% confidence interval around the difference between means.

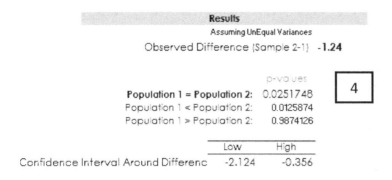

Results		
Assuming UnEqual Variances		
Observed Difference (Sample 2-1) -1.24		

	p-values	
Population 1 = Population 2:	0.0251748	
Population 1 < Population 2:	0.0125874	
Population 1 > Population 2:	0.9874126	

	Low	High
Confidence Interval Around Differenc	-2.124	-0.356

R solution

Enter the following command:

test.t.independent.fromsummary(6.1,.88,10,4.86,1.61,14,.9)

Use this command when you have summary data from this type of test. The inputs to the command are the mean of the first condition, the standard deviation of the first condition, the sample size of the first condition, the mean of the second condition, the standard deviation of the second condition, and the sample size of the second condition, followed by the desired level for the confidence interval (.9 for 90%). The result is:

```
RESULTS

t: 2.419817
df: 20
p: 0.02517479

90% confidence interval
Upper limit: 2.123807
Mean difference: 1.24
Lower limit: 0.3561934
Margin of error: 0.8838066
```

Exercise 2: Comparison of conversion rates (binary, independent)

From page(s): 98

Problem: An A/B test of two website designs investigated which would convert more users to register for a webinar. For Design A, 4 out of 109 converted. For Design B, 0 out of 88 converted. Is there enough evidence to conclude one design is better? What is the 90% confidence interval around the difference?

Answer: For these data, the appropriate test is an *N*-1 two-proportion test, with $z = 1.81$, $p = .07$. This means there is about a 93% chance the designs are different, which is probably strong enough evidence for most industrial circumstances. A 90% confidence interval around the observed difference of 3.67% ranges from about 0 to 7%.

Excel solution

1. Click on the "2 Completion Rates" link under the Compare Two Means or Proportions heading.

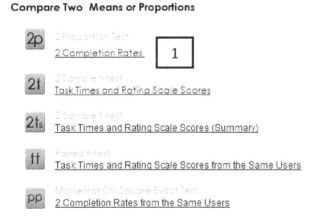

2. Enter the number of successes and the total number testes for each group.

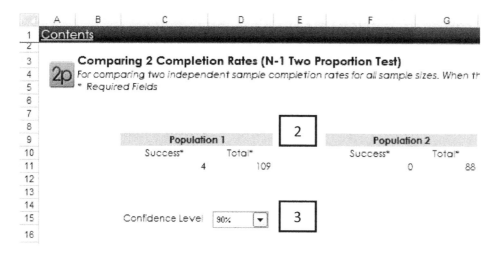

3. Set the confidence level to 90%.

4. The *p*-value (.07015) is in the Results section along with graphs of each conversion rate and the 90 % confidence interval around the difference (-.070 to 0).

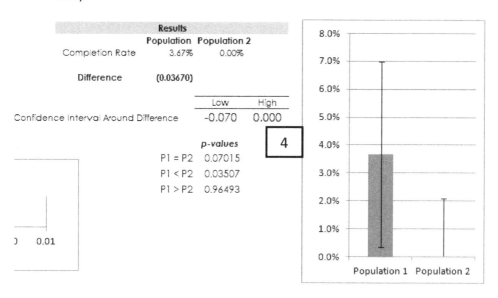

R solution

Enter the following command:

test.nminusonetwoproportion.givenxandn(4,109,0,88,.9)

Use this command when you know the number of conversions and sample sizes for the two conditions. The inputs to this command are the number of conversions for the first design, the sample size for the first design, the number of conversions for the second design, and the sample size for the second design, followed by the desired level for the confidence interval (.9 for 90%). The result is:

```
RESULTS

N-1 Two-Proportion z: 1.810954
p: 0.07014794

90% confidence interval of difference between proportions
p1: 0.03669725
p2: 0
P: 0.02030457
Adjusted value of p1: 0.0423767
Adjusted value of p2: 0.007569836
Adjusted difference: 0.03480686
Margin of error: 0.03496292
Upper limit: 0.06976978
Maximum likelihood estimate (observed difference): 0.03669725
Lower limit: -0.0001560615
```

Exercise 3: Comparison of recommendation scores (continuous, independent)

From page(s): 99

Problem: In a competitive analysis of travel websites, one set of 31 users completed tasks on Expedia.com and another set of 25 users completed the same tasks on Kayak.com. Users rated how likely they would be to recommend the website to a friend on an 11 point scale (0 to 10) with 10 being extremely likely. The mean score on Expedia.com was 7.32 (s = 1.87) and the mean score on Kayak.com was 5.72 (s = 2.99). Is there evidence that more people would likely recommend Expedia over Kayak.com? What is the plausible range for the difference between means using a 95% confidence interval?

Answer: The appropriate test is an independent groups *t*-test. With a mean difference of 1.6 and 38 degrees of freedom, the outcome is $t(38) = 2.33$, $p = .025$. A 95% confidence interval around the mean difference ranges from 0.2 to 3.0. These results significantly favor the Expedia.com website.

Excel solution

1. Click on the "Task Times and Rating Scale Scores (Summary)" link under the Compare Two Means or Proportions heading.

Compare Two Means or Proportions

2p 2 Proportion Test
2 Completion Rates

2t 2 Sample t-test
Task Times and Rating Scale Scores

2t$_s$ 2 Sample t-test
Task Times and Rating Scale Scores (Summary)   1

tt Paired t-test
Task Times and Rating Scale Scores from the Same Users

pp McNemar Chi-Square Exact Test
2 Completion Rates from the Same Users

2. Enter the mean, standard deviation and sample size for both groups in the Input section.

3. Set the confidence level to 95%.

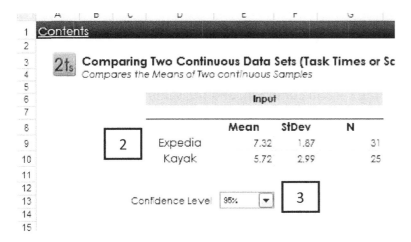

4. The *p*-value (.025) and 95% confidence interval around the difference between means are in the Results section.

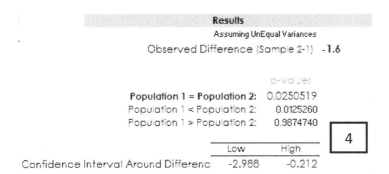

R solution

Enter the following command:

test.t.independent.fromsummary(7.32,1.87,31,5.72,2.99,25,.95)

Use this command when you have summary data from this type of test. The inputs to the command are the mean of the first condition, the standard deviation of the first condition, the sample size of the first condition, the mean of the second condition, the standard deviation of the second condition, and the sample size of the second condition, followed by the desired level for the confidence interval (.9 for 90%). The result is:

```
RESULTS

t: 2.332829
df: 38
p: 0.02505193

95% confidence interval
Upper limit: 2.988456
Mean difference: 1.6
Lower limit: 0.2115442
Margin of error: 1.388456
```

Exercise 4: Comparison of promotion rates (binary, independent)

From page(s): 99

Problem: Using the same set of data from Exercise 3, the responses were segmented into promoters, passive and detractors as shown in the table below. This process degrades a continuous measure into a discrete binary one (which is the typical approach when computing the Net Promoter Score). Is there evidence to conclude that there is a difference in the proportion of promoters (the top-two-box scores) between websites?

Website	Segment	Response Range	# of Responses
Expedia	Promoters	9-10	7
	Passive	7-8	14
	Detractors	0-6	10
Kayak	Promoters	9-10	5
	Passive	7-8	8
	Detractors	0-6	12

Answer: The appropriate test is the *N*-1 two-proportion test, with z = .232, p = .817. Given this sample there is only an 18.3% chance that the proportion of promoters is different between Expedia.com and Kayak.com. Note how the evidence for a difference has dropped when examining top-2-box scores compared to the difference between means in Exercise 3, with the plausible value of 0 almost exactly between the endpoints of the 90% confidence interval (ranging from -.16 to .20).

Excel solution

1. From the "2 Comp Rates" tab, enter 7 successes and 31 total for Expedia and 5 successes and 25 total for Kayak.

2. Set the Confidence Level to 90%.

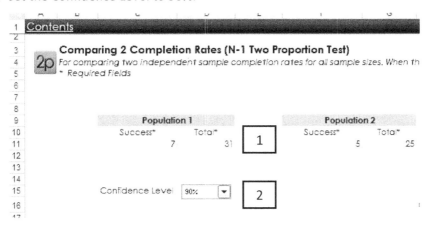

3. The *p*-value (.81664) along with the 90% confidence interval around the difference appears in the Results section.

James R. Lewis & Jeff Sauro

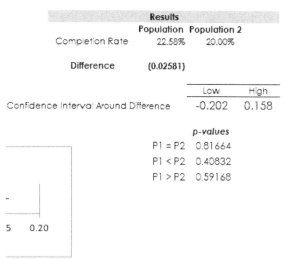

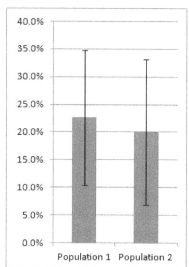

R solution

Enter the following command:

```
test.nminusonetwoproportion.givenxandn(7,31,5,25,.9)
```

Use this command when you know the number of promoters and sample sizes for the two conditions. The inputs to this command are the number of promoters for the first design, the sample size for the first design, the number of promoters for the second design, and the sample size for the second design, followed by the desired level for the confidence interval (.95 for 95%). The result is:

```
RESULTS

N-1 Two-Proportion z: 0.2318694
p: 0.8166394

90% confidence interval of difference between proportions
p1: 0.2258065
p2: 0.2
P: 0.2142857
Adjusted value of p1: 0.2372714
Adjusted value of p2: 0.2154000
Adjusted difference: 0.02187140
Margin of error: 0.1802361
Upper limit: 0.2021075
Maximum likelihood estimate (observed difference): 0.02580645
Lower limit: -0.1583647
```

Exercise 5: Comparison of success rates (binary, dependent)

From page(s): 100-101

Problem: The same fourteen users attempted to rent a car on two Rental Car websites: Budget.com and Enterprise.com. The order of presentation of the websites was counterbalanced, so half of the users worked with Budget first, and the other half with Enterprise. The table below shows which users were successful on which website. Is there enough evidence to conclude that the websites have different completion rates? How much of a difference, if any, likely exists between the completion rates (use a 90% level of confidence)?

User	Budget.com	Enterprise.com
1	1	1
2	1	1
3	1	0
4	1	0
5	0	1
6	1	1
7	1	1
8	0	0
9	1	1
10	1	1
11	1	1
12	1	0
13	1	1
14	1	1
Comp	86%	71%

Answer: The appropriate test for these data is a mid-*p* McNemar test. The table below shows the discordant pairs (cells b and c).

	Enterprise.com	Enterprise.com	Total
Budget.com	9 (a)	3 (b)	12 *(m)*
Budget.com Fail	1 (c)	1 (d)	2 *(n)*
Total	10 *(r)*	5 *(s)*	14 *(N)*

Three users performed worse on Enterprise.com and one performed better. The probability of this result if there really is no difference is .375. There's only a 62.5% chance the completion rates are different given the data from this sample. Although the observed completion rates are different, they aren't different enough for us to conclude that Budget.com's completion rate on this task is significantly different from Enterprise.com's. The 90% confidence interval for the difference in the proportions ranges from -9.5% to 35.5%. Because the interval includes 0, this also tells us there's less than a 90% chance that the completion rates are different.

Excel solution

1. Click the 2 Completion Rates from the Same Users link under the Compare Two Means or Proportions heading.

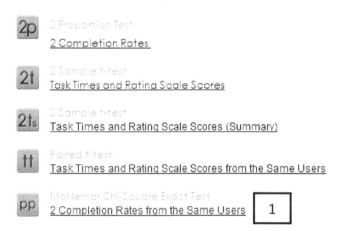

2. Clear out any previous values using the "Clear Values" button (macros must be enabled) and enter in the 1's or 0's for each user on both designs.

3. Set the confidence level (around the difference between proportions) to 90%.

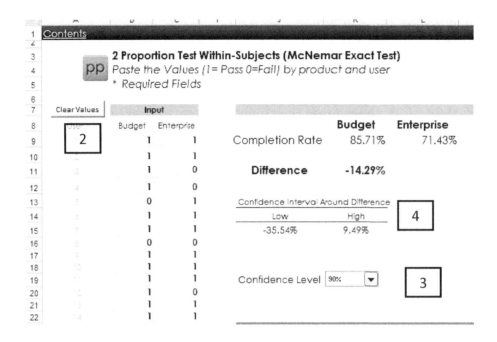

4. The confidence interval around the difference is in the Results section.

5. The *p*-value (.375) appears in the Results section.

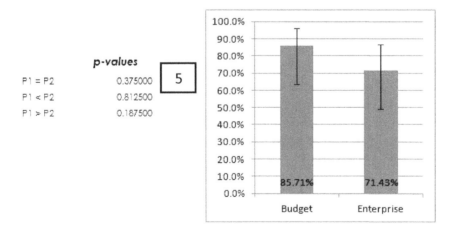

R solution

Enter the following command:

test.twobytwo.dependent(9,3,1,1,.9)

This command requires the dependent 2x2 table values of a, b, c, and d in that order, followed by the desired level for the confidence interval (.9 for 90%). The result is:

```
RESULTS

McNemar Mid Probability (recommended) ( 0.375 )

Alternate analyses (not recommended)
McNemar Exact Probability: 0.625
McNemar Chi-Squared: 1     df: 1      p: 0.3173105
McNemar z: -1     p: 0.3173105
McNemar Chi-Squared with Yates Correction: 0.25     df: 1     p: 0.6170751

90% CONFIDENCE INTERVAL

p1: 0.8571429
p2: 0.7142857
Adjusted value of p1: 0.8256741
Adjusted value of p2: 0.6954045
Adjusted difference in p: -0.1302696
Margin of error: 0.2251373
Upper limit: 0.09486766
Observed difference: -0.1428571
Lower limit: -0.3554069
```

Exercise 6: Comparison of SUS questionnaire scores (continuous, dependent)

From page(s): 101

Problem: After completing five tasks on both Budget.com and Enterprise.com, the fourteen users from Exercise 5 completed the System Usability Scale (see the following table). The mean SUS scores were 80.4 ($s = 11$) for Budget.com and 63.5 ($s = 15$) for Enterprise.com. Is there enough evidence to conclude that the SUS scores are different? What is the plausible range of mean differences for the entire user population using a 95% confidence interval?

User	Budget	Enterprise	Difference
1	90.0	65.0	25
2	85.0	82.5	2.5
3	80.0	55.0	25
4	92.5	67.5	25
5	82.5	82.5	0
6	80.0	37.5	42.5
7	62.5	77.5	-15
8	87.5	67.5	20
9	67.5	35.0	32.5
10	92.5	62.5	30
11	65.0	57.5	7.5
12	70.0	85.0	-15
13	75.0	55.0	20
14	95.0	60.0	35
Mean(sd)	80 (11)	64 (15)	16.8 (18)

Answer: Each user worked with each website, so the appropriate test is a paired *t*-test with 13 degrees of freedom. The outcome is statistically significant ($t(13) = 3.48$, $p = .004$), favoring Budget. A 95% confidence interval around the mean difference of 16.8 ranges from 6.4 to 27.2.

Excel solution

1. Click the "Task Times and Rating Scale Scores from the Same Users" link under the Compare Two Means or Proportions heading.

Compare Two Means or Proportions

2. Clear out any previous values using the "Clear Values" button (macros must be enabled) and enter in the 1's or 0's for each user on both designs.

3. Set the confidence level (around the difference between means) to 95%.

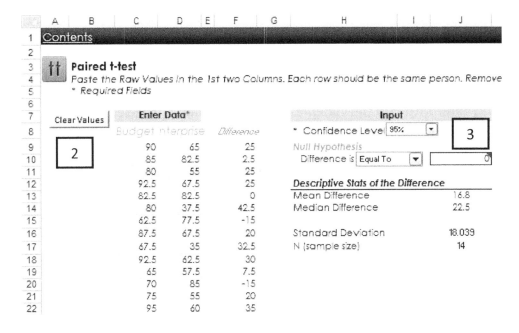

4. The *p*-value (.004) and confidence interval around the difference are in the Results section.

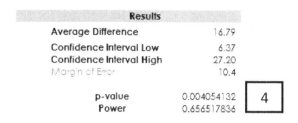

Results	
Average Difference	16.79
Confidence Interval Low	6.37
Confidence Interval High	27.20
Margin of Error	10.4
p-value	0.004054132
Power	0.656517836

4

Descriptive Statistics for each Group			
	Mean	StDev	N
Budget	80	11	14
Enterpris	64	15	14

R solution

Enter the following commands:

getdata.fromweb("table524.txt")

test.t.paired.fromarrays(Budget,Enterprise,.95)

The first command gets the data from a table stored on Jim's website, which puts the data for Budget and Enterprise into the variables of the same name. The second function uses those variables and the designated confidence level to compute the *t*-test and confidence interval. The result is:

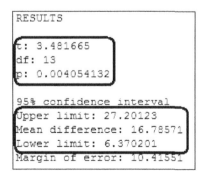

```
RESULTS

t: 3.481665
df: 13
p: 0.004054132

95% confidence interval
Upper limit: 27.20123
Mean difference: 16.78571
Lower limit: 6.370201
Margin of error: 10.41551
```

Chapter 6: What Sample Sizes Do We Need?

Part I – Summative Studies

Abstract

When planning user studies, practitioners should estimate the sample sizes required to meet their goals. This is most critical when the cost of adding to a sample is high. When estimating sample sizes, the appropriate method depends on the type of study. This chapter covers methods for user studies (such as summative usability studies) that use measurements that are continuous (such as time on task), multipoint scale (such as usability questionnaires) and discrete (such as successful task completions). The sample size estimation methods are derived from the formulas for z-tests, t-tests, and binomial tests.

Example 1: Estimate of continuous data

From page(s): 108

Summary: The times required to complete a particular task were 12, 14, 12, 20, and 16 minutes. With this information in hand, what would be the recommended sample size to estimate the mean time within 1.5 minutes with 95% confidence?

Answer: Sample size estimation for continuous data requires an estimate of the variance (or standard deviation) and decisions about the necessary level of confidence, power, and precision. Given that the variance of the five times is 11.2 (s = 3.347), to achieve a precision of ±1.5 (also known as the critical difference) with 95% confidence, the recommended sample size is 22. When estimating the values of parameters such as the mean rather than conducting a test against a benchmark or mean differences, set power to 50% and plan to use a two-tailed procedure.

Excel solution

1. Click the "For a Mean" link under the Sample Size for Margin of Error heading.

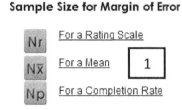

Sample Size for Margin of Error

Nr	For a Rating Scale
Nx̄	For a Mean 1
Np	For a Completion Rate

Sample Size for Problem Detection

Ni	Finding Problems in an Interface

2. Enter the critical difference (1.5) in the margin of error box, the estimate of the standard deviation (3.347).

3. Set the confidence level to 95% and be sure the tails are set to 2.

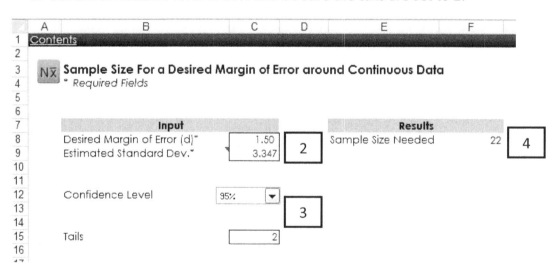

	A	B	C	D	E	F
1	Contents					
2						
3	Nx̄	**Sample Size For a Desired Margin of Error around Continuous Data**				
4		* Required Fields				
5						
6						
7		**Input**			**Results**	
8		Desired Margin of Error (d)*	1.50	2	Sample Size Needed	22 4
9		Estimated Standard Dev.*	3.347			
10						
11						
12		Confidence Level	95% ▼			
13				3		
14						
15		Tails	2			
16						

4. The estimated sample size needed is 22.

R solution

Enter the following command:

n.t.onesample.givenvar(.95,.5,11.2,1.5,2)

The first value for this command is the desired confidence level (.95 for 95%). Next is the appropriate level of power for estimation (.5 for 50%). The third value is for the variability, and the fourth is the designated critical difference. The last value designates a two-tailed procedure. The result is:

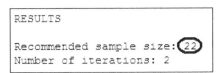

```
RESULTS

Recommended sample size: 22
Number of iterations: 2
```

If you have the standard deviation instead of the variance, you have two choices. You can square the standard deviation to get the variance and use the command above, or you can use the standard deviation in a command that is just like the one above, except that it requires the standard deviation in place of the variance (n.t.onesample.givensd).

This illustrates some aspects of the command naming convention used for the custom R functions. The "n" at the beginning denotes a sample size estimation command. The "t" indicates that it uses the *t*-distribution, so it's appropriate for continuous measures. The "onesample" is for single sets of data (either confidence intervals or comparisons against benchmarks), and "givenvar" or "givensd" depends on whether you have a variance or a standard deviation to use for the sample size estimation.

Example 2: Estimate of time (small sample)

From page(s): 109

Summary: Back in Chapter 3 we recommended using the geometric mean for estimates of typical completion times when the sample size is less than 25. Strictly speaking, estimates of sample sizes for studies using time as a measure when anticipating a sample size of less than 25 should use log-times rather than raw values. Using the same criteria as Example 1 but anticipating the use of log-times for the final time estimation, is the recommended sample size larger, smaller, or the same?

Answer: In this case, the recommended sample size is the same ($n = 22$). Note, however, that these time data are only slightly skewed. The more skewed the time data are, the greater the difference in the estimated sample sizes. Because the log transform applied to completion time data almost always reduces the estimate of the variance, it is often the case that you'll determine that you need a smaller sample size than you would if you used the raw (untransformed) data. If the cost of additional samples is low, then this won't matter much, but if it's high, then this could reduce the cost of the experiment without sacrificing any of the measurement goals. If you know you're going to use the log transform on your data, then you definitely want to do your sample size estimation with this in mind.

Excel solution

1. From the "Sample Size MOE Continuous" tab, first find the logarithm of each raw time using the Excel formula =LN().

2. Find the variance of the log values by using the formula = VAR().

3. Compute the arithmetic mean of the original times =AVERAGE().

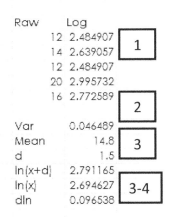

Raw	Log	
12	2.484907	1
14	2.639057	
12	2.484907	
20	2.995732	
16	2.772589	2
Var	0.046489	3
Mean	14.8	
d	1.5	
ln(x+d)	2.791165	3-4
ln(x)	2.694627	
dln	0.096538	

4. Convert the critical difference to the appropriate log transformed value by first computing the natural log of the mean of the original values plus the critical difference =LN(14.8 +1.5) =2.791165. Then subtract the log of the mean of the original values (2.694627) = 2.791165-2.694627 = .096538.

5. Enter the transformed critical difference in the Desired Margin of Error (*d*) field.

6. Take the square root of the variance of the log values =SQRT(.046489) = .215612 in the Estimated Standard Dev. Field.

7. Set the confidence level to 95% and the number of tails to 2.

Chapter 6: What Sample Sizes Do We Need? Part I – Summative Studies

192

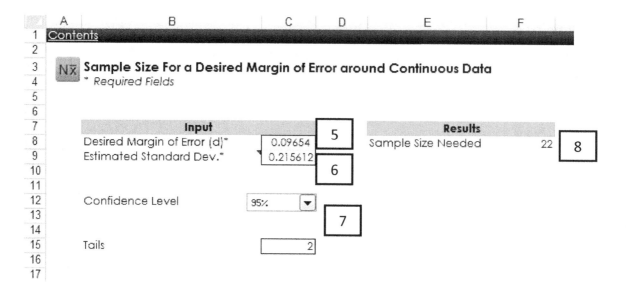

8. The estimated sample size needed is 22.

R solution

Enter the following commands:

```
times <- c(12,14,12,20,16)

log(times)

compute.logsummary.fromarray(times,1.5)

n.t.onesample.givenvar(.95,.5,.04648866,.09653793,2)
```

The first command assigns the times to a variable named "times." The second command shows the logs of those times (strictly speaking, you don't need to run this command, but it provides a check on intermediate computations that we show in the second edition of *Quantifying the User Experience: Practical Statistics for User Research*). The third command provides the information needed to put into the sample size command, which is the fourth command. The third command is important because it takes as input the array of times and the target value for the critical difference, and then produces the values to use in the fourth command for the variance and the critical difference. The result is:

```
> n.t.onesample.givenvar(.95,.5,11.2,1.5,2)

RESULTS

Recommended sample size: 22
Number of iterations: 2

> times <- c(12,14,12,20,16)
> log(times)
[1] 2.484907 2.639057 2.484907 2.995732 2.772589
> compute.logsummary.fromarray(times,1.5)

RESULTS

Arithmetic mean: 14.8
Median: 14
Geometric Mean: 14.51871
Mean of log data: 2.675438
Standard deviation of log data: 0.2156123
Variance of log data: 0.04648866
Standard error of the mean of the log data: 0.09642474
Sample size: 5
Value to use for log critical difference: 0.09653793

> n.t.onesample.givenvar(.95,.5,.04648866,.09653793,2)

RESULTS

Recommended sample size: 22
Number of iterations: 2
```

Example 3: A realistic example given estimate of variability (continuous)

From page(s): 110

Summary: This example illustrates the computation of a sample size requirement for the estimation of a value given an existing estimate of variability and realistic criteria. For speech recognition, it is important to track the recognizer's accuracy due to the usability problems that misrecognitions can cause. For this example, suppose the recognition variability (variance) from a previous similar evaluation is 5.5 (s = 2.345), the critical difference is ±1.5%, and the desired level of confidence is 90%. Set the power to 50% and plan to use a two-tailed procedure. What is the recommended sample size?

Answer: For these conditions, the recommended sample size is 9.

Excel solution

1. From the "Sample Size MOE Continuous" enter the desired margin of error (1.5) and estimate of the standard deviation (2.345).

2. Set the confidence level to 90% and the number of tails to 2.

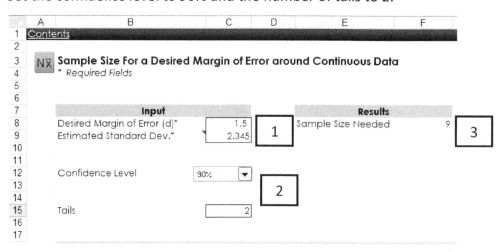

3. The estimated sample size needed is 9.

R solution

Enter the following command:

Chapter 6: What Sample Sizes Do We Need? Part I – Summative Studies

195

n.t.onesample.givenvar(.9,.5,5.5,1.5,2)

The result is:

```
RESULTS

Recommended sample size:⑨
Number of iterations: 3
```

Example 4: An unrealistic example (continuous)

From page(s): 110-111

Summary: Suppose a stakeholder wasn't satisfied with the criteria used in Example 1, and wanted a higher level of confidence (99%) and a smaller critical difference (0.5%). The variability remains the same at 5.5 (*s* = 2.345). Set power to 50% and plan to use a two-tailed procedure. Now what is the recommended sample size?

Answer: The new sample size recommendation is 150. There might be some settings in which usability investigators would consider 146 to 150 participants a reasonable and practical sample size for a moderated usability test, but they are rare. Confronted with these results, the hypothetical stakeholder would very likely want to reconsider the criteria.

Chapter 6: What Sample Sizes Do We Need? Part I – Summative Studies

196

Excel solution

1. From the "Sample Size MOE Continuous" enter the desired margin of error (.5) and estimate of the standard deviation (2.345).

2. Set the confidence level to 99% and the number of tails to 2.

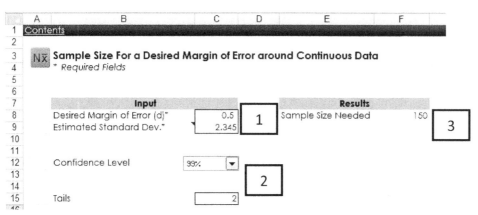

3. The estimated sample size needed is 150.

R solution

Enter the following command:

    n.t.onesample.givenvar(.99,.5,5.5,.5,2)

The result is:

```
RESULTS

Recommended sample size: 150
Number of iterations: 2
```

Example 5: No estimate of variability (continuous)

From page(s): 111-112

Summary: Suppose you don't have any idea what the measurement variability is, however, and it isn't possible to run a pilot study to get an initial estimate (no time or too expensive). To get around this problem you need to define the critical difference as a fraction of the standard deviation. Assume that with 80% confidence, you want to be able to detect an effect equal to or greater than one-third of a standard deviation. Set power to 50% and plan to use a two-tailed procedure. What is the recommended sample size?

Answer: The recommended sample size is 17.

Excel solution

1. From the "Sample Size MOE Continuous" enter the desired margin of error (.3) and estimate of the standard deviation (1).

2. Set the confidence level to 80% and the number of tails to 2.

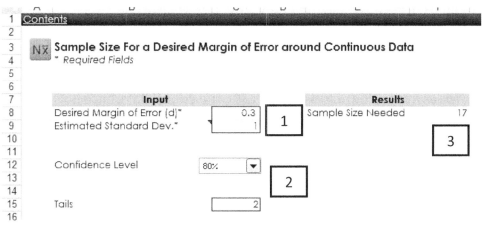

3. The estimated sample size needed is 17.

R solution

Enter the following command:

```
n.t.onesample.givensd(.80,.5,1,.33,2)
```

You don't know the standard deviation and are planning to set the critical difference to a third of the standard deviation. You can use this command to accomplish that goal by using 1 for the standard deviation and setting the critical difference to .33. The result is:

```
RESULTS

Recommended sample size: (17)
Number of iterations: 2
```

Example 6: Comparison with a benchmark (continuous)

From page(s): 112-113

Summary: Suppose you have a product requirement that the mean SUS for installation should be at least 75. In a preliminary evaluation, the mean SUS score was just 65. Development has fixed a number of usability problems found in that preliminary study, so you're ready to measure the SUS for installation again. The variability from the previous evaluation was 5.0 ($s = 2.236$), the critical difference is one point, and the desired level of confidence is 95%. For this exercise, continue setting power to 50%, but for comparison with a benchmark, plan to conduct a one-tailed test.

Answer: The recommended sample size is 16.

Excel solution

1. Select the "Comparing a Mean to a Criterion" link under the Sample Size for Comparisons: Power Analysis heading.

Sample Size for Comparisons : Power Analysis

N₂ₓ	Comparing 2 Independent Means
N₍ₓₓ₎	Comparing 2 Paired Means
N₍ₓc₎	Comparing a Mean to a Criterion
N₂ₚ	Comparing 2 Proportions (Completion Rates)
Npp	Comparing 2 Paired Proportions (Completion Rates)
Npc	Comparing a Proportion to a Criterion

2. Enter the desired margin of error (1) and estimate of the standard deviation (2.236) and set Power to 50%.

3. Set the confidence level to 95% and the number of tails to 1.

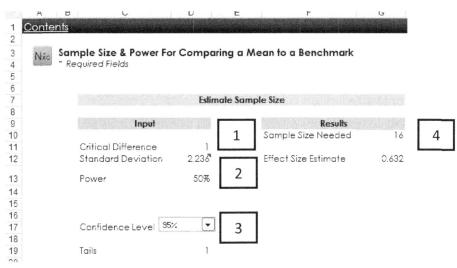

4. The estimated sample size needed is 16.

R solution

Enter the following command:

n.t.onesample.givenvar(.95,.5,5,1,1)

The result is:

```
RESULTS

Recommended sample size: (16)
Number of iterations: 2
```

Example 7: Within-subjects comparison of an alternative (continuous)

From page(s): 113-114

Summary: Suppose that you plan to obtain recognition accuracy scores from participants who have dictated test texts into your product under development and a competitor's current product. The difference score variability from a previous evaluation was 10.0 ($s = 3.162$). The critical difference is 2.5% and the desired level of confidence is 99%. For this example, continue setting power to 50%. For tests of alternatives, plan to conduct a two-tailed test.

Answer: The recommended sample size is 15.

Excel solution

1. Select the "Comparing 2 Paired Means" link under the Sample Size for Comparisons: Power Analysis heading.

2. Enter the desired margin of error (2.5) and estimate of the standard deviation (3.162) and set Power to 50%.

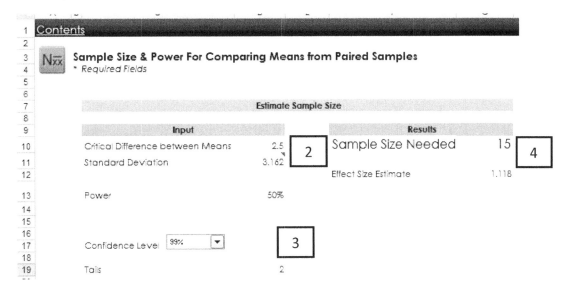

3. Set the confidence level to 95% and the number of tails to 2.

4. The estimated sample size needed is 15.

Chapter 6: What Sample Sizes Do We Need? Part I – Summative Studies

202

R solution

Enter the following command:

n.t.onesample.givenvar(.99,.5,10,2.5,2)

Even though there are two scores for each participant in a within-subjects test, the focus of the computations is on the set of difference scores, so you should use the "onesample" command. The result is:

```
RESULTS

Recommended sample size: 15
Number of iterations: 4
```

Example 8: Between-subjects comparison of an alternative (continuous)

From page(s): 114-115

Summary: Suppose that you need to conduct the experiment described in the previous example with independent groups of participants, keeping the measurement criteria the same: variability from a previous evaluation = 10.0 (s = 3.162), critical difference = 2.5%, desired level of confidence: 99%, desired power: 50%, two-tailed test.

Answer: The recommended sample size is 24 per group for a total sample size of 48.

Excel solution

1. Select the "Comparing 2 Independent Means" link under the Sample Size for Comparisons: Power Analysis heading.

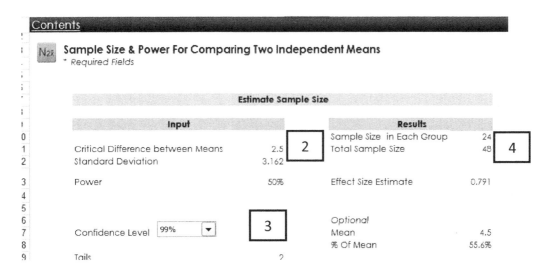

2. Enter the desired margin of error (2.5) and estimate of the standard deviation (3.162) and set Power to 50%.

3. Set the confidence level to 99% and the number of tails to 2.

4. The estimated sample size needed is 48 (24 in each group).

R solution

Enter the following command:

n.t.twosample.givenequalvar(.99,.5,10,2.5,2)

This command needs the same inputs as the "onesample" version – the confidence level, power, variance, critical difference, and number of tails for the test. Even though there are two samples, the procedure that this command uses assumes that the variances of the samples are equal – a reasonable assumption for much user research (for example, this should be the case if the groups contain participants from a single population who have received random assignment to treatment conditions). If you have evidence that the sample variances are unequal or a priori reason to anticipate unequal variances (for example, if comparing experts and novices), you should not use this command. The result is:

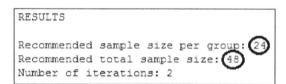

```
RESULTS

Recommended sample size per group: 24
Recommended total sample size: 48
Number of iterations: 2
```

Example 9: Increasing power beyond 50% (continuous)

From page(s): 115-117

Summary: The power of a test refers to its ability to detect a difference between observed measurements and hypothesized values if one exists. The power of a test is not an issue when you're just estimating the value of a parameter, but it is an issue when testing a hypothesis – either comparing a result to a benchmark or comparing alternatives. In the examples so far, we've set power to 50%. This means that the likelihood of getting enough evidence to just reject the null hypothesis at the recommended sample size is .5 – a coin toss. Researchers often want to have better odds than that, with a convention of setting power to 80%. Holding everything else the same and increasing the power of a study will always increase the recommended sample size. Suppose we recompute the sample size for the test conditions of Example 7, but this time with power set to 80%. The difference score variability from a previous evaluation was 10.0 (s = 3.162). The critical difference is 2.5% and the desired level of confidence is 99%. Plan to conduct a two-tailed test. Now what is the recommended sample size?

Answer: The recommended sample size is 22.

Excel solution

1. Select the "Comparing 2 Paired Means" link under the Sample Size for Comparisons: Power Analysis heading.

Sample Size for Comparisons : Power Analysis

$N_{2\bar{x}}$	Comparing 2 Independent Means
$N_{\bar{x}\bar{x}}$	Comparing 2 Paired Means 1
$N_{\bar{x}c}$	Comparing a Mean to a Criterion
N_{2p}	Comparing 2 Proportions (Completion Rates)
N_{pp}	Comparing 2 Paired Proportions (Completion Rates)
N_{pc}	Comparing a Proportion to a Criterion

2. Enter the desired margin of error (2.5) and estimate of the standard deviation (3.162) and set Power to 80%.

Chapter 6: What Sample Sizes Do We Need? Part I – Summative Studies

206

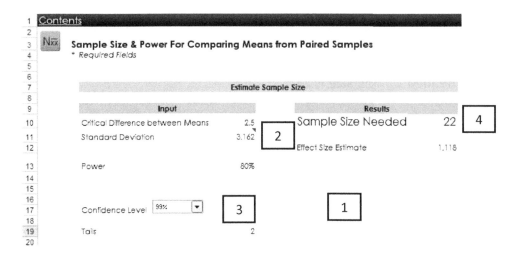

3. Set the confidence level to 99% and the number of tails to 2.

4. The estimated sample size needed is 22.

R solution

Enter the following command:

    n.t.onesample.givenvar(.99,.8,10,2.5,2)

The result is:

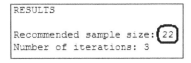

```
RESULTS

Recommended sample size: 22
Number of iterations: 3
```

Example 10: Large sample estimate of success rate with no prior estimate of *p* (binomial)

From page(s): 120

Summary: Assume you want to estimate the success rate of users logging into a website using a new login procedure. The success rate from a previous evaluation is not available, so use *p* = .5 (a choice that maximizes variance and consequently maximizes the recommended sample size). For a critical difference of .05 and 95% confidence, what is the recommended sample size (for estimation, set power to 50% and plan to use a two-tailed procedure)?

Answer: The recommended sample size is 385.

Excel solution

1. Select the "For a Completion Rate" link under the Sample Size for Margin of Error heading.

2. Enter the desired margin of error (5%).

3. Set the confidence level to 95% (this calculator assumes power of 50%).

4. Set the proportion to .5 and tails to 2.

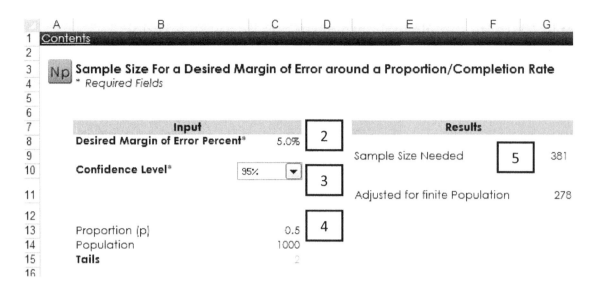

5. The estimated sample size needed is 381.

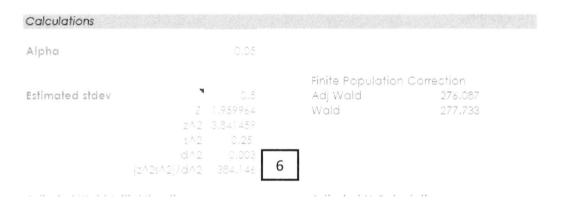

6. *Note*: This result differs slightly (381 vs. 385) because the calculator uses the small sample adjustment (from the Adjusted Wald interval) to generate the sample size. The large sample estimate (384.146) appears in the calculations for reference.

R solution

Enter the following command:

n.binomial.largesample(.95,.5,.5,.05,2)

This command is similar to the previous sample size commands. The functional arguments are the confidence (.95 for 95%, equivalent to setting the Type I test error criterion of alpha to .05), the power (.5 for 50%), the estimated value of p (.5), the critical difference to be able to detect (.05), and the number of tails for the test (2). The result is:

```
RESULT

Recommended sample size:(385)
```

Example 11: Large sample estimate of success rate with a prior estimate of p (binomial)

From page(s): 120

Summary: Suppose in Example 10 you did have a previous estimate of the success rate, with 95% successful logins (p = .95). For the same critical difference (.05), confidence (95%), and power (50%), what is the recommended sample size?

Answer: The recommended sample size is 73.

Excel solution

1. From the "Sample Size MOE Proportion" tab, enter the margin of error (.05)

2. Set the confidence level to 95%.

3. Enter .95 as the Proportion (p) and set the number of tails to 2.

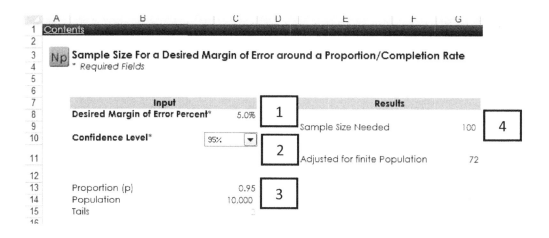

4. The estimated sample size needed is 100.

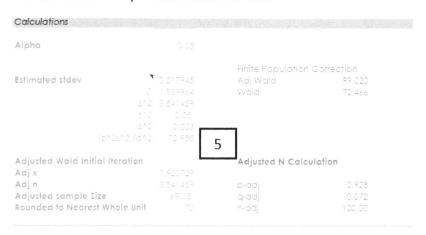

5. *Note*: The calculator sample size is difference because it is using the small sample adjustment (from the Adjusted Wald interval) to generate the sample size. The large sample estimate (72.988) appears in the calculator's calculations section for reference.

R solution

Enter the following command:

```
n.binomial.largesample(.95,.5,.95,.05,2)
```

The result is:

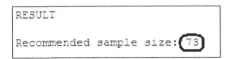

Example 12: Small sample estimate of success rate (binomial)

From page(s): 122-123

Summary: Suppose you have reason to believe that the current success rate for a particular task is .75, and want to see if that's correct. You know you won't be able to conduct a large-scale study; in fact, you probably won't be able to test more than 20 people. For this reason, you realistically set your target precision (critical difference) to .20, and balance that by setting your confidence to 95%. Plan to use a two-tailed procedure. What is the recommended sample size?

Answer: The recommended sample size is 17.

Excel solution

1. From the "Sample Size MOE Proportion" tab, enter the margin of error (.20)

2. Set the confidence level to 95%.

3. Enter .75 as the Proportion (*p*) and set the number of tails to 2.

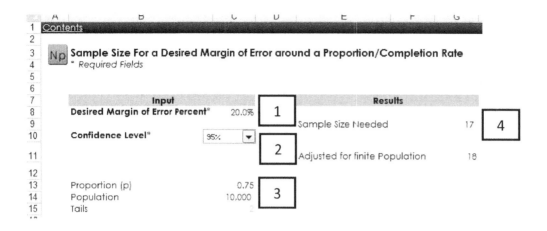

4. The estimated sample size needed is 17.

R solution

Enter the following command:

```
n.binomial.smallsample(.95,.5,.75,.2,2)
```

The result is:

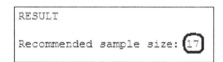

Example 13: Adjusted-Wald binomial confidence interval

From page(s): 123

Summary: To check the sample size recommendation from Example 12, we can construct an adjusted-Wald confidence interval to see if the precision is close to the desired critical difference. If n is going to equal 17 and the expected value of p is .75, then the expected value of x is np, which is 17(.75) = 12.75, which rounds to 13. We have to round the estimate up because x can only be a whole number. For this reason, the value of the resulting x/n will not usually equal the expected value of p, but it can get close – in this case it's 13/17 = .7647.

Answer: If we use these values of x and n to compute an adjusted-Wald binomial confidence interval, we find that the observed value of the critical difference (d) is .1936, just .0064 less (and therefore slightly more precise) than the target value of .20.

Excel solution

1. Click on the "Completion Rate" link under the Confidence Interval heading.

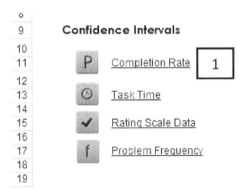

2. Enter the number of successes (13) and total tested (17).

3. Set the confidence level to 95%.

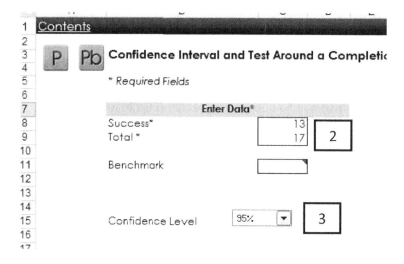

4. The margin of error (*d*) is 19.4%, as shown in the Results section.

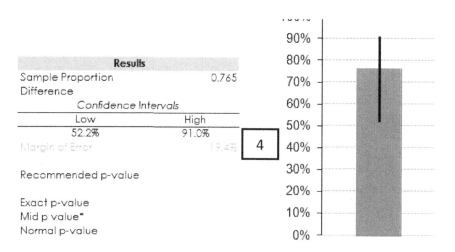

R solution

Enter the following command:

    ci.adjwald.fromsummary(13,17,.95)

The result is:

```
RESULTS

Adjusted p (Wilson):      0.7159158
Margin of error:         (0.1936148)
95% upper limit:          0.9095306
p (maximum likelihood):   0.7647059
95% lower limit:          0.522301
```

Web solution

As shown below, you can also get this information from the online calculator at
http://www.measuringu.com/wald.htm.

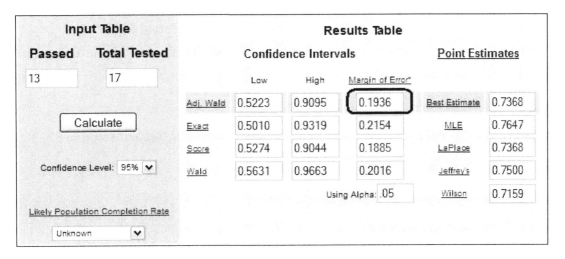

Example 14: Benchmark proportion (binomial)

From page(s): 123-124

Summary: Suppose a first design of the installation process for a new dictation program had a success rate of 55%, so for the next version you want to show that you've improved the success rate to at least 65%. You decide to use the standard levels of 95% confidence and 80% power and to set the required level of precision to 20%. For these test criteria, what is the recommended sample size?

Answer: The standard sample size estimate is 28. Using the "equivalent confidence" method (designed to ensure that the lower limit of the confidence interval will exceed the benchmark under the expected test conditions), the sample size estimate is 36.

Excel solution

1. Select the "Comparing a Proportion to a Criterion" link under the Sample Size for Comparisons: Power Analysis heading.

Sample Size for Comparisons : Power Analysis

N₂ₓ   Comparing 2 Independent Means

Nₓ̄ₓ   Comparing 2 Paired Means

Nₓ̄c   Comparing a Mean to a Criterion

N₂ₚ   Comparing 2 Proportions (Completion Rates)

Nₚₚ   Comparing 2 Paired Proportions (Completion Rates)

Nₚc   Comparing a Proportion to a Criterion | 1 |

2. Enter the Sample Proportion (85%) and test benchmark (65%).

3. Set Power to 80% confidence level to 95%.

4. Set the number of tails 1.

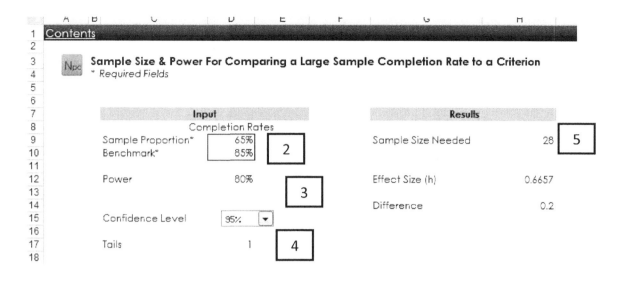

5. The estimated sample size needed is 28. *Note: The Excel calculator uses the standard approach for computing sample size, not the "equivalent confidence" method.*

R solution

Enter the following command:

    n.bench.rate(.65,.2,.95,.80)

For this command, you need to provide the benchmark (.65), the precision (.2), the confidence (.95 for 95%), and the power (.80 for 80%). The result is:

Chapter 6: What Sample Sizes Do We Need? Part I – Summative Studies

218

```
RESULTS

z(confidence): 1.644854
z(power): 0.8416212
z(combined): 2.486475
Equivalent confidence: 0.9935492

Standard estimate of n: 28

Initial estimate of n: 20
Initial adjusted p (Wilson): 0.7673536
Initial margin of error: 0.2053166
p (maximum likelihood): 0.85
Initial lower limit: 0.562037

Iteration: 1    n: 21   x: 18   p: 0.85714   xadj: 21.091   nadj: 27.183   padj: 0.77591   dadj: 0.19886   lower: 0.57705
Iteration: 2    n: 22   x: 19   p: 0.86364   xadj: 22.091   nadj: 28.183   padj: 0.78386   dadj: 0.19279   lower: 0.59108
Iteration: 3    n: 23   x: 20   p: 0.86957   xadj: 23.091   nadj: 29.183   padj: 0.79127   dadj: 0.18706   lower: 0.60421
Iteration: 4    n: 24   x: 20   p: 0.83333   xadj: 23.091   nadj: 30.183   padj: 0.76505   dadj: 0.19188   lower: 0.57317
Iteration: 5    n: 25   x: 21   p: 0.84     xadj: 24.091   nadj: 31.183   padj: 0.77259   dadj: 0.18664   lower: 0.58595
Iteration: 6    n: 26   x: 22   p: 0.84615   xadj: 25.091   nadj: 32.183   padj: 0.77965   dadj: 0.18167   lower: 0.59799
Iteration: 7    n: 27   x: 23   p: 0.85185   xadj: 26.091   nadj: 33.183   padj: 0.7863    dadj: 0.17694   lower: 0.60935
Iteration: 8    n: 28   x: 24   p: 0.85714   xadj: 27.091   nadj: 34.183   padj: 0.79255   dadj: 0.17245   lower: 0.6201
Iteration: 9    n: 29   x: 25   p: 0.86207   xadj: 28.091   nadj: 35.183   padj: 0.79844   dadj: 0.16817   lower: 0.63028
Iteration: 10   n: 30   x: 26   p: 0.86667   xadj: 29.091   nadj: 36.183   padj: 0.80401   dadj: 0.16409   lower: 0.63993
Iteration: 11   n: 31   x: 26   p: 0.83871   xadj: 29.091   nadj: 37.183   padj: 0.78239   dadj: 0.16825   lower: 0.61414
Iteration: 12   n: 32   x: 27   p: 0.84375   xadj: 30.091   nadj: 38.183   padj: 0.78809   dadj: 0.16444   lower: 0.62365
Iteration: 13   n: 33   x: 28   p: 0.84848   xadj: 31.091   nadj: 39.183   padj: 0.7935    dadj: 0.16080   lower: 0.6327
Iteration: 14   n: 34   x: 29   p: 0.85294   xadj: 32.091   nadj: 40.183   padj: 0.79864   dadj: 0.1573    lower: 0.64134
Iteration: 15   n: 35   x: 30   p: 0.85714   xadj: 33.091   nadj: 41.183   padj: 0.80353   dadj: 0.15395   lower: 0.64958
Iteration: 16   n: 36   x: 31   p: 0.86111   xadj: 34.091   nadj: 42.183   padj: 0.80818   dadj: 0.15074   lower: 0.65745

Recommended sample size: 36

Maximum tolerable number of failures given alpha = 0.05 with an observed mid-p significance level of 0.02311188 is: 7
```

Example 15: Independent proportions (binomial)

From page(s): 127-128

Summary: Suppose you've recently run a test comparing successful completion rates for the installation of the current version of a product and a new version in which you've made changes to improve the ease of installation. In that previous study, the successful completion rate for the current version was .7 and for the new version was .8. You've made some additional changes that should eliminate some of the problems participants had with the new version – enough that you think you should get a successful completion rate of at least .9 (90% success). For a test with 90% confidence and 80% power, what is the recommended sample size?

Answer: The appropriate test for this situation is the *N*-1 chi-squared test. The recommended sample size is 50 for each independent group for a total of 100.

Excel solution

1. Select the "Comparing 2 Proportions (Completion Rates)" link under the Sample Size for Comparisons: Power Analysis heading.

Sample Size for Comparisons : Power Analysis

N2x̄   Comparing 2 Independent Means

Nx̄x̄   Comparing 2 Paired Means

Nx̄c   Comparing a Mean to a Criterion

N2p   Comparing 2 Proportions (Completion Rates)   1

Npp   Comparing 2 Paired Proportions (Completion Rates)

Npc   Comparing a Proportion to a Criterion

2. Enter the two percentages (70% and 90%).

3. Set Power to 80% and the confidence level to 90%.

4. Set the number of tails 2.

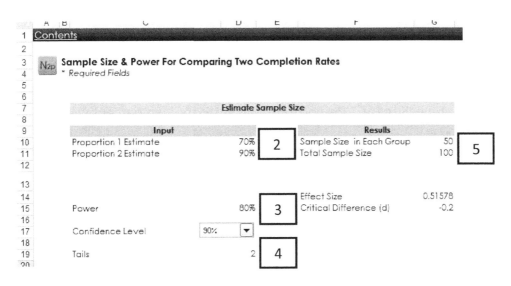

5. The estimated sample size needed is 50 in each group or a total of 100.

R solution

Enter the following command:

n.nminusonechisquared(.9,.8,.7,.9)

For this command, you need to provide the confidence (.9 for 90%, equivalent to setting alpha to .10), the power (.8 for 80%, equivalent to setting beta to .20), the current success rate (.7) and the expected success rate for the new version. The result is:

```
RESULTS

Recommended sample size per group: 50
Recommended total sample size: 100
```

Example 16: Independent proportions (binomial)

From page(s): 128

Summary: Assume that you don't have the time or money to run 100 participants, so you decide to relax confidence to 80%, keeping everything else the same as Example 15 (80% power, $p_1 = .7$, $p_2 = .9$). Now what is the recommended sample size?

Answer: The new sample size recommendation is 37 per group, for a total of 74.

Excel solution

1. From the "Sample Size for 2 Proportions" tab enter the two percentages (70% and 90%).

2. Set Power to 80% and the confidence level to **80%**.

3. Set the number of tails 2.

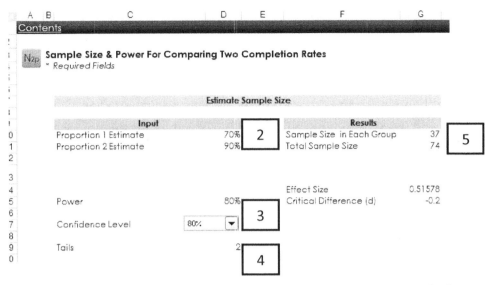

4. The estimated sample size needed is 37 in each group or a total of 74.

R solution

Enter the following command:

    n.nminusonechisquared(.8,.8,.7,.9)

The result is:

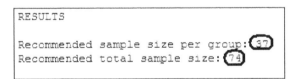

```
RESULTS

Recommended sample size per group: 37
Recommended total sample size: 74
```

Example 17: Independent proportions (binomial)

From page(s): 128

Summary: Assume that the requirement of 74 participants (Example 16) still exceeds your resources. What happens to the recommended sample size if you keep everything else the same (80% confidence, p_1 = .7, p_2 = .9), but lower the power to 50%?

Answer: The new sample size recommendation is 14 per group, for a total of 28.

Excel solution

1. From the "Sample Size for 2 Proportions" tab enter the two percentages (70% and 90%).

2. Set Power to **50**% and the confidence level to 80%.

3. Set the number of tails 2.

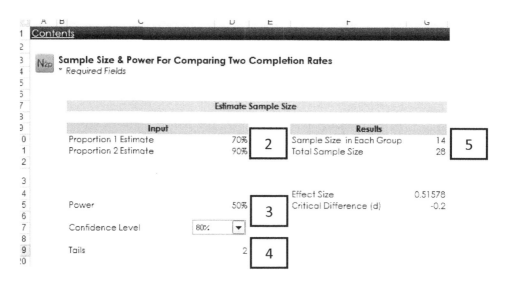

4. The estimated sample size needed is 14 in each group or a total of 28.

R solution

Enter the following command:

n.nminusonechisquared(.8,.5,.7,.9)

The result is:

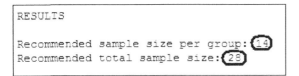

```
RESULTS

Recommended sample size per group: 14
Recommended total sample size: 28
```

Example 18: Dependent proportions (binomial)

From page(s): 131-132

Summary: Suppose you recently ran a pilot study in which you had 10 participants attempt to complete a car reservation with two websites using counterbalanced orders of presentation, with the overall success rates for Websites A and B equal to .8 and .9 respectively. In that study, one participant was successful with Website A but was unsuccessful with Website B (p_{12}=.10), and two were successful with Website B but not with Website A (p_{21}=.20), so the difference in the proportions was .10. If these results remained stable, how many participants would you need to run to achieve statistical significance with 95% confidence and 50% power?

Answer: The recommended sample size is 115. As a practical matter, if you estimate an odd number of participants, you should add one more so you can evenly counterbalance the order in which participants use the two products, so the final planned sample size should be 116.

Excel solution

1. Select the "Comparing 2 Paired Proportions (Completion Rates)" link under the Sample Size for Comparisons: Power Analysis heading.

2. Click on the link in the upper right "Estimated Sample Size from p12 and p21."

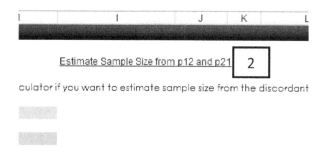

3. Enter the values for p_{12} (.1) and p_{21} (.2)

4. Set the Power to 50%.

5. Set the Confidence Level to 95% and number of tails to 2.

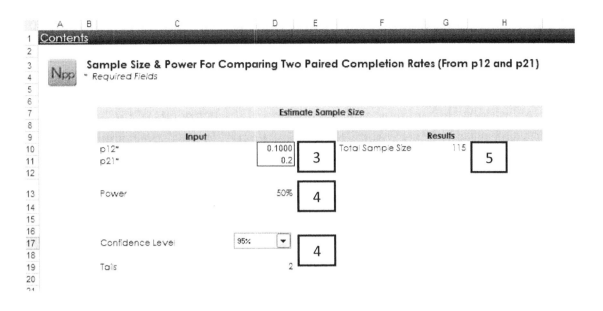

6. The estimated sample size needed is 115.

R solution

Enter the following command:

    n.mcnemar(.95,.5,.1,.2)

For this command, you need to provide the confidence (.95 for 95%), the power (.5 for 50%), the value of p_{12} (.1) and the value for p_{21} (.2). The result is:

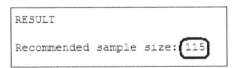

Example 19: CI around difference in dependent proportions (binomial)

From page(s): 132

Summary: As a check on the recommended sample size in Example 18, compute the resulting adjusted-Wald confidence interval. If one of the endpoints of the interval is close to 0 given this pattern of results, then the estimated sample size is appropriate. Is it?

Answer: For p_1=.8, p_2=.9, p_{12}=.1 and p_{21}=.2 with a sample size of 115, the resulting 95% adjusted-Wald confidence interval ranges from -.005 to .193, with the lower limit just below 0. Rounding to the nearest percentage, the interval for the difference in proportions ranges from about 0 to 19%, confirming the adequacy of the estimated sample size for the given conditions.

Excel solution

1. Select the "2 Completion Rates from the Sample Users" link under the Sample Size for Comparisons: Power Analysis heading.

Compare Two Means or Proportions

2p 2 Proportion Test
    2 Completion Rates

2t 2 Sample t-test
    Task Times and Rating Scale Scores

2ts 2 Sample t-test
    Task Times and Rating Scale Scores (Summary)

tt Paired t-test
    Task Times and Rating Scale Scores from the Same Users

pp McNemar Chi-Square Exact Test
    2 Completion Rates from the Same Users | 1 |

2. Click on the link in the upper right "Enter Summary Data."

Chapter 6: What Sample Sizes Do We Need? Part I – Summative Studies

227

ubjects (McNemar Exact Test)
0=Fail) by product and user   Enter Summary Data

2

3. Enter the total number of users that passed and failed by product for a total sample size of 115.

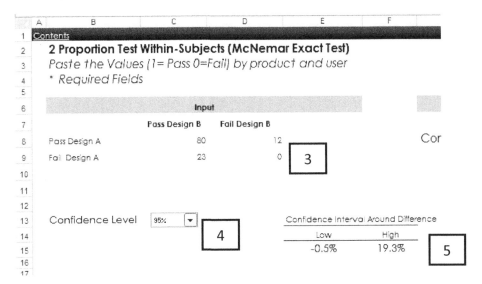

4. Set the confidence level to 95%.

5. The confidence interval around the difference is shown (-.5% to 19.3%).

R solution

Enter the following command:

```
ci.matchedproportions.difference(.8,.9,.1,.2,115,.95)
```

The result is:

```
RESULTS

95% CONFIDENCE INTERVAL

p1: 0.8
p2: 0.9
Adjusted value of p1: 0.7950717
Adjusted value of p2: 0.8891526
Adjusted difference: 0.09408084
Margin of error: 0.09906671
Upper limit: 0.1931475
Observed difference: 0.1
Lower limit: -0.004985873

TESTS OF SIGNIFICANCE

McNemar Mid Probability (recommended): 0.06524534

Alternate analyses (not recommended)
McNemar Exact Probability: 0.08953108
McNemar Chi-Squared: 3.457143    df: 1    p: 0.06297905
McNemar Chi-Squared with Yates Correction: 2.857143    df: 1    p: 0.09096895
```

If keeping all else the same and setting n to 116, the result is almost the same:

```
RESULTS

95% CONFIDENCE INTERVAL

p1: 0.8
p2: 0.9
Adjusted value of p1: 0.7968096
Adjusted value of p2: 0.8900926
Adjusted difference: 0.093283
Margin of error: 0.09823894
Upper limit: 0.1915219
Observed difference: 0.1
Lower limit: -0.004955932

TESTS OF SIGNIFICANCE

McNemar Mid Probability (recommended): 0.06524534

Alternate analyses (not recommended)
McNemar Exact Probability: 0.08953108
McNemar Chi-Squared: 3.457143    df: 1    p: 0.06297905
McNemar Chi-Squared with Yates Correction: 2.857143    df: 1    p: 0.09096895
```

Exercise 1: Estimate of continuous variable

From page(s): 135

Problem: Assume you've been using a single 100-point item as a post-task measure of ease-of-use in past usability tests. One of the tasks you routinely conduct is installation. For the most recent usability study of the current version of the software package, the variability of this measurement was 25 ($s = 5$). You're planning your first usability study with a new version of the software, and all you want to do is to get an estimate of this measure with 90% confidence and to be within ±2.5 points of the true value. How many participants do you need to run in the study?

Answer: The research problem in this exercise is to estimate a value without comparison to a benchmark or alternative. From the problem statement, the variability is 25 ($s = 5$), the critical difference (d) is 2.5, the desired level of confidence is 90%. Plan for a two-sided procedure with power set to 50%. The resulting sample size recommendation is 13.

Chapter 6: What Sample Sizes Do We Need? Part I – Summative Studies

230

Excel solution

1. Select the "For a Mean" link OR "For a Rating Scale" link under the Sample Size for Margin of Error heading. The only difference is the rating scale calculator provides estimates of the standard deviation based on historical rating scale data.

Sample Size for Margin of Error

Sample Size for Problem Detection

Ni   Finding Problems in an Interface

2. Enter the margin of error (2.5) and the estimate of the standard deviation (5).

3. Set the confidence level to 90% and the number of tails to 2.

4. The estimated sample size needed is 13.

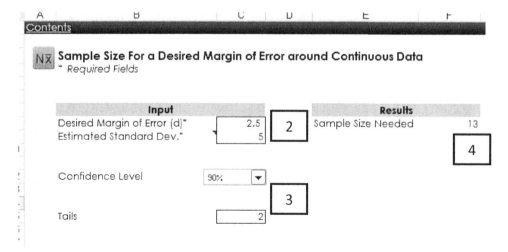

R solution

Enter the following command:

n.t.onesample.givenvar(.9,.5,25,2.5,2)

The result is:

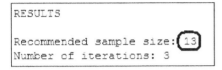

```
RESULTS

Recommended sample size: 13
Number of iterations: 3
```

Exercise 2: Test against benchmark (continuous)

From page(s): 136-137

Problem: Continuing with the situation described in Exercise 1, what if your research goal is to compare your result with a benchmark of having a result greater than 75? Also, assume that for this comparison you want a test with 80% power and want to be able to detect differences that are at least 2.5 points above the benchmark. The estimated variability of measurement is still 25 (s = 5) and desired confidence is still 90%. How many participants do you need to run in the study?

Answer: Relative to Exercise 1, we're moving from a simple estimation problem to a comparison with a benchmark, which means that we now need to consider the power of the test and, because we're testing against a benchmark, will use a one-sided rather than a two-sided procedure. Like the previous exercise, we'll use 90% confidence and 80% power. The sample size recommendation for this study is 20 participants.

Excel solution

1. Select the "Comparing a Mean to a Criterion" link under the Sample Size for Comparisons heading.

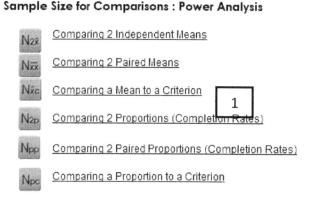

2. Enter the critical difference to detect (2.5) and the estimate of the standard deviation (5).

3. Set the Power to 80%.

4. Set the confidence level to 90% and the number of tails to 1.

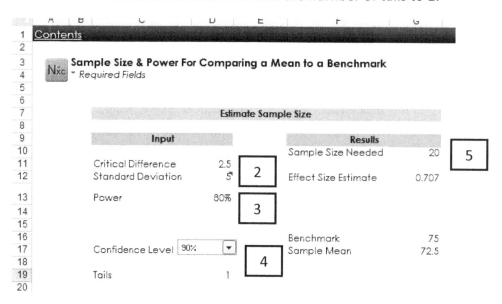

5. The estimated sample size needed is 20.

Enter the margin of error (2.5) and R solution

Enter the following command:

n.t.onesample.givenvar(.9,.8,25,2.5,1)

The result is:

```
RESULTS

Recommended sample size: 20
Number of iterations: 2
```

Exercise 3: Within-subjects test of difference (continuous)

From page(s): 136

Problem: Again continuing this example, what if you have improved the installation procedures for the new version, and want to test it against the previous version in a study where each participant performs the installation task with both the current and new versions, with the ability to detect a difference of at least 2.5 points? Assume that power and confidence remain at 80% and 90% respectively, and that the estimated variability is still 25 ($s = 5$). How many participants do you need to run in the study?

Answer: 3.   Relative to Exercise 2, we're moving from comparison with a fixed benchmark to a within-subjects comparison between alternative designs, so the test should be two-sided rather than one-sided. Continue to plan for 90% confidence, 80% power, critical difference of 2.5 points, and variability of 25 ($s = 5$). The recommended sample size is 27 participants.

Excel solution

1. Select the "Comparing 2 Paired Means" link under the Sample Size for Comparisons heading.

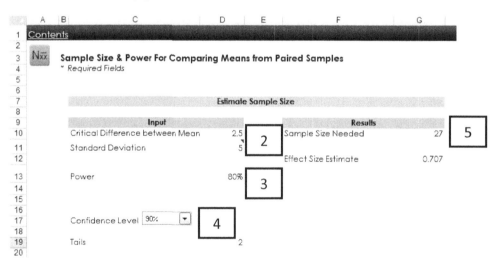

2. Enter the critical difference to detect (2.5) and the estimate of the standard deviation (5).

3. Set Power to 80%.

4. Set the confidence level to 90% and number of tails to 2.

5. The estimated sample size needed is 27.

R solution

Enter the following command:

    n.t.onesample.givenvar(.9,.8,25,2.5,2)

The result is:

```
RESULTS

Recommended sample size: (27)
Number of iterations: 2
```

Exercise 4: Between-subjects test of difference (continuous)

From page(s): 137

Problem: Next, assume that the installation procedure is so time-consuming that you cannot get participants to perform installation with both products, so you'll have to have the installations done by independent groups of participants. Assume that nothing else changes – power and confidence remain at 80% and 90% respectively, variance is still 25 ($s = 5$), and the critical difference is still 2.5. How many participants do you need to run in the study?

Answer: Relative to Exercise 3, we're moving from a within-subjects experimental design to one that is between-subjects. The sample size recommendation is for 51 participants per group (a total sample size of 102).

Excel solution

1. Select the "Comparing 2 Independent Means" link under the Sample Size for Comparisons heading.

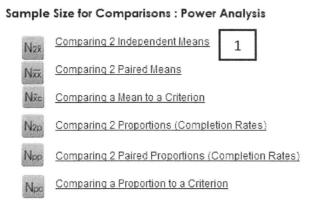

2. Enter the critical difference to detect (2.5) and the estimate of the standard deviation (5).

3. Set Power to 80%.

4. Set the confidence level to 90% and number of tails to 2.

5. The estimated sample size needed is 102 (51 per group).

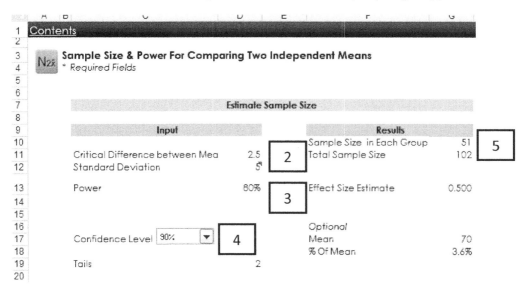

R solution

Enter the following command:

n.t.twosample.givenequalvar(.9,.8,25,2.5,2)

The result is:

```
RESULTS

Recommended sample size per group: 51
Recommended total sample size: 102
Number of iterations: 3
```

Exercise 5: Within-subjects test of difference (continuous)

From page(s): 137-138

Problem: Continuing with the situation described in the previous exercise, suppose your resources (time and money) will only allow you to run a total of 20 participants to compare the alternative installation procedures. What can you do to reduce the estimated sample size?

Answer: Keeping many of the conditions of the situations the same, over the course of the first four exercises, we've gone from needing a sample size of 13 to simply estimate the ease-of-use score within a specified level of precision, to 20 to compare it against a benchmark, to 27 to perform a within-subjects usability test, to 102 to perform a between-subjects usability test. Clearly, the change that led to the greatest increase in the sample size estimate was the shift from a within- to a between-subjects comparison of alternatives, so one way to reduce the estimated sample size is to strive to run within-subjects studies rather than between-subjects when you must compare alternatives. The other aspects of experimental design that you can control are the choices for confidence level, power, and critical difference. Let's assume that you were able to change your plan to a within-subjects study. Furthermore, you have worked with your stakeholders to relax the requirement for the critical difference (*d*) from 2.5 to 3.5. These two changes – switching from a between- to a within-subjects design and increasing the critical difference by just one point – lead to a study design for which you should only need 15 participants. Note that if the critical difference were relaxed to 5 points, the required sample size would be just 8 participants.

Excel solution

1. Select the "Comparing 2 Paired Means" link under the Sample Size for Comparisons heading.

Sample Size for Comparisons : Power Analysis

N₂ₓ   Comparing 2 Independent Means

Nₓₓ   Comparing 2 Paired Means   1

Nₓᶜ   Comparing a Mean to a Criterion

N₂ₚ   Comparing 2 Proportions (Completion Rates)

Nₚₚ   Comparing 2 Paired Proportions (Completion Rates)

Nₚᶜ   Comparing a Proportion to a Criterion

2. Enter the critical difference to detect (3.5) and the estimate of the standard deviation (5).

3. Set Power to 80%.

4. Set the confidence level to 90% and number of tails to 2.

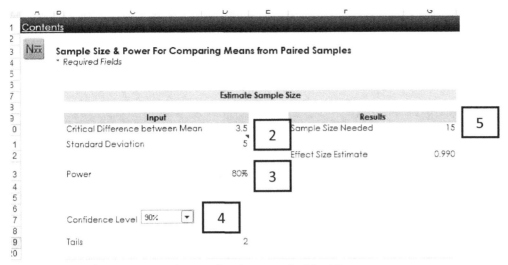

5. The estimated sample size needed is 15.

6. Change the critical difference to 5.

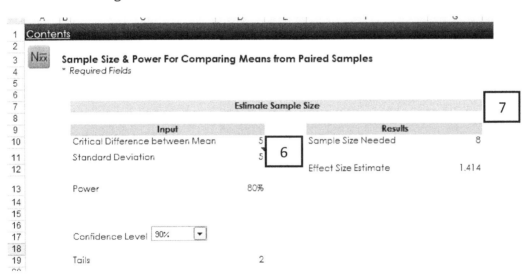

7. The estimated sample size needed is now 8.

R solution

Enter the following commands:

        n.t.onesample.givenvar(.9,.8,25,3.5,2)

        n.t.onesample.givenvar(.9,.8,25,5,2)

The result is:

```
> n.t.onesample.givenvar(.9,.8,25,3.5,2)

RESULTS

Recommended sample size: 15
Number of iterations: 2

> n.t.onesample.givenvar(.9,.8,25,5,2)

RESULTS

Recommended sample size: 8
Number of iterations: 3
```

Exercise 6: Estimate of success rate (binomial)

From page(s): 138

Problem: Suppose that in addition to your subjective assessment of ease-of-use, you have also been measuring installation successes and failures using small-sample moderated usability studies. For the most recent usability study, the installation success rate was 65%. Using this as your best estimate of future success rates, what sample size do you need if you want to estimate with 90% confidence the new success rate within ±15 percentage points of the true value?

Answer: For this question, the variable of interest is a binomial pass/fail measurement, so the appropriate approach is the sample size method based on the adjusted-Wald binomial confidence interval. We have the three pieces of information that we need to proceed: the success rate from the previous evaluation (*p*) was .65, the critical difference (*d*) is .15, and the desired level of confidence is

90%. The recommended sample size for these test criteria is 26. To check, set the expected number of successes (x) to .65(26), which rounds to 17. A 90% adjusted-Wald binomial confidence interval for 17/26 has an observed p of .654, an adjusted p of .639, and a margin of error of .147, just a little more precise than the target precision of .15.

Excel solution

1. From the "Sample Size MOE Proportion" tab, enter the margin of error (.15)

2. Set the confidence level to 90%.

3. Enter .65 as the Proportion (p) and set the number of tails to 2.

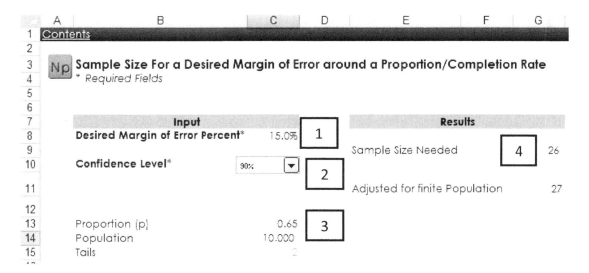

4. The estimated sample size needed is 26.

5. The associated 90% adjusted-Wald binomial confidence interval shows a margin of error of 14.7%.

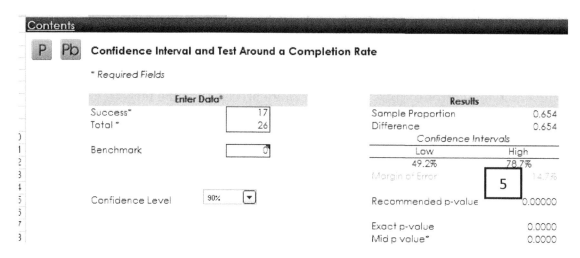

R solution

Enter the following commands:

n.binomial.smallsample(.9,.5,.65,.15,2)

ci.adjwald.fromsummary(17,26,.9)

The result is:

```
> n.binomial.smallsample(.9,.5,.65,.15,2)

RESULT

Recommended sample size: 26

> ci.adjwald.fromsummary(17,26,.9)

RESULTS

Adjusted p (Wilson):        0.6393459
Margin of error:            0.1474205
90% upper limit:            0.7867664
p (maximum likelihood):     0.6538462
90% lower limit:            0.4919255
```

James R. Lewis & Jeff Sauro

Exercise 7: Comparison of independent proportions (binomial)

From page(s): 138

Problem: You're pretty confident that your new installation process will be much more successful than the current process – in fact, you think you should have about 85% correct installation – much better than the current success rate of 65%. The current installation process is lengthy, typically taking 2-3 days to complete with verification of correct installation, so each participant will perform just one installation. You want to be able to detect the expected difference of 20 percentage points between the success rates with 80% confidence and 80% power, and are planning to run the same number of participants with the current and new installation procedures. How many participants (total including both groups) do you need to run?

Answer: Because in this problem you're planning to compare success rates between independent groups, the appropriate test is the *N*-1 chi-squared test. From the conditions of the problem, we have the information needed to do the sample size estimation: the expected values of p_1 and p_2 (.65 and .85 respectively, for an average $p = .75$ and $d = .20$), planned 80% confidence, and planned 80% power. The resulting sample size recommendation is 43 participants per group, for a total of 86 participants. This is outside the scope of most moderated usability tests. Relaxing the power to 50% would reduce the recommended sample size to 16 per group (total sample size of 32).

Excel solution

1. Select the "Comparing 2 Proportions (Completion Rates)" link under the Sample Size for Comparisons heading.

Sample Size for Comparisons : Power Analysis

2. Enter the two proportions.

3. Set confidence to 80%

4. Set Power to 80% and the number of tails to 2.

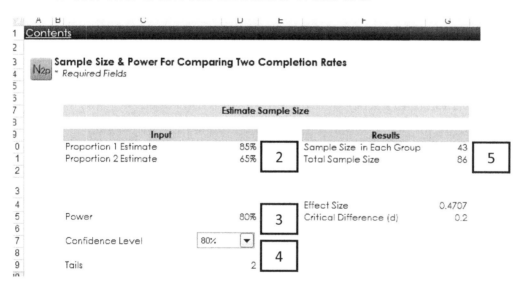

5. The estimated sample size needed is 86 (43 in each group).

6. Adjust Power down to 50% (below).

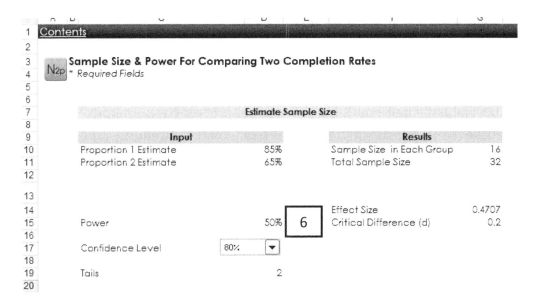

7. The estimated sample size needed is now 32 (16 in each group).

R solution

Enter the following commands:

n.nminusonechisquared(.8,.8,.65,.85)

n.nminusonechisquared(.8,.5,.65,.85)

The result is:

```
> n.nminusonechisquared(.8,.8,.65,.85)

RESULTS

Recommended sample size per group: 43
Recommended total sample size: 86

> n.nminusonechisquared(.8,.5,.65,.85)

RESULTS

Recommended sample size per group: 16
Recommended total sample size: 32
```

Exercise 8: Comparison of dependent proportions (binomial)

From page(s): 139

Problem: For another product (Product B for "Before"), the current installation procedure is fairly short (about a half-hour), but that current process has numerous usability issues that have led to an estimated 50% failure rate on first attempts. You've tracked down the most serious usability issues and now have a prototype of an improved product (Product A for "After"). In a pilot study with 10 participants, you had 4 participants succeed with both products, 1 failed with both, 4 were successful with Product A but not B, and 1 was successful with Product B but not A. What are the resulting estimates for p_1, p_2, p_{12}, and p_{21}? If you want to run a larger-scale test with 95% confidence and 80% power, how many participants should you plan to run if you expect this pattern of results to stay about the same?

Answer: The appropriate statistical test for this type of study is the McNemar Test (using mid-p) or, equivalently, a confidence interval using the adjusted-Wald method for matched proportions. From the pilot study, the estimates for the different key proportions are $p_1 = .8$, $p_2 = .5$, $p_{12} =.4$, and $p_{21} = .1$, so $d = .3$. The resulting recommended sample size is 42.

You can check this estimate by computing a confidence interval to see if it includes or excludes 0. Because the power of the test is 80%, you need to compute an equivalent confidence to use that combines the nominal power and confidence of the test. The composite z for this problem is 2.8 (1.96 + .84), so the equivalent confidence to use for a two-sided confidence interval is 99.4915%. The closest integer values for a, b, c, and d are, respectively, 17, 17, 4, and 4, for the following values:

- p_1: 34/42 = .81

- p_2: 21/42 = .5

- p_{12}: 17/42 = .405

- p_{21}: 4/42 = .095

The resulting confidence interval ranges from -.55 to -.015 – close to but not including 0.

For a sample size of 40, the expected values of p_1, p_2, p_{12}, and p_{21} are exactly .8, .5, .4, and .1 respectively, and the resulting confidence interval ranges from -.549 to .0025, just barely including 0. The bounds of these confidence intervals support the sample size estimate of 42, but if samples were expensive, 40 would probably be adequate.

Excel solution

1. Select the "Comparing 2 Paired Proportions (Completion Rates)" link under the Sample Size for Comparisons: Power Analysis heading.

2. Click on the link in the upper right "Estimated Sample Size from p12 and p21."

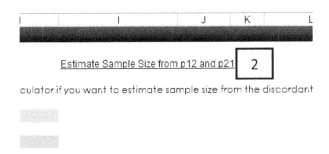

3. Enter the values for p_{12} (.4) and p_{21} (.1).

4. Set the Power to 80%.

5. Set the Confidence Level to 95% and number of tails to 2.

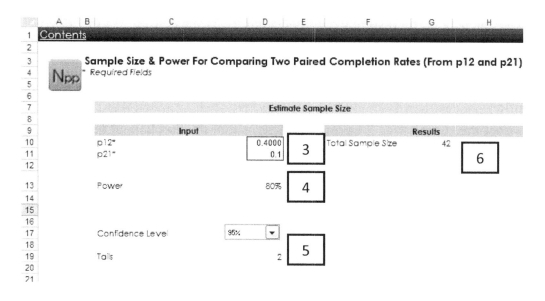

6. The estimated sample size needed is 42.

R solution

Enter the following commands:

n.mcnemar(.95,.8,.4,.1)

compute.equivalentconfidence(.95,.80,2)

ci.matchedproportions.difference(.81,.5,.405,.095,42,.994915)

ci.matchedproportions.difference(.8,.5,.4,.1,40,.994915)

The results are:

```
> n.mcnemar(.95,.8,.4,.1)

RESULT

Recommended sample size: 42

> compute.equivalentconfidence(.95,.80,2)

RESULTS

z(confidence): 1.959964
z(power): 0.8416212
z(combined): 2.801585

Equivalent confidence: 0.9949148
```

Chapter 6: What Sample Sizes Do We Need? Part I – Summative Studies

250

```
> ci.matchedproportions.difference(.81,.5,.405,.095,42,.994915)

RESULTS

99.4915% CONFIDENCE INTERVAL

p1: 0.81
p2: 0.5
Adjusted value of p1: 0.7830734
Adjusted value of p2: 0.5
Adjusted difference: -0.2830734
Margin of error: 0.2678804
Upper limit: -0.01519298
Observed difference: -0.31
Lower limit: -0.5509539

TESTS OF SIGNIFICANCE

McNemar Mid Probability (recommended): 0.00434351

Alternate analyses (not recommended)
McNemar Exact Probability: 0.00719738
McNemar Chi-Squared: 8.047619    df: 1    p: 0.00455635
McNemar Chi-Squared with Yates Correction: 6.857143    df: 1    p: 0.008828761

> ci.matchedproportions.difference(.8,.5,.4,.1,40,.994915)

RESULTS

99.4915% CONFIDENCE INTERVAL

p1: 0.8
p2: 0.5
Adjusted value of p1: 0.7731962
Adjusted value of p2: 0.5
Adjusted difference: -0.2731962
Margin of error: 0.2756976
Upper limit: 0.002501418
Observed difference: -0.3
Lower limit: -0.5488938

TESTS OF SIGNIFICANCE

McNemar Mid Probability (recommended): 0.00719738

Alternate analyses (not recommended)
McNemar Exact Probability: 0.01181793
McNemar Chi-Squared: 7.2    df: 1    p: 0.007290358
McNemar Chi-Squared with Yates Correction: 6.05    df: 1    p: 0.01390630
```

Chapter 7: What Sample Sizes Do We Need?

Part II – Formative Studies

Abstract

The purpose of formative user research is to discover and enumerate the events of interest in the study (for example, the problems that participants experience during a formative usability study). The statistical methods used to estimate sample sizes for formative research draw upon techniques not routinely taught in introductory statistics classes. This chapter covers techniques based on the binomial probability model and discusses issues associated with violation of the assumptions of the binomial model when averaging probabilities across a set of problems or participants while maintaining a focus on practical aspects of iterative design.

Example 1: Sample size for formative usability study

From page(s): 145

Summary: Suppose you decide to run a formative usability study and, for the tasks you use and the types of participants you observe, you want to have an 80% chance of observing, at least once, problems that have a probability of occurrence of .15. How many participants should you plan to observe?

Answer: The recommended sample size is 10.

Excel solution

1. Select the "Finding Problems in an Interface" link under the Sample Size for Problem Detection heading.

Sample Size for Margin of Error

Nr — For a Rating Scale

Nx̄ — For a Mean

Np — For a Completion Rate

Sample Size for Problem Detection

Ni — Finding Problems in an Interface   1

2. Enter the estimate of the problem occurrence at .15.

3. Set the chance of detecting the problem to 80%.

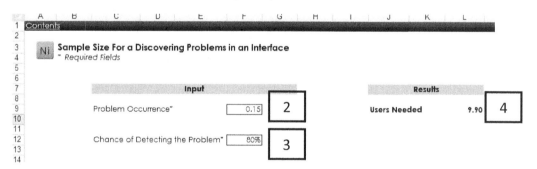

4. The estimated sample size needed is 9.9 (round up to 10).

R solution

Enter the following command:

n.atleastonce(.8,.15)

To use this command, you need to provide the problem discovery goal (.8 for 80%) and the desired problem discovery likelihood (.15 in this example). The result is:

```
RESULT

Recommended sample size: 10
```

Example 2: Analysis of 0-1 problem discovery matrix

From page(s): 152-156

Summary: Suppose you've run four participants in a usability study and have created a list of observed problems and matched them with the participants who experienced them, as shown in the following matrix (derived from Table 7.5 in the second edition of *Quantifying the User Experience: Practical Statistics for User Research*).

p	1	2	4	5	6	7	8
1	1	1	1	0	1	1	1
2	1	1	1	0	1	0	1
3	1	1	1	1	1	0	0
4	1	1	1	0	0	1	0

The first row in the matrix is a header row that includes numbers assigned to the different observed usability problems. The next four rows are for the four participants. The first column in the matrix is the participant numbers. The remaining columns are for the observed problems. A "1" indicates a participant experienced that problem; a "0" indicates that the participant did not experience the problem.

Chapter 7: What Sample Sizes Do We Need? Part II – Formative Studies

254

As covered in *Quantifying the User Experience: Practical Statistics for User Research* (2nd ed.), small-sample estimates of problem discovery rates tend to be highly inflated. For the matrix above, what are the initially estimated (observed) problem discovery rate (p_{est}), the adjusted problem discovery rate (p_{adj}), the estimated proportion of problems discovered so far (p_{sofar}), the estimated number of problems available for discovery ($N_{available}$), and the estimated number of undiscovered problems ($N_{undiscovered}$)?

Answer: The results are p_{est} = .71, p_{adj} = .48, p_{sofar} = .93, $N_{available}$ = 8, and $N_{undiscovered}$ = 1.

Excel solution

1. From the "Sample Size Problems" tab used in the previous example, scroll down to the "Compute Adjusted Value of Problem Occurrence p*" section and clear out any values in the matrix by clicking the "Clear Values" button (macros must be enabled).

2. Enter the values from the matrix by problem and user.

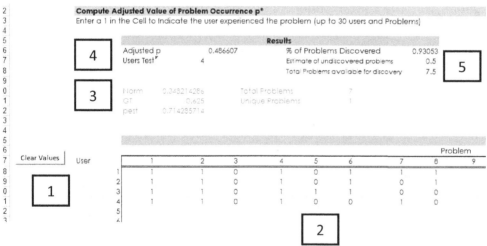

3. The value of p_{est} =.714 is at the bottom of the Results section.

4. The value of p_{adj} =.4866 appears at the top of the Results section.

5. The Results section also displays the estimates of p_{sofar} = .93053, $N_{available}$ = 7.5 (round up to 8), and $N_{undiscovered}$ = .5 (round up to 1).

R solution

Enter the following command:

> analyze.01matrix.fromweb("table705.txt")

This version of the command gets the designated 0-1 matrix file from Jim's website. To get a file on your local computer, you'd use the "analyze.01matrix.fromfile" command. The result is:

```
RESULTS

Number of participants: 4
Number of known problems: 7
Number of known problems that occurred just once: 1
Observed p: 0.7142857
pdef: 0.3482143
pGT: 0.625
Adjusted p: 0.4866071
Estimated proportion of discovery (so far): 0.9305297
Estimated number of problems available for discovery: 8
Estimated number of undiscovered problems: 1
```

Example 3: Analysis of 0-1 problem discovery matrix

From page(s): 156

Summary: Imagine a usability study of five tasks using a prototype speech recognition application with weather, news, and e-mail/calendar functions. Participant 1 experienced no usability problems; Participant 2 had one problem in each of Tasks 2, 4, and 5; and Participant 3 had the same problem as Participant 2 in Task 2, and different problems in Tasks 1, 4, and 5 (results shown in the following matrix). Doing an analysis similar to that of Exercise 2, what are the results?

p	1	2	3	4	5	6
1	0	0	0	0	0	0
2	0	1	0	1	1	0
3	1	1	1	0	0	1

Answer: The results are p_{est} = .39, p_{adj} = .125, p_{sofar} = .33, $N_{available}$ = 19, and $N_{undiscovered}$ = 13.

Excel solution

1. From the "Sample Size Problems" tab used in the previous example, scroll down to the "Compute Adjusted Value of Problem Occurrence p*" section and clear out any values in the matrix by clicking the "Clear Values" button (macros must be enabled).

2. Enter the values from the matrix by problem and user.

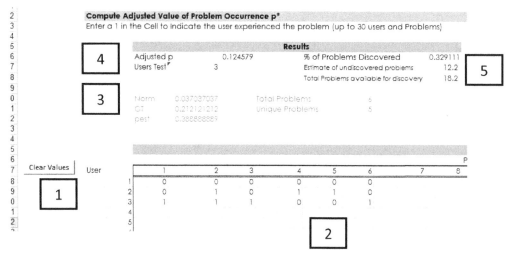

3. The value of p_{est} =.3888 is at the bottom of the Results section.

4. The value of p_{adj} =.124579 is at the top of the Results section.

5. The Results section also displays the estimates of p_{sofar} = .32911, $N_{available}$ = 18.2 (round up to 19), and $N_{undiscovered}$ = 12.2 (round up to 13).

R solution

Enter the following command:

```
analyze.01matrix.fromweb("cs1.txt")
```

The result is:

```
RESULTS

Number of participants: 3
Number of known problems: 6
Number of known problems that occurred just once: 5
Observed p: 0.3888889
pdef: 0.0370304
pGT: 0.2121212
Adjusted p: 0.1245791
Estimated proportion of discovery (so far): 0.3291110
Estimated number of problems available for discovery: 19
Estimated number of undiscovered problems: 13
```

Example 4: Additional problem discovery analyses

From page(s): 156

Summary: Suppose rather than having the 0-1 problem discovery matrix, you have the following data from an analysis of the original matrix:

- Number of participants (n) = 7

- Number of different usability problems discovered (N) = 33

- Initial estimate of p: .27

- Adjusted estimate of p: .15

Given this information, what are the estimated proportion of problems discovered so far (p_{sofar}), the estimated number of problems available for discovery ($N_{available}$), and the estimated number of undiscovered problems ($N_{undiscovered}$).

Answer: The results are p_{sofar} = .68, $N_{available}$ = 49, and $N_{undiscovered}$ = 16.

Excel solution

1. In an Excel sheet type the following : = 1 - (1-.15)^7

2. =33/.68

3. =49-33

5		
6	0.679422912	1
7	48.52941176	2
8	16	
9		3
10		

R solution

Enter the following commands:

1 - (1-.15)^7

33/.68

49-33

These are standard R math commands. The first computes p_{sofar} given the adjusted estimate of p (.15) and the number of participants run so far (7). The second computes $N_{available}$ given the number of different events (problems) observed so far and p_{sofar}. The third provides the estimate of the number of events (problems) remaining for discovery ($N_{undiscovered}$) given the estimate of $N_{available}$ (49) and the number of different events (problems) observed so far (33). The result is:

```
> 1 - (1-.15)^7
[1] 0.6794229
>
> 33/.68
[1] 48.52941
>
> 49-33
[1] 16
```

Exercise 1: Sample size for formative usability study

From page(s): 179

Problem: Assume you need to conduct a single-shot (not iterative) formative usability study that can detect about 85% of the problems that have a probability of occurrence of .25 for the specific participants and tasks used in the study (in other words, not 85% of ALL possible usability problems, but 85% of the problems discoverable with your specific method).   How many participants should you plan to run?

Answer: You should plan to run 7 participants.

Excel solution

1. Select the "Finding Problems in an Interface" link under the Sample Size for Problem Detection heading.

Sample Size for Margin of Error

Nr   For a Rating Scale

Nx̄   For a Mean

Np   For a Completion Rate

Sample Size for Problem Detection

 Ni   Finding Problems in an Interface   1

2. Enter the estimate of the problem occurrence at .25.

3. Set the chance of detecting the problem to 85%.

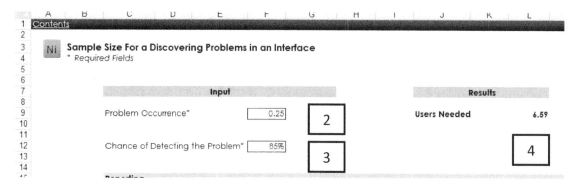

4. The estimated sample size needed is 6.59 (round up to 7).

R solution

Enter the following command:

    n.atleastonce(.85,.25)

The result is:

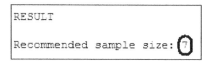

Exercise 2: Sample size for formative usability study

From page(s): 180

Problem: Suppose you decide that you will maintain your goal of 85% discovery, but need to set the target value of *p* to .20. Now how many participants do you need?

Answer: You should plan to run 9 participants.

Excel solution

1. From the "Sample Size Problems" tab, enter the estimate of the problem occurrence at .20.

2. Set the chance of detecting the problem to 85%.

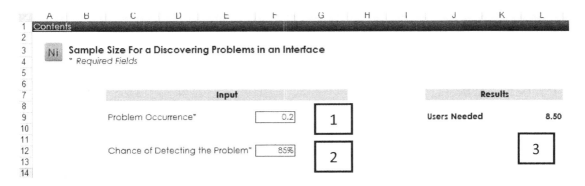

3. The estimated sample size needed is 8.5 (round up to 9).

R solution

Enter the following command:

n.atleastonce(.85,.2)

The result is:

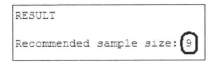

```
RESULT

Recommended sample size: (9)
```

Exercise 3: Probability of discovery of events of given *p* and *n*

From page(s): 180

Problem: You just ran a formative usability study with 4 participants. What percentage of the problems of *p* = .50 are you likely to have discovered? What about *p* = .01; .90; .25?

Answer: For *n* = 4 and *p* = .50, it's 94%. For *p* = .01, it's 4% expected discovery; for *p* = .90, it's 99.99%; for *p* = .25, it's 68%.

Excel solution

1. Select the "Problem Frequency" link under the Confidence Intervals heading.

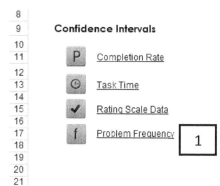

2. Scroll down and enter the sample size of 4.

3. Enter in the values of .5, .10, .9 and .25 (other values are shown for comparison).

4. The results show the likelihood (as percentages) of uncovering each problem for the given frequencies.

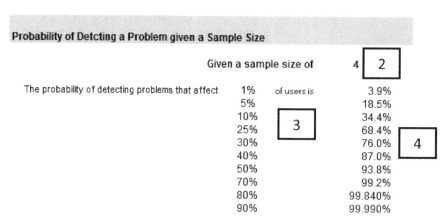

R solution

Enter the following commands:

```
p.atleastonce(.5,4)

p.atleastonce(.01,4)

p.atleastonce(.9,4)
```

p.atleastonce(.25,4)

For this command, you need to provide the probability of the event and the sample size (number of trials). The result is:

```
> p.atleastonce(.5,4)

RESULT

Probability of an event of p = 0.5 happening at least once in 4 trials: 0.9375

> p.atleastonce(.01,4)

RESULT

Probability of an event of p = 0.01 happening at least once in 4 trials: 0.03940399

> p.atleastonce(.9,4)

RESULT

Probability of an event of p = 0.9 happening at least once in 4 trials: 0.9999

> p.atleastonce(.25,4)

RESULT

Probability of an event of p = 0.25 happening at least once in 4 trials: 0.6835938
```

Exercises 4-6: Analysis of 0-1 problem discovery matrix

From page(s): 180

Problem: The following matrix shows the results of a formative usability evaluation of an interactive voice response application in which six participants completed four tasks, with the discovery of twelve distinct usability problems. For this matrix, what is the observed value of p across these problems and participants? What is the adjusted value of p? Using the adjusted value of p, what is the estimated total number of the problems available for discovery with these tasks and types of participants? What is the estimated number of undiscovered problems? How confident should you be in this estimate? Should you run more participants, or is it reasonable to stop?

p	1	2	3	4	5	6	7	8	9	10	11	12
1	0	0	1	0	0	0	0	0	0	0	1	0
2	1	0	1	1	0	0	0	0	1	0	1	0
3	0	0	0	0	1	0	0	0	0	0	1	0
4	0	1	0	0	0	1	0	0	0	0	1	0
5	0	1	1	0	0	0	0	0	0	1	0	1
6	0	0	0	0	0	0	1	1	0	0	1	1

Answer: The initial estimate (observed value) of p is .28. The adjusted estimate is .13. For these six participants the estimated discovery (so far) is .57. The estimated number of problems available for discovery is 22, and the estimated number of undiscovered problems is about 10. Because a sample size of 6 is in the range of over-optimism when using the binomial model, there are probably more than 10 problems remaining for discovery. Given the results shown in Table 7.9 in *Quantifying the User Experience: Practical Statistics for User Research* (2nd ed.), it's reasonable to believe that there could be an additional 2 to 7 undiscovered problems, so it's unlikely that there are more than 17 undiscovered problems. This low rate of problem discovery (p_{adj} = .13) is indicative of an interface in which there are few high-frequency problems to find. If there are resources to continue testing, it might be more productive to change the tasks in an attempt to create the conditions for discovering a different set of problems and, possibly, more frequently-occurring problems.

Excel solution

1. Select the "Finding Problems in an Interface" link under the Sample Size for Problem Detection heading.

Sample Size for Margin of Error

 For a Rating Scale

 For a Mean

 For a Completion Rate

Sample Size for Problem Detection

 Finding Problems in an Interface   1

2. Clear out any previous values (macros must be enabled).

3. Enter the values from the matrix by problem and user.

Compute Adjusted Value of Problem Occurrence p*
Enter a 1 in the Cell to indicate the user experienced the problem (up to 30 users and Problems)

	Results		
Adjusted p	0.12963	% of Problems Discovered	0.565265
Users Test	6	Estimate of undiscovered problems	9.2
		Total Problems available for discov	21.2

Norm	0.092592593	Total Problems	12
GT	0.166666667	Unique Problems	8
pest	0.277777778		

[boxes labeled: 5, 4, 2, 6, 3]

User	Problem											
	1	2	3	4	5	6	7	8	9	10	11	12
1	0	0	1	0	0	0	0	0	0	0	1	0
2	1	0	1	1	0	0	0	0	1	0	1	0
3	0	0	0	0	1	0	0	0	0	0	1	0
4	0	1	0	0	0	1	0	0	0	0	1	0
5	0	1	1	0	0	0	0	0	0	1	0	1
6	0	0	0	0	0	0	1	1	0	0	1	1

[Clear Values]

4. The value of p_{est} =.2778 is at the bottom of the Results section.

5. The value of p_{adj} =.12963 is at the top of the Results section.

6. The Results section also displays the estimates of p_{sofar} = .565 $N_{available}$ = 21.2 (round up to 22), and $N_{undiscovered}$ = 9.2 (round up to 10).

R solution

Enter the following command:

```
analyze.01matrix.fromweb("table711.txt")
```

The result is:

```
RESULTS

Number of participants: 6
Number of known problems: 12
Number of known problems that occurred just once: 8
Observed p: 0.2777778
pdef: 0.0925926
pGT: 0.1666667
Adjusted p: 0.1296296
Estimated proportion of discovery (so far): 0.565265
Estimated number of problems available for discovery: 22
Estimated number of undiscovered problems: 10
```

Chapter 8: Standardized Usability Questionnaires

Abstract

Standardized usability questionnaires are questionnaires designed for the assessment of perceived usability, typically with a specific set of questions presented in a specified order using a specified format with specific rules for producing scores based on the answers of respondents. For usability testing, standardized questionnaires are available for assessment of a product at the end of a study (post-study – for example, QUIS, SUMI, PSSUQ, and SUS) and after each task in a study (post-task – for example, ASQ, Expectation Ratings, SEQ, SMEQ, and Usability Magnitude Estimation). Standardized questionnaires are also available for the general assessment of website usability (for example, WAMMI and SUPR-Q). All of these questionnaires have undergone psychometric qualification, including assessment of reliability, validity, and sensitivity, making them valuable tools for usability practitioners.

Exercise 1: Analysis of matrix of PSSUQ data

From page(s): 240-241

Problem: You've run a study using the PSSUQ (standard Version 3), with the results shown in the following table. What are each participant's overall and subscale scores, and what are the mean overall and subscale scores for the study?

	Participant					
	1	2	3	4	5	6
Item 1	1	2	2	2	5	1
Item 2	1	2	2	1	5	1
Item 3	1	2	3	1	4	1
Item 4	1	1	2	1	4	1
Item 5	1	1	2	1	5	1
Item 6	1	1	4	1	4	3
Item 7	1	2	NA	1	6	1
Item 8	3	1	NA	1	6	1
Item 9	3	1	1	1	5	1
Item 10	1	3	2	1	4	1
Item 11	2	2	2	1	4	1
Item 12	1	1	2	1	4	1
Item 13	1	1	2	2	4	1
Item 14	1	1	2	3	4	1
Item 15	1	1	3	1	4	1
Item 16	1	1	2	1	4	1

Answer: The following table shows the overall and subscale PSSUQ scores for each participant and the mean overall and subscale scores for the study (averaged across participants). Even though there is some missing data, only two cells in the table are empty (designated with NA), so it's OK to just average the available data.

	Participant						
	1	**2**	**3**	**4**	**5**	**6**	**Mean**
Item 1	1	2	2	2	5	1	2.17
Item 2	1	2	2	1	5	1	2.00
Item 3	1	2	3	1	4	1	2.00
Item 4	1	1	2	1	4	1	1.67
Item 5	1	1	2	1	5	1	1.83
Item 6	1	1	4	1	4	3	2.33
Item 7	1	2	NA	1	6	1	2.20
Item 8	3	1	NA	1	6	1	2.40
Item 9	3	1	1	1	5	1	2.00
Item 10	1	3	2	1	4	1	2.00
Item 11	2	2	2	1	4	1	2.00
Item 12	1	1	2	1	4	1	1.67
Item 13	1	1	2	2	4	1	1.83
Item 14	1	1	2	3	4	1	2.00
Item 15	1	1	3	1	4	1	1.83
Item 16	1	1	2	1	4	1	1.67
Overall	1.31	1.44	2.21	1.25	4.50	1.13	1.97
SysUse	1.00	1.50	2.50	1.17	4.50	1.33	2.00
InfoQual	1.83	1.67	1.75	1.00	4.83	1.00	2.01
IntQual	1.00	1.00	2.33	2.00	4.00	1.00	1.89

Excel solution

1. Select the "Rating Scale Data" link under the Confidence Intervals section.

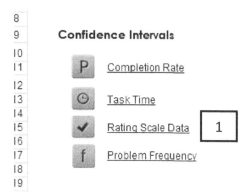

2. Clear out any previous values (macros must be enabled) and enter the values for each of the 16 items.

3. Set the confidence level to 95%.

4. The mean, standard deviation and sample size appear in the Descriptive statistics section.

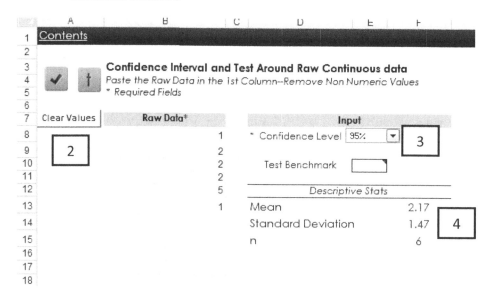

5. The confidence interval is in the Results section.

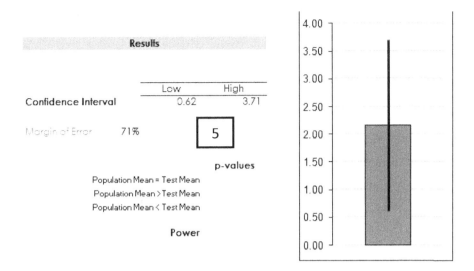

	Low	High
Confidence Interval	0.62	3.71

Results

Margin of Error   71%   5

p-values

Population Mean = Test Mean
Population Mean > Test Mean
Population Mean < Test Mean

Power

6. Repeat this procedure for all items, subscales and the overall score.

R solution

Enter the following command:

analyze.pssuq.fromweb("table810.txt",.95)

This command gets the designated data file from Jim's website (based on Table 8.10 in the second edition of *Quantifying the User Experience: Practical Statistics for User Research*) and computes confidence intervals using the designated level (in this case, .95 for 95%). To analyze a file on your local computer, you'd use the "analyze.pssuq.fromfile" command. The result is:

```
RESULTS OF PSSUQ ANALYSIS

Scales

Overall mean: 1.97      95% confidence interval: 0.612 - 3.33      Comparisons: Mean lower than norm; interval consistent with norm
SysUse  mean: 2         95% confidence interval: 0.601 - 3.4       Comparisons: Mean lower than norm; interval consistent with norm
InfoQual mean: 2.01     95% confidence interval: 0.513 - 3.51      Comparisons: Mean lower than norm; interval consistent with norm
IntQual mean: 1.89      95% confidence interval: 0.644 - 3.13      Comparisons: Mean lower than norm; interval consistent with norm

Items

Item 01 mean: 2.17      95% confidence interval: 0.622 - 3.71      Comparisons: Mean lower than norm; interval consistent with norm
Item 02 mean: 2         95% confidence interval: 0.374 - 3.63      Comparisons: Mean lower than norm; interval consistent with norm
Item 03 mean: 2         95% confidence interval: 0.673 - 3.33      Comparisons: Mean lower than norm; interval consistent with norm
Item 04 mean: 1.67      95% confidence interval: 0.396 - 2.94      Comparisons: Mean lower than norm; interval consistent with norm
Item 05 mean: 1.83      95% confidence interval: 0.152 - 3.51      Comparisons: Mean lower than norm; interval consistent with norm
Item 06 mean: 2.33      95% confidence interval: 0.753 - 3.91      Comparisons: Mean lower than norm; interval consistent with norm
Item 07 mean: 2.2       95% confidence interval: -0.0751 - 4.48    Comparisons: Mean lower than norm; interval consistent with norm
Item 08 mean: 2.4       95% confidence interval: 0.101 - 4.7       Comparisons: Mean lower than norm; interval consistent with norm
Item 09 mean: 2         95% confidence interval: 0.244 - 3.76      Comparisons: Mean lower than norm; interval consistent with norm
Item 10 mean: 2         95% confidence interval: 0.673 - 3.33      Comparisons: Mean lower than norm; interval consistent with norm
Item 11 mean: 2         95% confidence interval: 0.85 - 3.15       Comparisons: Mean lower than norm; interval consistent with norm
Item 12 mean: 1.67      95% confidence interval: 0.396 - 2.94      Comparisons: Mean lower than norm; interval consistent with norm
Item 13 mean: 1.83      95% confidence interval: 0.606 - 3.06      Comparisons: Mean lower than norm; interval consistent with norm
Item 14 mean: 2         95% confidence interval: 0.673 - 3.33      Comparisons: Mean lower than norm; interval consistent with norm
Item 15 mean: 1.83      95% confidence interval: 0.438 - 3.23      Comparisons: Mean lower than norm; interval consistent with norm
Item 16 mean: 1.67      95% confidence interval: 0.396 - 2.94      Comparisons: Mean lower than norm; interval consistent with norm
```

```
Scales

Overall mean: 1.97
SysUse  mean: 2
InfoQual mean: 2.01
IntQual mean: 1.89

Items

Item 01 mean: 2.17
Item 02 mean: 2
Item 03 mean: 2
Item 04 mean: 1.67
Item 05 mean: 1.83
Item 06 mean: 2.33
Item 07 mean: 2.2
Item 08 mean: 2.4
Item 09 mean: 2
Item 10 mean: 2
Item 11 mean: 2
Item 12 mean: 1.67
Item 13 mean: 1.83
Item 14 mean: 2
Item 15 mean: 1.83
Item 16 mean: 1.67
```

Exercise 2: More analysis of matrix of PSSUQ data

From page(s): 240-241

Problem: Given the published information about normative patterns in responses to the PSSUQ, are you surprised by the mean score of Item 7 relative to the other items for the data in the table above? What about the relative values of InfoQual and IntQual? Based on the typical values for the PSSUQ, does this product seem to be above or below average in perceived usability?

Answer: Regarding Item 7, generally, its scores tend to be higher (poorer) than those for other items, but in this set of data, the mean item scores are fairly uniform, ranging from 1.67 to 2.40, with 2.20 for Item 7, making it one of the higher scoring items but not as much higher as is usual, which is a bit surprising. The same is true for the relative pattern of the subscales. Typically, InfoQual is about half a point higher than IntQual, but for these data the difference is only about .15. Based on the typical values for the PSSUQ, the mean Overall score is usually about 2.82, so with an Overall score of 1.98, this product seems to be above average in perceived usability – at least, in reference to the products evaluated to produce the current PSSUQ norms. To determine if it is significantly better than average, you'd need to compute a confidence interval on the data from the study to see if the interval included or excluded the benchmark. It turns out that the 95% confidence interval for Overall ranges from .622 to 3.33 – a fairly wide interval due to the small sample size and relatively high variability – so even though the mean is lower than the norm, the interval is consistent with the norm. Thus, this Overall score is not statistically significantly different from the norm of 2.82.

Excel solution

1. Select the "Rating Scale Scores against a Criterion" link under the Confidence Intervals section.

Test a Mean or Proportion to Criteron

Pb   1 Proportion Binomial Test / zTest
     Completion Rate against a Criterion

tₗₒg 1-Sample t-test using Log Transformation
     Task Time against a Criterion

t   1-Sample t-test
     Rating Scale Scores against a Criterion   [1]

tₛ   1-Sample t-test
     Rating Scale Scores against a Criterion (Summary)

2. Clear out any previous values (macros must be enabled) and enter the values for the Overall score.

3. Set the confidence level to 95%.

4. Enter the benchmark of 2.82.

5. The mean, standard deviation and sample size appear in the Descriptive Stats section.

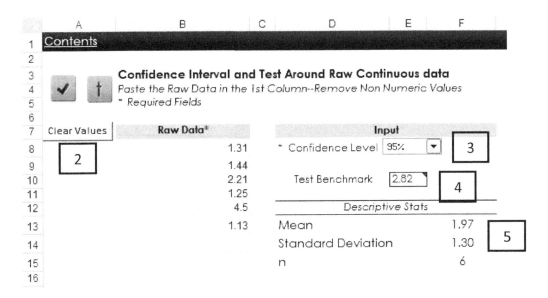

6. The range of the confidence interval and the *p*-value (.17) against the test are in the Results section.

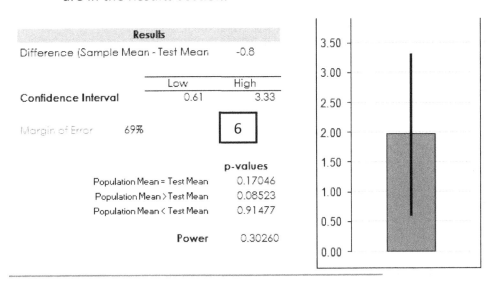

R solution

Enter the following command:

analyze.pssuq.fromweb("table810.txt",.95)

The result is:

```
RESULTS OF PSSUQ ANALYSIS

Scales

Overall mean: 1.97      95% confidence interval: 0.612 - 3.33    Comparisons: Mean lower than norm; interval consistent with norm
SysUse  mean: 2         95% confidence interval: 0.601 - 3.4     Comparisons: Mean lower than norm; interval consistent with norm
InfoQual mean: 2.01     95% confidence interval: 0.513 - 3.51    Comparisons: Mean lower than norm; interval consistent with norm
IntQual mean: 1.89      95% confidence interval: 0.644 - 3.13    Comparisons: Mean lower than norm; interval consistent with norm

Items

Item 01 mean: 2.17      95% confidence interval: 0.622 - 3.71    Comparisons: Mean lower than norm; interval consistent with norm
Item 02 mean: 2         95% confidence interval: 0.374 - 3.63    Comparisons: Mean lower than norm; interval consistent with norm
Item 03 mean: 2         95% confidence interval: 0.673 - 3.33    Comparisons: Mean lower than norm; interval consistent with norm
Item 04 mean: 1.67      95% confidence interval: 0.396 - 2.94    Comparisons: Mean lower than norm; interval consistent with norm
Item 05 mean: 1.83      95% confidence interval: 0.152 - 3.51    Comparisons: Mean lower than norm; interval consistent with norm
Item 06 mean: 2.33      95% confidence interval: 0.753 - 3.91    Comparisons: Mean lower than norm; interval consistent with norm
Item 07 mean: 2.2       95% confidence interval: -0.0751 - 4.48  Comparisons: Mean lower than norm; interval consistent with norm
Item 08 mean: 2.4       95% confidence interval: 0.101 - 4.7     Comparisons: Mean lower than norm; interval consistent with norm
Item 09 mean: 2         95% confidence interval: 0.244 - 3.76    Comparisons: Mean lower than norm; interval consistent with norm
Item 10 mean: 2         95% confidence interval: 0.673 - 3.33    Comparisons: Mean lower than norm; interval consistent with norm
Item 11 mean: 2         95% confidence interval: 0.85 - 3.15     Comparisons: Mean lower than norm; interval consistent with norm
Item 12 mean: 1.67      95% confidence interval: 0.396 - 2.94    Comparisons: Mean lower than norm; interval consistent with norm
Item 13 mean: 1.83      95% confidence interval: 0.606 - 3.06    Comparisons: Mean lower than norm; interval consistent with norm
Item 14 mean: 2         95% confidence interval: 0.673 - 3.33    Comparisons: Mean lower than norm; interval consistent with norm
Item 15 mean: 1.83      95% confidence interval: 0.438 - 3.23    Comparisons: Mean lower than norm; interval consistent with norm
Item 16 mean: 1.67      95% confidence interval: 0.396 - 2.94    Comparisons: Mean lower than norm; interval consistent with norm
```

```
Overall mean: 1.97

95% confidence interval: 0.612 - 3.33

Comparisons: Mean lower than norm; interval consistent with norm
```

Exercise 3: Analysis of matrix of SUS data

From page(s): 240-242

Problem: Suppose you've run a study using the standard version of the SUS, with the following results. What are the SUS scores for each participant and their average for the product?

	Participant				
	1	**2**	**3**	**4**	**5**
Item 1	3	2	5	4	5
Item 2	1	1	2	2	1
Item 3	4	4	4	5	5
Item 4	1	3	1	1	1
Item 5	3	4	4	4	5
Item 6	1	2	2	2	1
Item 7	4	3	4	3	5
Item 8	1	2	1	1	1
Item 9	4	4	5	3	5
Item 10	2	1	2	3	1

Answer: The following table shows the recoded item values and SUS scores for each participant and the mean SUS score for the study averaged across participants.

	Participants					
	1	2	3	4	5	
Item 1	2	1	4	3	4	
Item 2	4	4	3	3	4	
Item 3	3	3	3	4	4	
Item 4	4	2	4	4	4	
Item 5	2	3	3	3	4	
Item 6	4	3	3	3	4	
Item 7	3	2	3	2	4	
Item 8	4	3	4	4	4	
Item 9	3	3	4	2	4	
Item 10	3	4	3	2	4	
						Mean
Overall	80	70	85	75	100	82.00
Pred-LTR	8	7	8	7	10	Grade: A

Excel solution

1. For scoring SUS, we recommend using the Practical Guide to the System Usability Scale Calculator (available for purchase at: http://www.measuringu.com/products/SUSpack) which reduces errors in coding and item reversal and generates the percentile rank and grade automatically.

2. To score by hand, enter the values in a spreadsheet. For the odd items enter the formula =5-B4 , where B4 is the value in cell B4. For even items enter =B5-1 where B5 is the value in cell B5.

3. Add up all the items for each user, for example, =SUM(I3:I13) would be the sum for user 1.

4. Multiply the summed score by 2.5 to get the SUS score per user.

		Orginal								Recoded			
	1	2	3	4	5			1	2	3	4	5
Item 1	3	2	5	4	5			2	1	4	3	4
Item 2	1	1	2	2	1			4	4	3	3	4
Item 3	4	4	4	5	5			3	3	3	4	4
Item 4	1	3	1	1	1			4	2	4	4	4
Item 5	3	4	4	4	5			2	3	3	3	4
Item 6	1	2	2	2	1			4	3	3	3	4
Item 7	4	3	4	3	5			3	2	3	2	4
Item 8	1	2	1	1	1			4	3	4	4	4
Item 9	4	4	5	3	5			3	3	4	2	4
Item 10	2	1	2	3	1			3	4	3	2	4
Sum								32	28	34	30	40
Times 2.5								80	70	85	75	100

(Boxed markers on page: **2**, **3**, **4**)

R solution

Enter the following command:

```
analyze.sus.fromweb("table811.txt",.9)
```

This command gets the designated data file from Jim's website (based on Table 8.9 in the second edition of *Quantifying the User Experience: Practical Statistics for User Research*) and computes confidence intervals using the designated level (in this case, .9 for 90%). To analyze a file on your local computer, you'd use the "analyze.sus.fromfile" command. The result is:

```
RESULTS OF SUS ANALYSIS

Overall

Overall SUS mean: 82      90% confidence interval: 71 - 93
Percentiles: 92.6         90% confidence interval: 59.8 - 100
Curve grades: A           90% confidence interval: C - A+
Estimated NPS: 20%

Subscales

Usable scale: 81.2        90% confidence interval: 69.9 - 92.6
Learnable scale: 85       90% confidence interval: 75 - 95
```

Exercise 4: More analysis of matrix of SUS data

From page(s): 241-242

Problem: Given the published information about typical SUS scores, is the average SUS for the data in the table above generally above or below average? What grade would it receive using the Sauro/Lewis SUS grading curve? If you computed a 90% confidence interval, what would the grade range be? If these participants also responded to the NPS Likelihood to Recommend item, are any of them likely to be Promoters? Using those estimated Likelihood to Recommend ratings, what is the estimated Net Promoter Score (NPS)?

Answer: Based on the data collected by Sauro (2011), the mean SUS score across a large number of usability studies is 68, so the mean from this study is above average. On the Sauro/Lewis SUS grading curve, scores between 80.8 and 84.0 get an A (see Table 8.6 in the second edition of *Quantifying the User Experience: Practical Statistics for User Research*). A 90% confidence interval on these data ranges from about 71 to 93, so the corresponding grade range is from C to A+ (at least you know it's probably not a D), and because the confidence interval does not include 68, the result is significantly above average ($p < .10$). If these participants also responded to the NPS Likelihood to Recommend item, only one of them is likely to be a Promoter (responding with a 9 or 10 to the Likelihood to Recommend question). The simplified regression equation for estimating Likelihood to Recommend from SUS is LTR = SUS/10, so the predicted Likelihood to Recommend responses for these five participants are, respectively, 8, 7, 8, 7, and 10. Given these LTR scores, there are 0% Detractors and 20% (1/5) Promoters, for a roughly estimated NPS of 20% (%Promoters minus %Detractors).

Excel solution

1. Select the "Rating Scale Scores against a Criterion" link under the Confidence Intervals section.

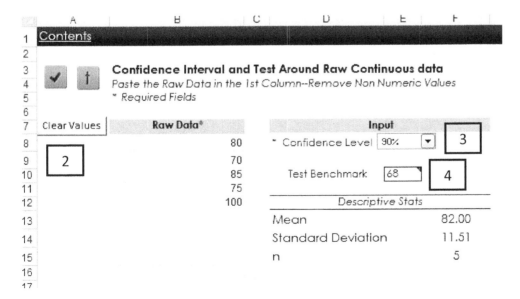

2. Clear out any previous values (macros must be enabled) and enter the 5 SUS scores.

3. Set the confidence level to 90%.

4. Enter the benchmark of 68.

5. The *p*-value (.05301) and 90% confidence interval appear in the Results section.

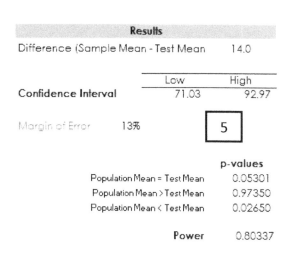

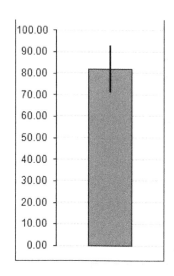

R solution

Enter the following command:

analyze.sus.fromweb("table811.txt",.9)

The result is:

```
RESULTS OF SUS ANALYSIS

Overall

Overall SUS mean: 82      90% confidence interval: 71 - 93
Percentiles: 92.6         90% confidence interval: 59.8 - 100
Curve grades: A           90% confidence interval: C - A+
Estimated NPS: 20%

Subscales

Usable scale: 81.2        90% confidence interval: 69.9 - 92.6
Learnable scale: 85       90% confidence interval: 75 - 95
```

Chapter 9: Six Enduring Controversies in Measurement and Statistics

Abstract

This chapter contains discussions of six enduring controversies in measurement and statistics, specifically:

- Is it OK to average data from multipoint scales?
- Do you need to test at least 30 users?
- Should you always conduct a two-tailed test?
- Can you reject the null hypothesis when p > .05?
- Can you combine usability metrics into single scores?
- What if you need to run more than one test?

Because many usability practitioners deeply depend on the use of measurement and statistics to guide their design recommendations, they inherit these controversies. In this chapter we summarize both sides of each issue and discuss what we, as pragmatic usability practitioners, recommend.

Exercise 1: Sample size for within-subjects comparison of continuous measure

From page(s): 274 (Chapter Review Question 2 in text)

Problem: Suppose you're planning a within-subjects comparison of the accuracy of two dictation products, with the following criteria (similar to Example 5 in Chapter 6):

- Difference score variability from a previous evaluation = 10.0

- Critical difference = 3.0

- Desired level of confidence (two-tailed): 90%

- Desired power: 90%

What sample size should you plan for the test? If it turns out to be less than 30 (and it will), what should you say to someone who criticizes your plan by claiming "you have to have a sample size of at least 30 to be statistically significant?"

Answer: You should plan for a sample size of 12. If challenged because this is less than 30, your response should acknowledge the general rule of thumb (no need to get into a fight), but point out that you've used a statistical process to get a more accurate estimate based on the needs of the study, the details of which you'd be happy to share with the critic. After all, no matter how good a rule of thumb might (or might not) be, when it states a single specific number, it's very unlikely to be exactly right.

Excel solution

1. Select the "Comparing 2 Paired Means" link under the Confidence Intervals section.

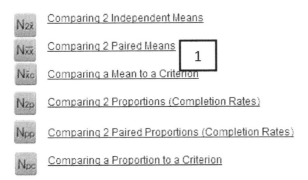

2. Enter the critical difference (3) and standard deviation (=SQRT(10) = 3.1622277).

3. Set the Power to 90%.

4. Set the confidence level to 90% and number of tails to 2.

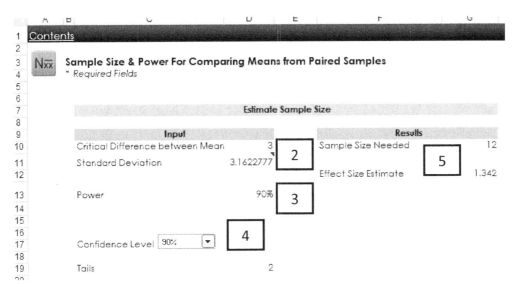

5. The estimated sample size needed is 12.

R solution

Enter the following command:

n.t.onesample.givenvar(.9,.9,10,3,2)

This command takes, in order, the desired level of confidence (.9 for 90%), the desired level of power (.9 for 90%), the estimated variance, the desired precision (critical difference) and the appropriate number of tails for the test (2). The result is:

```
RESULTS

Recommended sample size: (12)
Number of iterations: 2
```

Exercise 2: Likelihood of getting *x* significant results when alpha = .05

From page(s): 275 (Chapter Review Question 6 in text)

Problem: Suppose you've run a formative usability study comparing your product against five competitive products with four measures and five tasks, for a total of 100 tests, using α = .05, with the results shown in the table below (an asterisk indicates a significant result). Are you likely to have seen this many significant results out of 100 tests by chance if the null hypothesis is true? How would you interpret the findings by product?

Task	Measure	Product A	Product B	Product C	Product D	Product E
1	1	*	*	*	*	*
1	2					
1	3					
1	4				*	*
2	1			*	*	*
2	2					
2	3					
2	4				*	*
3	1		*			*
3	2					
3	3					

3	4					*
4	1				*	*
4	2			*		
4	3					
4	4					
5	1				*	*
5	2					
5	3					
5	4					*
# Sig?		1	2	3	6	9

Answer: For the full set of 100 tests, there were 21 significant results (α = .05). The critical value of x (number of significant tests) for 100 tests if the null hypothesis is true is 9, so it seems very unlikely that the overall null hypothesis is true (in fact, the probability is just .00000002). For a study like this, the main purpose is usually to understand where a control product is in its competitive usability space, so the focus is on differences in products rather than differences in measures or tasks. For the subsets of 20 tests by product, the critical value of x is 3, so you should be relatively cautious in how you use the significant results for Products A and B, but can make stronger claims with regard to the statistically significant differences between the control product and Products C, D, and E (slightly stronger for C, much stronger for D and E). The following table shows the probabilities for these hypothetical product results.

Product	x (# sig)	P(x or more)
A	1	0.642
B	2	0.264
C	3	0.075
D	6	0.0003
E	9	0.0000002

Excel solution

1. Open an excel sheet and use the following formula =1-BINOMDIST(C4-1,20,0.05,TRUE) where C4 is the number of significant outcomes. Repeat this for values of 1, 2, 3, 6, and 9.

2. For 21 out of 100, enter =1-BINOMDIST(21-1,100,0.05,TRUE).

	Probability	
1	0.641514078	1
2	0.264160475	
3	0.075483674	
6	0.000329294	
9	1.97934E-07	
21	2.08106E-08	2

R solution

Enter the following commands:

p.xormore(21,100,.05,.10)

p.xormore(1,20,.05,.10)

p.xormore(2,20,.05,.10)

p.xormore(3,20,.05,.10)

p.xormore(6,20,.05,.10)

p.xormore(9,20,.05,.10)

For this command, you need to provide the number of statistically significant results, the total number of tests, the criterion used to determine statistical significance (alpha), and the criterion to use to establish the critical value of x (the value of x at which the likelihood of x or more events is less than the criterion). The result is:

```
> p.xormore(21,100,.05,.10)

RESULTS

Probability of 21 or more significant outcomes given 100 tests with alpha of 0.05 is: 2.081061e-08
For the criterion of 0.1 the critical value of x is: 9

> p.xormore(1,20,.05,.10)

RESULTS

Probability of 1 or more significant outcomes given 20 tests with alpha of 0.05 is: 0.6415141
For the criterion of 0.1 the critical value of x is: 3

> p.xormore(2,20,.05,.10)

RESULTS

Probability of 2 or more significant outcomes given 20 tests with alpha of 0.05 is: 0.2641605
For the criterion of 0.1 the critical value of x is: 3

> p.xormore(3,20,.05,.10)

RESULTS

Probability of 3 or more significant outcomes given 20 tests with alpha of 0.05 is: 0.07548367
For the criterion of 0.1 the critical value of x is: 3

> p.xormore(6,20,.05,.10)

RESULTS

Probability of 6 or more significant outcomes given 20 tests with alpha of 0.05 is: 0.0003292943
For the criterion of 0.1 the critical value of x is: 3

> p.xormore(9,20,.05,.10)

RESULTS

Probability of 9 or more significant outcomes given 20 tests with alpha of 0.05 is: 1.979338e-07
For the criterion of 0.1 the critical value of x is: 3
```

Chapter 10: An Introduction to Correlation, Regression, and ANOVA

Abstract

The previous chapters have covered the fundamentals that practitioners need to conduct usability testing and other user research. There is a world of more advanced statistical methods that can inform user research. In this chapter we provide an introduction to three related methods: correlation, regression, and analysis of variance (ANOVA)—methods that allow user researchers to answer some common questions such as

- **Correlation**: Are two measurements associated or independent? For example, is there a significant correlation between perceived usability and likelihood-to-recommend?
- **Regression**: Can I use one variable to predict the other with reasonable accuracy? For example, if I know the perceived usability as measured with the System Usability Scale (SUS), can I accurately predict likelihood-to-recommend?
- **ANOVA**: Are there any significant differences among a set of more than two means? For example, are the mean SUS scores for five websites all the same, or is at least one of them different?

Example 1: Correlation magnitude, significance, and confidence interval

From page(s): 279-283

Summary: For the following UMUX-LITE and SUS data, compute the correlation, its statistical significance, the associated 95% confidence interval, and the coefficient of determination.

Participant	UMUX-LITE	SUS
1	55.4	72.5
2	87.9	82.5
3	66.2	50.0
4	82.5	82.5
5	22.9	10.0
6	44.6	65.0
7	44.6	62.5

Answer: The UMUX-LITE and SUS correlated significantly ($r(5) = 0.80$, $p = 0.03$). The 95% confidence interval ranged from about 0.11 to 0.97. The coefficient of determination is about 64%.

Excel solution

1. Select the "Simple Regression" link under the Correlation & Regression section.

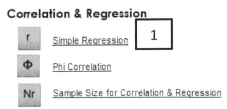

Correlation & Regression

r	Simple Regression	1
Φ	Phi Correlation	
Nr	Sample Size for Correlation & Regression	

2. Enter the raw values (also available in the Additional Data tab) into the input fields.

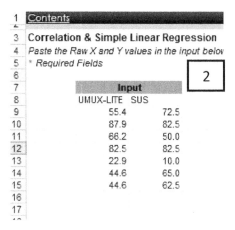

3. Set alpha to .05 (located in the results section).

4. The correlation, p-value, 95% confidence interval around r and R-Squared value are shown in the results section.

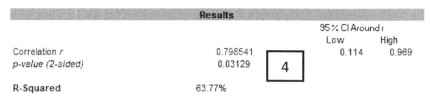

R solution

Enter the following commands:

```
sus <- c(72.5, 82.5, 50, 82.5, 10, 65, 62.5)

umux <- c(55.4, 87.9, 66.2, 82.5, 22.9, 44.6, 44.6)

test.correlation(sus, umux, .95)
```

The first two commands enter the UMUX-LITE and SUS scores as arrays. There must be an equal number of scores in each array. The correlation function takes as input the names of the two arrays and the level of confidence desired for the confidence interval. The result is:

```
> umux <- c(55.4, 87.9, 66.2, 82.5, 22.9, 44.6, 44.6)
> sus <- c(72.5, 82.5, 50, 82.5, 10, 65, 62.5)
> test.correlation(umux, sus, .95)

RESULTS

r: 0.7985414
df: 5
p: 0.0312869

95% Confidence Interval
Upper limit: 0.9689333
r: 0.7985414
Lower limit: 0.1140928

R-squared: 63.77%
```

Example 2: Sample size estimation for correlation

From page(s): 284

Summary: For the previous example, the confidence interval around the correlation was very wide. Suppose you wanted to improve the accuracy of the estimate around 0.80, keeping confidence at 95% and constraining the margin of error to 0.2. Assuming everything else stays the same, what sample size would you need?

Answer: You would need a sample size of 18.

Excel solution

1. Select the "Sample Size for Correlation & Regression" link under the Correlation & Regression section.

Correlation & Regression

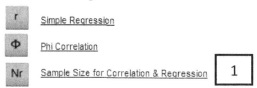

2. Under the Correlation section, enter the expected value of the correlation (.8) and the desired margin of error (.2)

3. Set the confidence level (95%).

4. The estimated sample size needed is 18.

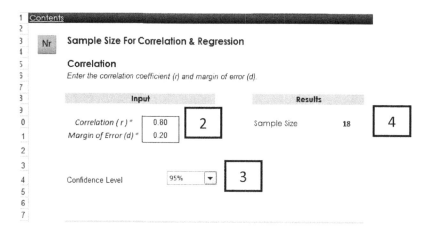

R solution

Enter the following command:

    n.correlation(.8,.2,.95)

For this command, you need to enter the expected value of the correlation, the desired margin of error, and the desired confidence level. The result is:

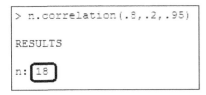

```
> n.correlation(.8,.2,.95)

RESULTS

n: 18
```

Example 3: Phi correlation magnitude, significance, and confidence interval

From page(s): 286-287

Summary: Use the phi coefficient to compute the correlation between binary variables. The following table shows the purchase histories for two books. Given this data, what is the magnitude of the phi coefficient, its statistical significance, and 95% confidence interval?

	Book B	
Book A	Y	N
Y	6 (a)	2 (b)
N	3 (c)	4 (d)

Answer: The magnitude of the phi coefficient is 0.327. At 95% confidence, the result is not statistically significant ($\chi^2(1) = 1.63$, $p = .20$). The 95% confidence interval ranges from -0.22 to 0.72.

Excel solution

1. Select the "Phi Correlation" link under the Correlation & Regression section.

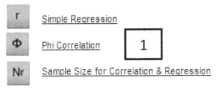

2. Paste the raw values (1's and 0's only) by participant in the Input columns.

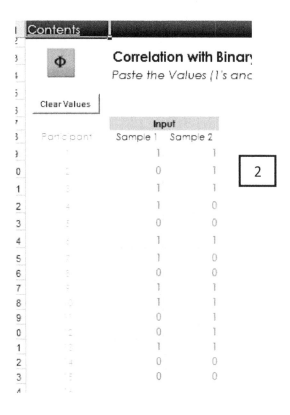

3. The phi correlation is shown (.327).

4. The Chi-Square value (1.607) and significance of the correlation are shown (p = .204).

5. The 95% confidence interval around the correlation is also shown (-.222 to .719).

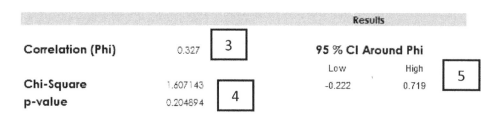

R solution

Enter the following command:

test.phi(6,2,3,4,.95)

For this command, you need to enter the counts for *a*, *b*, *c*, and *d* and the desired confidence level. The count for *a* is the number of joint agreements (in this example, the number of people who had purchased both Books A and B); the count for *d* is the number of joint disagreement (the number of people who purchased neither Book A nor Book B), and *b* and *c* are the discordant counts (for *b*, the number of people who bought Book A but did not buy Book B and, for *c*, the number of people who bought Book B but did not buy Book A). The result is:

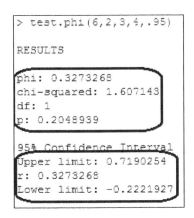

```
> test.phi(6,2,3,4,.95)

RESULTS

phi: 0.3273268
chi-squared: 1.607143
df: 1
p: 0.2048939

95% Confidence Interval
Upper limit: 0.7190254
r: 0.3273268
Lower limit: -0.2221927
```

Example 4: Regression slope and intercept: Slope, intercept, and predicted value with confidence intervals

From page(s): 288-291

Summary: Suppose you want to use linear regression to predict SUS scores (*y*) from UMUX-LITE scores (*x*) for the data used in Example 1 (shown again below). What is the regression formula? What are the 95% confidence intervals around the slope and the intercept? If you set UMUX-LITE to 68, what is the predicted value of SUS (and what is the 95% confidence interval around that estimated value)?

Participant	UMUX-LITE (x)	SUS (y)
1	55.4	72.5
2	87.9	82.5
3	66.2	50.0
4	82.5	82.5
5	22.9	10.0
6	44.6	65.0
7	44.6	62.5

Answer: The regression formula is SUS = 0.875(UMUX-LITE) + 10.18. The 95% confidence interval around the slope ranges from about 0.12 to 1.63 and the 95% confidence interval around the intercept ranges from about -36.49 to 56.84. For a UMUX-LITE of 68, the predicted value of SUS is 69.71 with a 95% confidence interval ranging from about 51.81 to 87.61.

Excel solution

1. Select the "Simple Regression" link under the Correlation & Regression section.

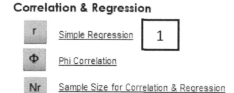

2. Enter the raw values.

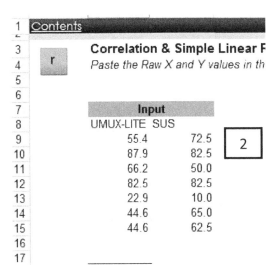

Correlation & Simple Linear F

Paste the Raw X and Y values in th

Input	
UMUX-LITE	SUS
55.4	72.5
87.9	82.5
66.2	50.0
82.5	82.5
22.9	10.0
44.6	65.0
44.6	62.5

3. The slope (.8754) and intercept (10.177) are provided.

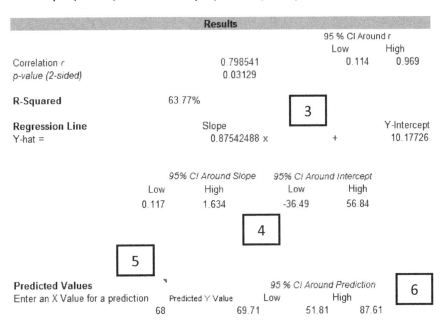

Results

		95 % CI Around r	
		Low	High
Correlation r	0.798541	0.114	0.969
p-value (2-sided)	0.03129		

R-Squared   63.77%

Regression Line   Slope   Y-Intercept
Y-hat =   0.87542488 x   +   10.17726

	95% CI Around Slope		95% CI Around Intercept	
	Low	High	Low	High
	0.117	1.634	-36.49	56.84

Predicted Values   95 % CI Around Prediction
Enter an X Value for a prediction   Predicted Y Value   Low   High
                                    68   69.71   51.81   87.61

4. The 95% confidence interval around the slope and intercept are also provided in the results section.

5. Enter the X value of 68 to predict the Y value.

6. The predicted value is displayed (69.71) along with the 95% confidence interval around the prediction (51.81 to 87.61).

R solution

Enter the following commands:

sus <- c(72.5, 82.5, 50, 82.5, 10, 65, 62.5)

umux <- c(55.4, 87.9, 66.2, 82.5, 22.9, 44.6, 44.6)

analyze.regression(sus, umux, .95, 68)

The first two commands set up the arrays of values for the variables in the analysis. The inputs to the analyze.regression command are the array with the y values (the variable to be predicted), the array with the x values (the predictor variable), the level of confidence for the various confidence intervals, and a specific value of x to use to predict y. If you're not interested in predicting a value of y from a particular value of x, just use 0 -- this will provide the predicted value of and confidence interval around the x-intercept. The output also provides the population variabilities for the x and error (e) values -- you don't need them in this exercise, but you will need them for the sample size estimation exercises for regression.

```
> sus <- c(72.5, 82.5, 50, 82.5, 10, 65, 62.5)
> umux <- c(55.4, 87.9, 66.2, 82.5, 22.9, 44.6, 44.6)
> analyze.regression(sus, umux, .95,68)

RESULTS

Slope and Intercept
Slope: 0.8754249
Intercept: 10.17726

95% Confidence Interval for Slope
Standard error: 0.2951138
Upper limit: 1.634039
Slope: 0.8754249
Lower limit: 0.1168106

95% Confidence Interval for Intercept
Standard error: 18.15335
Upper limit: 56.84194
Intercept: 10.17726
Lower limit: -36.48742

Overall Significance of Model
r: 0.7985414
df: 5
p: 0.0312869

95% Confidence Interval for Correlation
Upper limit: 0.9689333
r: 0.7985414
Lower limit: 0.1140928

95% Confidence Interval for R-squared
Upper limit: 93.88%
R-squared: 63.77%
Lower limit: 1.3%

95% Confidence Interval for Predicted Value
Standard error: 6.963498
Upper limit: 87.60639
Predicted value of y given x = 68 : 69.70615
Lower limit: 51.80591

Values for Sample Size Estimation
Mean of x: 57.72857
Population variability of x: 451.2678
Population variability of error: 196.5094
```

Example 5: Sample size estimation for linear regression based on slope

From page(s): 293

Summary: To estimate the sample size needed to constrain the estimate of the slope to a specified size, you need an estimate of the population variability of x, an estimate of the population variability of the error (e), the desired level of confidence, and the smallest acceptable margin of error around the estimated slope. For the example we've been using in this chapter, the 95% confidence interval around the slope of 0.874 ranged from about 0.12 to 1.63 -- a margin of error of ±0.76. Suppose the data you've collected so far is from a pilot study with $n = 7$, and that for the final study you need, with 95% confidence, to have a margin of error of ±0.25. From the pilot study, your estimates of the population variances of x and e were, respectively, 451.48 and 196.91. Assuming everything else stays the same, what sample size would you need to achieve the desired accuracy?

Answer: The estimated sample size requirement is $n = 32$.

Excel solution

1. Select the "Sample Size for Correlation & Regression" link under the Correlation & Regression section.

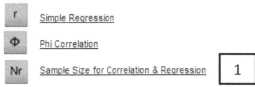

2. Under the heading "Regression (Slope) Sample size, enter the alpha level (alpha=.05), margin of error (d=.25) estimate of the standard deviation of the X values (Sx = 21.25) and the expected population error standard deviation (Se=14.03). NOTE: The Excel calculator uses the standard deviation as input whereas the R functions use the variance.

Regression (Slope) Sample Size

Enter alpha, margin of error (d) and the standard deviation of the X scores, error standard deviation.

	Input			Results	
alpha *	0.05				
d *	0.25	**2**	Sample Size **32**	**3**
s_x *	21.25				
s_e *	14.03				

3. The sample sizes needed (32) is displayed in the results section.

R solution

Enter the following command:

        n.slope(451.48, 196.91, .25, .95)

The inputs to the function are, in order, the expected population variance of the *x* scores, the expected population error variance, the desired margin of error, and the desired level of confidence.

```
> n.slope(451.48, 196.91, .25, .95)

RESULTS

Recommended sample size: 32
Number of iterations: 2
```

Example 6: Sample size estimation for linear regression based on intercept

From page(s): 294

Summary: To estimate the sample size needed to constrain the *y* intercept (or any other predicted value) to a specified size, you need an estimate of the population variability of *x*, an estimate of the population variability of the error (*e*), the smallest acceptable margin of error around the estimated value, the desired level of confidence, the value of *x* for which you want to predict *y* (which is 0 when estimating the *y*-intercept), and the mean of *x*.

For the example we've been using in this chapter, the 95% confidence interval around the intercept of 10.18 ranged from about -36.49 to 56.84 – a margin of error of ±46.7. Suppose the data you've collected so far is from a pilot study with $n = 7$, and that for the final study you need, with 95% confidence, to have a margin of error of ±5. From the pilot study, your estimates of the population variances of x and e were, respectively, 451.48 and 196.91. The mean of x was 57.7. Assuming everything else stays the same, what sample size would you need to achieve the desired accuracy?

Answer: The estimated sample size requirement is $n = 258$.

Excel solution

1. Select the "Sample Size for Correlation & Regression" link under the Correlation & Regression section.

Correlation & Regression

r	Simple Regression
Φ	Phi Correlation
Nr	Sample Size for Correlation & Regression 1

2. Enter the alpha level (alpha=.05), margin of error (d=5), estimate of the standard deviation of the X values (Sx = 21.25) and the expected population error standard deviation (Se=14.03), predicted value of X (x=0) and mean of x values (Mean(x) = 57.7) NOTE: The Excel calculator uses standard deviations as input whereas the R function uses variances.

Regression (Intercept) Sample Size

Enter alpha, margin of error (d) and the standard deviation of the X scores, error standard deviation, mean of $\rangle$

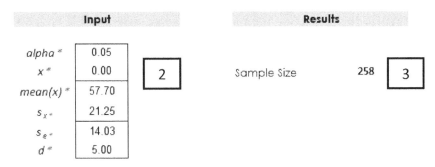

Input				Results	
alpha *	0.05				
x *	0.00	**2**	Sample Size	258	**3**
mean(x) *	57.70				
S_x *	21.25				
S_e *	14.03				
d *	5.00				

3. The sample size needed (258) is displayed in the results section.

R solution

Enter the following command:

    n.prediction(451.48, 196.91, 5, .95, 0, 57.7)

To get the following result:

```
> n.prediction(451.48, 196.91, 5, .95, 0, 57.7)

RESULTS

Recommended sample size: 258
Number of iterations: 2
```

Example 7: One-way ANOVA

From page(s): 298

Summary: Assume that you have the following ratings of the quality of four artificial voices, with four ratings per voice from 16 different participants in the study (higher ratings are better). In other words, this is a between-subjects design, so each participant heard and rated one of the four voices. Does a one-way ANOVA indicate any significant difference among the ratings of these artificial voices?

Voice A	Voice B	Voice C	Voice D
4.2	3.9	3.4	4.9
5.7	2.1	4.0	5.9
5.3	4.3	2.6	6.0
5.7	3.3	3.8	6.8

Answer: At least one of the means is significantly different from at least one of the others ($F(3, 12) = 10.6$, $p = 0.001$).

Excel solution

1. Select the 2+ Large Sample Means under the Analysis of Variance (ANOVA) heading.

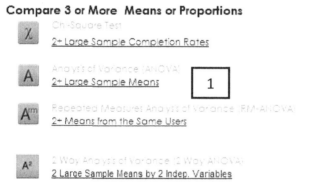

Compare 3 or More Means or Proportions

Ch-Square Test
2+ Large Sample Completion Rates

Analysis of Variance (ANOVA)
2+ Large Sample Means   1

Repeated Measures Analysis of Variance (RM-ANOVA)
2+ Means from the Same Users

2 Way Analysis of Variance (2 Way ANOVA)
2 Large Sample Means by 2 Indep. Variables

2. Enter the data for each voice.

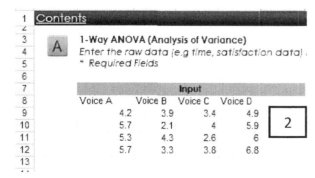

Contents

1-Way ANOVA (Analysis of Variance)
Enter the raw data (e.g time, satisfaction data).
* Required Fields

	Input		
Voice A	Voice B	Voice C	Voice D
4.2	3.9	3.4	4.9
5.7	2.1	4	5.9
5.3	4.3	2.6	6
5.7	3.3	3.8	6.8

3. The F statistics (10.61) and p-value (p = .0011) are shown in the results section.

Results					
Summary Table					
Source	df	SS	MS	F	p
Factor (Between Group	3	19.19188	6.39729	10.61	0.0011
Error (Within Groups)	12	7	1		3
Total	15	26.42938			

Fcritical Value
            3.490294819

R solution

Enter the following commands:

```
x <- c('A', 'A', 'A', 'A', 'B', 'B', 'B', 'B', 'C', 'C', 'C', 'C', 'D', 'D', 'D', 'D')

y <- c(4.2, 5.7, 5.3, 5.7, 3.9, 2.1, 4.3, 3.3, 3.4, 4.0, 2.6, 3.8, 4.9, 5.9, 6.0, 6.8)

x_name <- "cond"

y_name <- "rating"

voices.df <- data.frame(x,y)

names(voices.df) <- c(x_name,y_name)

aov.out <- aov(rating ~ cond, data=voices.df)

summary(aov.out)
```

The first six commands put the data into an R "data frame" so each rating is associated with the rated voice -- in this form, you can use standard R functions for ANOVA (of which there are several). The fifth command uses a standard R function named aov, which does one-way ANOVA -- placing the output of the ANOVA into a variable named aov.out. The last command produces a summary (shown below) of the ANOVA with the values for F, p, and degrees of freedom needed to report the result of the analysis.

```
> x <- c('A', 'A', 'A', 'A', 'B', 'B', 'B', 'B', 'C', 'C', 'C', 'C', 'D', 'D', 'D', 'D')
> y <- c(4.2, 5.7, 5.3, 5.7, 3.9, 2.1, 4.3, 3.3, 3.4, 4.0, 2.6, 3.8, 4.9, 5.9, 6.0, 6.8)
> x_name <- "cond"
> y_name <- "rating"
> voices.df <- data.frame(x,y)
> names(voices.df) <- c(x_name,y_name)
> aov.out <- aov(rating ~ cond, data=voices.df)
> summary(aov.out)
            Df Sum Sq Mean Sq F value  Pr(>F)
cond         3 19.192   6.397   10.61 0.00108 **
Residuals   12  7.237   0.603
---
Signif. codes:  0 '***' 0.001 '**' 0.01 '*' 0.05 '.' 0.1 ' ' 1
```

Example 8: Multiple comparisons

From page(s): 298-300

Summary: There are many ways to conduct multiple comparisons. A full discussion is outside the scope of this book. We're going to focus on three variations of multiple *t*-testing, varying from liberal (more Type I errors but fewer Type II errors) to conservative (fewer Type I errors but more Type II errors). All three approaches start with the results of standard *t*-tests. The most liberal approach is to use the specified level of significance (e.g., .05) to decide which results are statistically significant. The most conservative approach (Bonferroni adjustment) is to divide the specified level of significance by the number of comparisons. An intermediate approach (Benjamini-Hochberg adjustment) is to take the *p*-values from all the comparisons and rank them from lowest to highest. Then create a new threshold for statistical significance for each comparison by dividing the rank by the number of comparisons and then multiplying this by the initial significance threshold (alpha).

The Benjamini–Hochberg method positions itself between unadjusted testing and the Bonferroni method by adopting a sliding scale for the threshold of statistical significance. The first threshold will always be the same as the Bonferroni threshold, and the last threshold will always be the same as the unadjusted value of α. The thresholds in between the first and last comparisons rise in equal steps from the Bonferroni to the unadjusted threshold.

Rather than controlling the family-wise error rate to a specified level, the Benjamini–Hochberg method controls the false discovery rate—the proportion of rejected null hypotheses that are incorrect rejections (false discoveries)—rather than allowing only one Type I error. For this reason, if there is a need to adjust thresholds of significance, we recommend the Benjamini—Hochberg procedure due to its placement between liberal (unadjusted) and conservative (Bonferroni) approaches.

Continuing with the example from the previous exercise, the ANOVA indicated a difference among the means. For these three methods (unadjusted, Benjamini-Hochberg, and Bonferroni), which means would you conclude are significantly different from one another? (Note that this is an exercise to illustrate these three methods -- in practice, you should choose the method appropriate for your situation before you run the multiple comparisons.)

Answer: Without adjustment, you'd conclude that four comparisons were significantly different (Voice A vs. Voice B, Voice A vs. Voice C, Voice B vs. Voice D, and Voice C vs. Voice D). Using the Benjamini-Hochberg method, you'd conclude that the same four comparisons were significant. With the more conservative Bonferroni approach, you'd only conclude that two of the comparisons were significant (Voice B vs. Voice D and Voice C vs. Voice D).

Excel solution
1. Select the "Correction for Multiple Comparisons" in the Extras section.

Extras

Interpreting Rating Scales

Correction for Multiple Comparisons | 1 |

Estimate Survey Sample Size

2. Enter the p-values for each comparison and sort from lowest to highest.

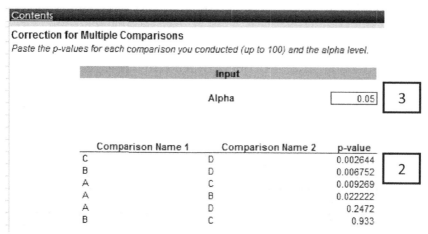

3. Enter the alpha rejection level (.05).

4. The total number of comparisons are shown (6), the Bonferonni Threshold (p = .008333) and the comparisons that are significant are flagged "Sig" for the BH comparison (4 marked Sig.) and Bonferonni (2 marked Sig).

Results

Total Comparisons	6
Bonferonni Threshold	0.008333333

Rank	BH Threshold	BH Significant	Bonferonni Significant
1	0.008	Sig.	Sig.
2	0.017	Sig.	Sig.
3	0.025	Sig.	
4	0.033	Sig.	
5	0.042		
6	0.050		

R solution

Enter the following commands:

A <- c(4.2, 5.7, 5.3, 5.7)

B <- c(3.9, 2.1, 4.3, 3.3)

C <- c(3.4, 4.0, 2.6, 3.8)

```
D <- c(4.9, 5.9, 6.0, 6.8)

t.test(A,B,var.equal = TRUE)

t.test(A,C,var.equal = TRUE)

t.test(A,D,var.equal = TRUE)

t.test(B,C,var.equal = TRUE)

t.test(B,D,var.equal = TRUE)

t.test(C,D,var.equal = TRUE)

compute.mcadjustments(6, .05)
```

The first four commands put the data into the four voice variables (A, B, C, and D). The next six commands perform all possible pairwise *t*-tests with those four variables (using the standard R command for independent *t*-tests and, to match the values in *Quantifying the User Experience*, assuming equal variance). The last command produces the adjusted *p*-values for the Bonferroni and Benjamini-Hochberg methods. The results are:

```
> A <- c(4.2, 5.7, 5.3, 5.7)
> B <- c(3.9, 2.1, 4.3, 3.3)
> C <- c(3.4, 4.0, 2.6, 3.8)
> D <- c(4.9, 5.9, 6.0, 6.8)
>
> t.test(A,B,var.equal = TRUE)

        Two Sample t-test

data: [A and B]
t = 3.0603, df = 6, p-value = [0.02222]
alternative hypothesis: true difference in means is not equal to 0
95 percent confidence interval:
 0.3658012 3.2841988
sample estimates:
mean of x mean of y
    5.225     3.400

> t.test(A,C,var.equal = TRUE)

        Two Sample t-test

data: [A and C]
t = 3.7718, df = 6, p-value = [0.009269]
alternative hypothesis: true difference in means is not equal to 0
95 percent confidence interval:
 0.623499 2.926501
sample estimates:
mean of x mean of y
    5.225     3.450

> t.test(A,D,var.equal = TRUE)

        Two Sample t-test

data: [A and D]
t = -1.2818, df = 6, p-value = [0.2472]
alternative hypothesis: true difference in means is not equal to 0
95 percent confidence interval:
 -1.9635069  0.6135069
sample estimates:
mean of x mean of y
    5.225     5.900
```

```
> t.test(B,C,var.equal = TRUE)

        Two Sample t-test

data:  B and C
t = -0.0876, df = 6, p-value = 0.933
alternative hypothesis: true difference in means is not equal to 0
95 percent confidence interval:
 -1.446742  1.346742
sample estimates:
mean of x mean of y
     3.40      3.45


> t.test(B,D,var.equal = TRUE)

        Two Sample t-test

data:  B and D
t = -4.0467, df = 6, p-value = 0.006752
alternative hypothesis: true difference in means is not equal to 0
95 percent confidence interval:
 -4.011682 -0.988318
sample estimates:
mean of x mean of y
      3.4       5.9


> t.test(C,D,var.equal = TRUE)

        Two Sample t-test

data:  C and D
t = -4.9247, df = 6, p-value = 0.002644
alternative hypothesis: true difference in means is not equal to 0
95 percent confidence interval:
 -3.667323 -1.232677
sample estimates:
mean of x mean of y
     3.45      5.90
```

```
> compute.mcadjustments(6, .05)

RESULTS

Bonferroni adjustment for critical value of p: 0.008333333

Benjamini-Hochberg adjustments for critical values of p
Rank 1: 0.008333333
Rank 2: 0.01666667
Rank 3: 0.025
Rank 4: 0.03333333
Rank 5: 0.04166667
Rank 6: 0.05
```

As a final step in the analysis, put the results of the t-tests into a table in order of p-value, smallest first, as shown below. An asterisk in the table indicates a statistically significant result for the indicated method (unadjusted when $p < .05$, Benjamini-Hochberg when $p <$ B-H Criterion, and Bonferroni when $p < .008$).

Comparison	t(df)	p	B-H Criterion	Unadjusted	B-H	Bonferroni
C-D	-4.92 (6)	0.003	0.008	*	*	*
B-D	-4.09 (6)	0.007	0.017	*	*	*
A-C	3.77 (6)	0.009	0.025	*	*	
A-B	3.06 (6)	0.022	0.033	*	*	
A-D	-1.28 (6)	0.247	0.042			
B-C	-0.88 (6)	0.933	0.05			

Example 9: Two-way ANOVA

From page(s): 304-305

Summary: One of the key advantages of ANOVA is its ability to assess the effects of more than one variable individually (main effect) and together (interaction). For example, consider an unpublished study in which male and female participants used the MOS-R to rate the quality of two artificial voices, one male and one female (higher ratings are better). The social psychological principle of "similarity attraction" might apply to user reactions to artificial voices such that males would prefer a male voice and females a female voice. If the similarity attraction hypothesis held, the expectation was that there would be a significant interaction between the gender of the artificial voice (Voice) and the gender of the person rating the voice (Rater). Given the data in the following table, does there appear to be an interaction?

Participant	Voice	Rater	Rating	Participant	Voice	Rater	Rating
1	M	M	3.6	9	F	M	4.2
2	M	M	6.1	10	F	M	3.4
3	M	M	5.7	11	F	M	3.2
4	M	M	4.2	12	F	M	3.7
5	M	F	6.0	13	F	F	4.4
6	M	F	3.4	14	F	F	4.2
7	M	F	5.7	15	F	F	4.6
8	M	F	5.7	16	F	F	2.7

Answer: Although there was a significant main effect for the overall difference in ratings for the two artificial voices ($F(1, 12) = 6.55$, $p = 0.025$), there was no significant effect for the gender of the participant ($F(1, 12) = 0.44$, $p = 0.52$) and the interaction was not statistically significant ($F(1, 12) = 0.003$, $p = .96$). There did not appear to be a Voice x Rater interaction.

Excel solution

1. Under the Section, Compare 3 or More Means or Proportions, select the "2 Large Sample Means by 2 Indep. Variable" for a 2-Way ANOVA.

2. Enter the data for each variable (Voice and Rater).

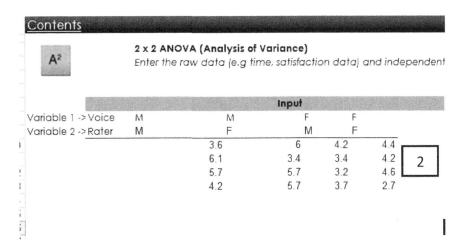

		Input		
Variable 1 -> Voice	M	M	F	F
Variable 2 -> Rater	M	F	M	F
		3.6	6	4.2	4.4
		6.1	3.4	3.4	4.2
		5.7	5.7	3.2	4.6
		4.2	5.7	3.7	2.7

3. The F statistics (6.5474, .4426, .0026) and p-values (.02506, .51845, .96003) are shown in the Results section.

Results						
Summary Table						
Source	SS	df	MS	F	p	3
Total	18.13	15	1.21			
Factor (Between Groups)	6.675	3	2.23			
Voice	6.25	1	6.25	6.5474	**0.02506**	
Rater	0.42	1	0.42	0.4426	**0.51845**	
Interaction	0.0025	1	0.00	0.0026	**0.96003**	
Error (Within Groups)	11.46	12	0.95			

R solution

Enter the following commands:

```
x <- c('M', 'M', 'M', 'M', 'M', 'M', 'M', 'M', 'F', 'F', 'F', 'F', 'F', 'F', 'F', 'F')

y <- c('M', 'M', 'M', 'M', 'F', 'F', 'F', 'F', 'M', 'M', 'M', 'M', 'F', 'F', 'F', 'F')

z <- c(3.6, 6.1, 5.7, 4.2, 6.0, 3.4, 5.7, 5.7, 4.2, 3.4, 3.2, 3.7, 4.4, 4.2, 4.6, 2.7)

x_name <- "voice"

y_name <- "rater"

z_name <- "rating"

voices.df <- data.frame(x,y,z)

names(voices.df) <- c(x_name,y_name,z_name)

aov.out <- aov(rating ~ voice*rater, data=voices.df)

summary(aov.out)
```

The first eight commands put the data into an R "data frame" so each rating is associated with the gender of the artificial voice and the rater's gender -- in this form, you can use standard R functions for ANOVA (of which there are several). The ninth command uses a standard R function named aov, which does two-way ANOVA

-- placing the output of the ANOVA into a variable named aov.out. The last command produces a summary (shown below) of the ANOVA with the values for F, p, and degrees of freedom needed to report the result of the analysis.

```
> x <- c('M', 'M', 'M', 'M', 'M', 'M', 'M', 'M', 'F', 'F', 'F', 'F', 'F', 'F', 'F', 'F')
> y <- c('M', 'M', 'M', 'M', 'F', 'F', 'F', 'F', 'M', 'M', 'M', 'M', 'F', 'F', 'F', 'F')
> z <- c(3.6, 6.1, 5.7, 4.2, 6.0, 3.4, 5.7, 5.7, 4.2, 3.4, 3.2, 3.7, 4.4, 4.2, 4.6, 2.7)
> x_name <- "voice"
> y_name <- "rater"
> z_name <- "rating"
> voices.df <- data.frame(x,y,z)
> names(voices.df) <- c(x_name,y_name,z_name)
> aov.out <- aov(rating ~ voice*rater, data=voices.df)
> summary(aov.out)
            Df Sum Sq Mean Sq F value Pr(>F)
voice        1  6.250   6.250   6.547 0.0251 *
rater        1  0.422   0.422   0.443 0.5185
voice:rater  1  0.003   0.003   0.003 0.9600
Residuals   12 11.455   0.955
---
Signif. codes:  0 '***' 0.001 '**' 0.01 '*' 0.05 '.' 0.1 ' ' 1
```

Exercise 1: Correlation

From page(s): 311

Summary: Assume that you have concurrently collected data from ten usability studies for the SUS and a single-item measure of perceived effort (7-point scale with 1 = "No undue effort" and 7 = "Far too much effort"). The following table shows the means from the ten experiments. You think they're probably correlated, but you're not sure to what extent. For this question (a) calculate the correlation and assess its statistical significance, (b) then determine the 95% confidence interval around the estimated correlation, and (c) compute and interpret the coefficient of determination.

Experiment	SUS	Effort
1	68.1	4.0
2	50.0	4.2
3	70.8	4.0
4	85.2	6.4
5	92.4	6.6
6	69.9	3.9
7	45.7	3.5
8	82.3	6.2
9	78.6	5.8
10	55.5	4.0

Answer: The linear correlation is statistically significant ($r(8) = 0.858$, $p = 0.001$). The 95% confidence interval ranges from 0.498 to 0.966. The coefficient of determination, R^2, is 73.7%, suggesting that variability in mean SUS accounts for much of the variability in mean Effort, but with about 27.3% of variability left unexplained (either due to error, the effect of some other variable(s), or systematic nonlinear components).

Excel solution

1. Select the "Simple Regression" link under the Correlation & Regression section.

Correlation & Regression

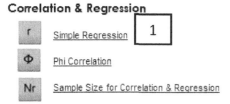

James R. Lewis & Jeff Sauro

2. Enter the raw values (also available in the Additional Data tab) into the input fields.

Contents

Correlation & Simple Linear F

Paste the Raw X and Y values in th

Input		
UMUX-LITE	SUS	
68.10	4.00	
50.00	4.20	2
70.80	4.00	
85.20	6.40	
92.40	6.60	
69.90	3.90	
45.70	3.50	
82.30	6.20	
78.60	5.80	
55.50	4.00	

3. Set alpha to .05 (located in the results section).

Alpha	0.05	3

Calculations

4. The correlation, p-value, 95% confidence interval around r and R-Squared value are shown in the results section.

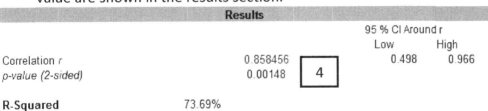

	Results		95 % CI Around r	
			Low	High
Correlation *r*		0.858456	0.498	0.966
p-value (2-sided)		0.00148	4	
R-Squared		73.69%		

R solution

Enter the following commands:

sus <- c(68.1, 50.0, 70.8, 85.2, 92.4, 69.9, 45.7, 82.3, 78.6, 55.5)

effort <- c(4.0, 4.2, 4.0, 6.4, 6.6, 3.9, 3.5, 6.2, 5.8, 4.0)

test.correlation(sus, effort, .95)

The first two commands define the values for SUS and Effort. The third command computes the correlation between SUS and Effort, with the following output:

```
> sus <- c(68.1, 50.0, 70.8, 85.2, 92.4, 69.9, 45.7, 82.3, 78.6, 55.5)
> effort <- c(4.0, 4.2, 4.0, 6.4, 6.6, 3.9, 3.5, 6.2, 5.8, 4.0)
> test.correlation(sus, effort, .95)

RESULTS

r: 0.8584555
df: 8
p: 0.001475057

95% Confidence Interval
Upper limit: 0.9659694
r: 0.8584555
Lower limit: 0.4980029

R-squared: 73.69%
```

Exercise 2: Regression

From page(s): 311

Summary: Based on the results from Exercise 1, you've decided that you'd like to establish a company-wide target for future usability tests that use the perceived effort item. It is common to set a target for the SUS to 80, which is an A- on the Sauro–Lewis curved grading scale. For this question, (a) determine the regression equation that would allow prediction of Effort from SUS, (b) use the equation to compute the value of Effort that corresponds to a SUS of 80, and (c) compute the 90% confidence interval around that estimated Effort value.

Answer: The regression equation for predicting Effort from SUS is Effort = 0.122 + 0.068(SUS). The predicted value for Effort after setting SUS to 80 is about 5.5. The 90% confidence interval around that predicted value ranges from 5.1 to 6.0.

Excel solution

1. Select the "Simple Regression" link under the Correlation & Regression section.

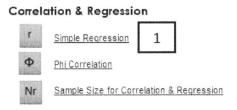

2. Enter the raw values.

Input	
UMUX-LITE	SUS
68.10	4.00
50.00	4.20
70.80	4.00
85.20	6.40
92.40	6.60
69.90	3.90
45.70	3.50
82.30	6.20
78.60	5.80
55.50	4.00

3. The slope (.0678) and intercept (.121894) are provided.

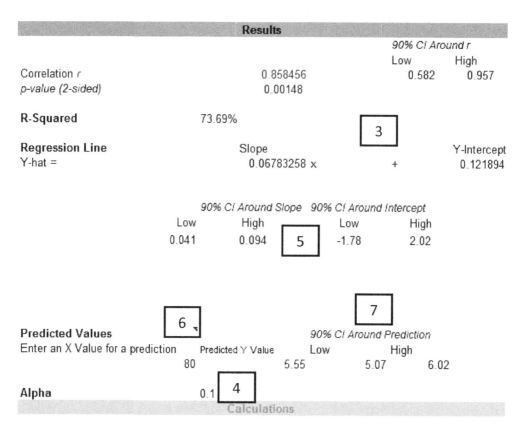

	Results			
			90% CI Around r	
			Low	High
Correlation r	0.858456		0.582	0.957
p-value (2-sided)	0.00148			

R-Squared   73.69%

3

| **Regression Line** | Slope | | Y-Intercept |
| Y-hat = | 0.06783258 x | + | 0.121894 |

	90% CI Around Slope		90% CI Around Intercept	
	Low	High	Low	High
	0.041	0.094	-1.78	2.02

5

7

6

Predicted Values			90% CI Around Prediction	
Enter an X Value for a prediction	Predicted Y Value	Low	High
80	5.55	5.07	6.02

Alpha   0.1   4

Calculations

4. Change the Alpha value to .10 in the bottom of the results section.

5. The 90% confidence interval around the slope and intercept are also provided.

6. Enter the X value of 80 to predict the Y value.

7. The predicted value is displayed (5.55) along with the 90% confidence interval around the prediction (5.07 to 6.02).

R solution

Enter the following commands:

```
sus <- c(68.1, 50.0, 70.8, 85.2, 92.4, 69.9, 45.7, 82.3, 78.6, 55.5)

effort <- c(4.0, 4.2, 4.0, 6.4, 6.6, 3.9, 3.5, 6.2, 5.8, 4.0)
```

analyze.regression(effort, sus, .90, 80)

The first two commands set up the arrays of values for the variables in the analysis. The inputs to the analyze.regression command are the array with the y values (the variable to be predicted), the array with the x values (the predictor variable), the level of confidence for the various confidence intervals, and a specific value of x to use to predict y. (If you're not interested in predicting a value of y from a particular value of x, just use 0 -- this will provide the predicted value of and confidence interval around the x-intercept.)

```
> sus <- c(68.1, 50.0, 70.8, 85.2, 92.4, 69.9, 45.7, 82.3, 78.6, 55.5)
> effort <- c(4.0, 4.2, 4.0, 6.4, 6.6, 3.9, 3.5, 6.2, 5.8, 4.0)
> analyze.regression(effort, sus, .90, 80)

RESULTS

Slope and Intercept
Slope: 0.06783258
Intercept: 0.1218943

90% Confidence Interval for Slope
Standard error: 0.01432841
Upper limit: 0.09447695
Slope: 0.06783258
Lower limit: 0.04118821

90% Confidence Interval for Intercept
Standard error: 1.022782
Upper limit: 2.023807
Intercept: 0.1218943
Lower limit: -1.780018

Overall Significance of Model
r: 0.8584555
df: 8
p: 0.001475057

90% Confidence Interval for Correlation
Upper limit: 0.9570131
r: 0.8584555
Lower limit: 0.5821756

90% Confidence Interval for R-squared
Upper limit: 91.59%
R-squared: 73.69%
Lower limit: 33.89%

90% Confidence Interval for Predicted Value
Standard error: 0.2560359
Upper limit: 6.024612
Predicted value of y given x = 80 : 5.548501
Lower limit: 5.07239

Values for Sample Size Estimation
Mean of x: 69.85
Population variability of x: 216.2825
Population variability of error: 0.3552282
```

Exercise 3: Sample size estimation for linear regression based on estimated value

From page(s): 312

Summary: Suppose you wanted to control your estimate of the appropriate Effort target to within 0.1. Given the results in (2) and continuing to use 90% confidence, what sample size (number of studies with concurrent collection of SUS and Effort) would you probably need? The results from (2) that you need are the mean of x (69.85), the population variability of x (216.2825), and the population variability of e (0.3552282).

Answer: If you want to control the estimate of Effort to ±0.1, assuming everything except the sample size stays the same, you'd need data from about 146 studies.

Excel solution

1. Select the "Sample Size for Correlation & Regression" link under the Correlation & Regression section.

2. Enter the alpha level (alpha=.10), margin of error (d=.10), estimate of the standard deviation of the X values (Sx = 14.71) and the expected population error standard deviation (Se=.60), predicted value of X (x=80) and mean of x values (Mean(x) = 69.85) NOTE: The Excel calculator uses the standard deviations as input whereas the R functions use the variances. Simply take the square root of the values in the exercise (=SQRT(216.2825) and =SQRT(0.3552282))

Regression (Intercept) Sample Size

on. Enter alpha, margin of error (d) and the standard deviation of the X scores, error standard deviati

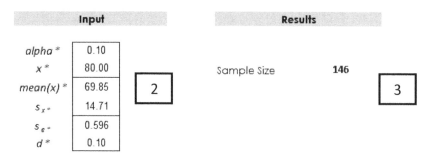

Input		
alpha *	0.10	
x *	80.00	
mean(x) *	69.85	2
S_x =	14.71	
S_e =	0.596	
d *	0.10	

Results		
Sample Size	146	3

3. The sample sizes needed (146) is displayed in the results section.

R solution

Enter the following command:

n.prediction(216.2825, 0.3552282, 0.1, .90, 80, 69.85)

To get the following result:

```
> n.prediction(216.2825, 0.3552282, 0.1, .90, 80, 69.85)

RESULTS

Recommended sample size: 146
Number of iterations: 2
```

Exercise 4: Phi correlation magnitude and significance

From page(s): 312

Summary: Convert the values in the table from Exercise 1 to binary data where SUS scores greater than 79.9 are "1" and all others are 0, and Effort scores greater than 5.5 are "1" and all others are 0. Then compute phi to estimate the correlation between SUS and Effort and assess its statistical significance.

Answer: The following table shows the summary of the data in a 2 × 2 matrix. The resulting value of phi is a statistically significant 0.802 ($\chi^2(1) = 6.43$, $p = 0.01$).

	SUS	
Effort	1	0
1	3 (a)	1 (b)
0	0 (c)	6 (d)

Excel solution

1. Select the "Phi Correlation" link under the Correlation & Regression section.

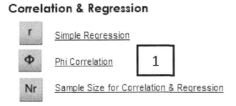

2. Paste the raw values (1's and 0's only) by participant in the Input columns.

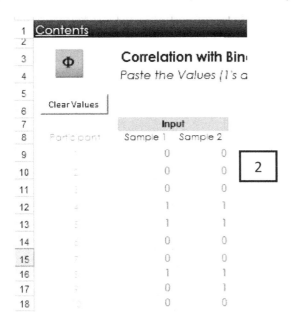

3. The phi correlation is shown (.802).

4. The Chi-Square value (6.43) and significance of the correlation are shown (p = .011).

5. The 95% confidence interval around the correlation is also shown (.348 to .951).

Results		

Correlation (Phi)   0.802   3

Chi-Square   6.428571

p-value   0.011230   4

95 % CI Around Phi

Low	High
0.348	0.951	5

R solution

Enter the following command:

    test.phi(3, 1, 0, 6, .95)

For this command, you need to enter the counts for *a*, *b*, *c*, and *d* and the desired confidence level. The result is:

```
> test.phi(3, 1, 0, 6, .95)

RESULTS

phi: 0.8017837
chi-squared: 6.428571
df: 1
p: 0.01122989

95% Confidence Interval
Upper limit: 0.9512142
r: 0.8017837
Lower limit: 0.3476692
```

Chapter 10: An Introduction to Correlation, Regression, and ANOVA

Exercise 5: One-way ANOVA with multiple comparisons

From page(s): 312-313

Summary: Suppose you have used a survey to collect SUS scores from respondents who have used a major hotel website or mobile app to book a reservation, with the results shown in the following table. Does the omnibus *F*-test for a one-way ANOVA indicate that at least one of the means is different from the others? Which one(s)?

Company A Website	Company A Mobile	Company B Website	Company B Mobile
72.5	62.5	82.5	100.0
85.0	72.5	72.5	80.0
70.0	77.5	87.5	90.0
80.0	57.5	70.0	80.0
60.0	82.5	80.0	85.0
80.0	50.0	75.0	80.0
80.0	67.5	97.5	92.5
85.0	70.0	57.5	75.0
65.0	52.5	70.0	100.0
75.0	82.5	85.0	77.5

Answer: The result of the ANOVA was significant ($F(3, 36) = 5.576$, $p = 0.003$), indicating that at least one of the means is different from at least one of the other means. The following table shows the observed significance levels (*p*-values) for the six comparisons and, using $\alpha = 0.05$, the results for multiple comparisons without adjustment, using the Benjamini–Hochberg adjustment, and using the Bonferroni adjustment ($\alpha/6 = 0.008$). For the Benjamini–Hochberg method the *p*-values from the six comparisons were ranked from lowest to highest. The new statistical significance thresholds were created by dividing the rank by the number of comparisons and then multiplying this by alpha (0.05). For six comparisons, the lowest *p*-value (with a rank of 1) is compared against a new threshold of $(1/6)*0.05 = 0.008$, the second is compared against $(2/6)*0.05 = 0.017$, and so forth. Two comparisons were statistically significant without adjustment and when using the Benjamini–Hochberg method (A Mobile vs. B Mobile and A Web vs. B Mobile). Only one comparison (A Mobile vs. B Mobile) was significant when using the Bonferroni adjustment. There are other comparisons that also have relatively low values of p (all but A Web vs. B Web) that might bear consideration, especially for a researcher working in an industrial context in which Type II errors are as or more important than Type I errors.

Comparison	p	B-H Criterion	Unadjusted	B-H	Bonferroni
A Mob - B Mob	0.001	0.008	*	*	*
A Web - B Mob	0.014	0.017	*	*	
A Mob - B Web	0.062	0.025			
B Web - B Mob	0.089	0.033			
A Web - A Mob	0.108	0.042			
A Web - B Web	0.58	0.05			

Excel solution

1. Select the 2+ Large Sample Means under the Analysis of Variance (ANOVA) heading.

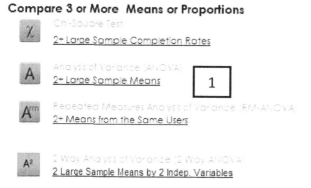

Compare 3 or More Means or Proportions

Chi-Square Test
2+ Large Sample Completion Rates

Analysis of Variance (ANOVA)
2+ Large Sample Means   1

Repeated Measures Analysis of Variance (RM-ANOVA)
2+ Means from the Same Users

2 Way Analysis of Variance (2 Way ANOVA)
2 Large Sample Means by 2 Indep. Variables

2. Enter the data for each group.

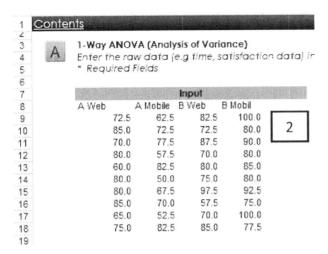

		Input		
A Web	A Mobile	B Web	B Mobil	
72.5	62.5	82.5	100.0	
85.0	72.5	72.5	80.0	2
70.0	77.5	87.5	90.0	
80.0	57.5	70.0	80.0	
60.0	82.5	80.0	85.0	
80.0	50.0	75.0	80.0	
80.0	67.5	97.5	92.5	
85.0	70.0	57.5	75.0	
65.0	52.5	70.0	100.0	
75.0	82.5	85.0	77.5	

3. The F statistic (5.58) and p-value (p = .003) are shown in the results section.

		Results				
Summary Table						
Source	df	SS	MS	F	p	
Factor (Between Group	3	1743.125	581.042	5.58	0.003	
Error (Within Groups)	36	3.751	104			3
Total	39	5494.375				

Fcritical Value
    2.866265551

4. To analyze the multiple comparisons (after running separate t-tests to obtain the p-values), select the "Correction for Multiple Comparisons" in the Extras section.

Extras

5. Enter the p-values for each comparison and sort from lowest to highest.

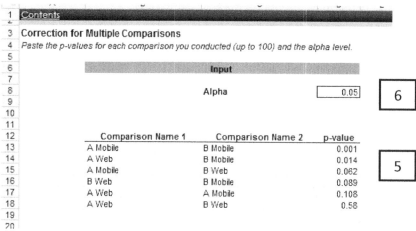

6. Enter the alpha rejection level (.05).

7. The total number of comparisons are shown (6), the Bonferonni Threshold (p = .008333) and the comparisons that are significant are flagged "Sig" for the BH comparison (2 marked Sig.) and Bonferonni (1 marked Sig).

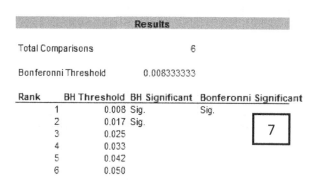

R solution

For the ANOVA, enter the following commands:

```
x <- c('WebA', 'WebA', 'WebA', 'WebA', 'WebA', 'WebA', 'WebA', 'WebA',
'WebA', 'WebA', 'MobA', 'MobA', 'MobA', 'MobA', 'MobA', 'MobA', 'MobA',
'MobA', 'MobA', 'MobA', 'WebB', 'WebB', 'WebB', 'WebB', 'WebB', 'WebB',
'WebB', 'WebB', 'WebB', 'WebB', 'MobB', 'MobB', 'MobB', 'MobB', 'MobB',
'MobB', 'MobB', 'MobB', 'MobB', 'MobB')

y <- c(72.5, 85.0, 70.0, 80.0, 60.0, 80.0, 80.0, 85.0, 65.0, 75.0, 62.5, 72.5, 77.5,
57.5, 82.5, 50.0, 67.5, 70.0, 52.5, 82.5, 82.5, 72.5, 87.5, 70.0, 80.0, 75.0, 97.5,
57.5, 70.0, 85.0, 100.0, 80.0, 90.0, 80.0, 85.0, 80.0, 92.5, 75.0, 100.0, 77.5)

x_name <- "Cond"

y_name <- "SUS"

survey.df <- data.frame(x,y)

names(survey.df) <- c(x_name,y_name)

aov.out <- aov(SUS ~ Cond, data=survey.df)

summary(aov.out)
```

The first six commands put the data into an R "data frame" which is the input into the fifth command (a standard R function named aov) that places the output of the ANOVA into a variable named aov.out. The last command produces a summary (shown below) of the ANOVA with the values for *F*, *p*, and degrees of freedom needed to report the result of the analysis.

```
          Df Sum Sq Mean Sq F value  Pr(>F)
Cond       3   1743   581.0   5.576 0.00301 **
Residuals 36   3751   104.2
```

For the multiple comparisons, enter the following commands:

```
WebA <- c(72.5, 85.0, 70.0, 80.0, 60.0, 80.0, 80.0, 85.0, 65.0, 75.0)

MobA <- c(62.5, 72.5, 77.5, 57.5, 82.5, 50.0, 67.5, 70.0, 52.5, 82.5)
```

```
WebB <- c(82.5, 72.5, 87.5, 70.0, 80.0, 75.0, 97.5, 57.5, 70.0, 85.0)

MobB <- c(100.0, 80.0, 90.0, 80.0, 85.0, 80.0, 92.5, 75.0, 100.0, 77.5)

t.test(WebA,MobA,var.equal = TRUE)

t.test(WebA,WebB,var.equal = TRUE)

t.test(WebA,MobB,var.equal = TRUE)

t.test(MobA,WebB,var.equal = TRUE)

t.test(MobA,MobB,var.equal = TRUE)

t.test(WebB,MobB,var.equal = TRUE)

compute.mcadjustments(6, .05)
```

The first four commands put the data into the four survey variables (WebA, MobA, WebB, and MobB). The next six commands perform all possible pairwise *t*-tests with those four variables (using the standard R command for independent *t*-tests and, to match the values in *Quantifying the User Experience*, assuming equal variance). The last command produces the adjusted *p*-values for the Bonferroni and Benjamini-Hochberg methods. The results (for comparison withe the results table above) are:

```
> t.test(WebA,MobA,var.equal = TRUE)

        Two Sample t-test

data:  WebA and MobA
t = 1.7011, df = 18, p-value = 0.1061
alternative hypothesis: true difference in means is not equal to 0
95 percent confidence interval:
 -1.821757 17.321757
sample estimates:
mean of x mean of y
    75.25      67.50

> t.test(WebA,WebB,var.equal = TRUE)

        Two Sample t-test

data:  WebA and WebB
t = -0.5651, df = 18, p-value = 0.579
alternative hypothesis: true difference in means is not equal to 0
95 percent confidence interval:
 -11.793925   6.793925
sample estimates:
mean of x mean of y
    75.25      77.75

> t.test(WebA,MobB,var.equal = TRUE)

        Two Sample t-test

data:  WebA and MobB
t = -2.7422, df = 18, p-value = 0.01339
alternative hypothesis: true difference in means is not equal to 0
95 percent confidence interval:
 -18.986058  -2.513942
sample estimates:
mean of x mean of y
    75.25      86.00

> t.test(MobA,WebB,var.equal = TRUE)

        Two Sample t-test

data:  MobA and WebB
t = -1.9982, df = 18, p-value = 0.06103
alternative hypothesis: true difference in means is not equal to 0
95 percent confidence interval:
 -21.026829   0.526829
sample estimates:
mean of x mean of y
    67.50      77.75
```

```
> t.test(MobA,MobB,var.equal = TRUE)

        Two Sample t-test

data:  MobA and MobB
t = -3.9343, df = 18, p-value = 0.0009722
alternative hypothesis: true difference in means is not equal to 0
95 percent confidence interval:
 -28.379051  -8.620949
sample estimates:
mean of x mean of y
     67.5      86.0

> t.test(WebB,MobB,var.equal = TRUE)

        Two Sample t-test

data:  WebB and MobB
t = -1.8036, df = 18, p-value = 0.08806
alternative hypothesis: true difference in means is not equal to 0
95 percent confidence interval:
 -17.860108   1.360108
sample estimates:
mean of x mean of y
    77.75     86.00

> compute.mcadjustments(6, .05)

RESULTS

Bonferroni adjustment for critical value of p: 0.008333333

Benjamini-Hochberg adjustments for critical values of p
Rank 1: 0.008333333
Rank 2: 0.01666667
Rank 3: 0.025
Rank 4: 0.03333333
Rank 5: 0.04166667
Rank 6: 0.05
```

Exercise 6: Two-way ANOVA with multiple comparisons

From page(s): 313-315

Summary: Continuing to use the data from Question 5, switch to a two-way ANOVA to assess the main effects of Company (A vs. B) and Channel (website vs. mobile app) and their interaction. Interpret the results.

Answer: The main effect of Company was significant ($F(1,36) = 10.58$, $p = 0.002$), the main effect of Channel was not ($F(1, 36) = 0.01$, $p = 0.939$), and they interacted significantly ($F(1, 36) = 6.14$, $p = 0.018$). The following table shows the results of these multiple comparisons without adjustment (all using $\alpha = 0.05$), with Benjamini–Hochberg adjustment, and with Bonferroni adjustment ($0.05/4 = 0.013$). For the Benjamini–Hochberg method, the p-values from the four comparisons were ranked from lowest to highest. The new statistical significance thresholds were created by dividing the rank by the number of comparisons and multiplying by alpha (0.05). For four comparisons, the lowest p-value, with a rank of 1 is compared against a new threshold of $(1/4)*0.05 = 0.013$ and so forth. In this example, all three methods (unadjusted, Benjamini–Hochberg, and Bonferroni) indicated that only the comparison of Company A Mobile versus Company B Mobile was statistically significant.

Comparison	p	B-H Criterion	Unadjusted	B-H	Bonferroni
A Mob - B Mob	0.001	0.013	*	*	*
B Web - B Mob	0.089	0.025			
A Web - A Mob	0.108	0.038			
A Web - B Web	0.58	0.05			

Excel solution

1. Under the Section, Compare 3 or More Means or Proportions, select the "2 Large Sample Means by 2 Indep. Variable" for a 2-Way ANOVA.

Compare 3 or More Means or Proportions

χ. Chi-Square Test
2- Large Sample Completion Rates

A Analysis of Variance (ANOVA)
2- Large Sample Means

A^rm Repeated Measures Analysis of Variance (RM-ANOVA)
2- Means from the Same Users

A² 2 Way Analysis of Variance (2 Way ANOVA)
2 Large Sample Means by 2 Indep. Variables

2. Enter the data for each variable (Company and Channel).

Contents

A² **2 x 2 ANOVA (Analysis of Variance)**
Enter the raw data (e.g time, satisfaction data) and independent var

		Input		
Variable 1 -> Compan A	A	B	B
Variable 2 -> Channel Web	Mobile	Web	Mobile
72.5	62.5	82.5	100.0
85.0	72.5	72.5	80.0
70.0	77.5	87.5	90.0
80.0	57.5	70.0	80.0
60.0	82.5	80.0	85.0
80.0	50.0	75.0	80.0
80.0	67.5	97.5	92.5
85.0	70.0	57.5	75.0
65.0	52.5	70.0	100.0
75.0	82.5	85.0	77.5

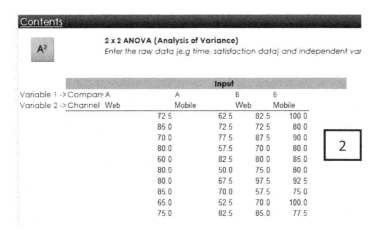

3. The F statistics (10.58, .006, 6.142) and p-values (.00249, .9387, .01802) are shown in the Results section.

Results

Summary Table

Source	SS	df	MS	F	p
Total	5,494.38	39	140.88		
Factor (Between Groups)	1743.125	3	581.04		
Company	1,102.50	1	1,102.50	10.58	**0.00249**
Channel	0.63	1	0.63	0.006	**0.9387**
Interaction	640.0000	1	640.00	6.142	**0.01802**
Error (Within Groups)	3,751.25	36	104.20		

4. To analyze the multiple comparisons, select the "Correction for Multiple Comparisons" in the Extras section.

Extras

5. Enter the p-values for each comparison and sort from lowest to highest.

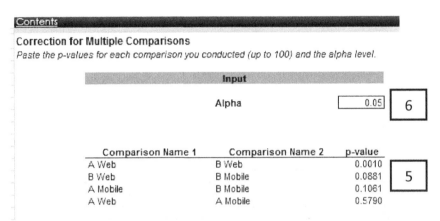

6. Enter the alpha rejection level (.05).

7. The total number of comparisons are shown (4), the Bonferonni Threshold (p = .0125) and the comparisons that are significant are flagged "Sig" for the BH comparison (1 marked Sig.) and Bonferonni (1 marked Sig).

Results			
Total Comparisons		4	
Bonferonni Threshold		0.0125	

Rank	BH Threshold	BH Significant	Bonferonni Significant
1	0.013	Sig.	Sig.
2	0.025		
3	0.038		
4	0.050		

7

R solution

For the ANOVA, enter the following commands:

```
x <- c('A', 'A', 'A', 'A', 'A', 'A', 'A', 'A', 'A', 'A', 'A', 'A', 'A', 'A', 'A', 'A', 'A', 'A', 'A', 'A',
'B', 'B', 'B', 'B', 'B', 'B', 'B', 'B', 'B', 'B', 'B', 'B', 'B', 'B', 'B', 'B', 'B', 'B', 'B', 'B')

y <- c('Web', 'Web', 'Web', 'Web', 'Web', 'Web', 'Web', 'Web', 'Web', 'Web',
'Mob', 'Mob', 'Mob', 'Mob', 'Mob', 'Mob', 'Mob', 'Mob', 'Mob', 'Mob', 'Web',
'Web', 'Web', 'Web', 'Web', 'Web', 'Web', 'Web', 'Web', 'Web', 'Mob', 'Mob',
'Mob', 'Mob', 'Mob', 'Mob', 'Mob', 'Mob', 'Mob', 'Mob')

z <- c(72.5, 85.0, 70.0, 80.0, 60.0, 80.0, 80.0, 85.0, 65.0, 75.0, 62.5, 72.5, 77.5,
57.5, 82.5, 50.0, 67.5, 70.0, 52.5, 82.5, 82.5, 72.5, 87.5, 70.0, 80.0, 75.0, 97.5,
57.5, 70.0, 85.0, 100.0, 80.0, 90.0, 80.0, 85.0, 80.0, 92.5, 75.0, 100.0, 77.5)

x_name <- "Company"

y_name <- "Channel"

z_name <- "SUS"

survey.df <- data.frame(x,y,z)

names(survey.df) <- c(x_name,y_name,z_name)

aov.out <- aov(SUS ~ Company*Channel, data=survey.df)

summary(aov.out)
```

The first eight commands put the data into an R "data frame" so you can use standard R functions for ANOVA (of which there are several). The ninth command uses a standard R function named aov, which does two-way ANOVA -- placing the output of the ANOVA into a variable named aov.out. The last command produces a summary (shown below) of the ANOVA with the values for F, p, and degrees of freedom needed to report the result of the analysis.

```
                 Df Sum Sq Mean Sq  F value    Pr(>F)
Company           1   1103  1102.5   10.580  0.00249  **
Channel           1      1     0.6    0.006  0.93870
Company:Channel   1    640   640.0    6.142  0.01802  *
Residuals        36   3751   104.2

---
Signif. codes:   0 '***' 0.001 '**' 0.01 '*' 0.05 '.' 0.1 ' ' 1
```

For the multiple comparisons, enter the following commands:

WebA <- c(72.5, 85.0, 70.0, 80.0, 60.0, 80.0, 80.0, 85.0, 65.0, 75.0)

MobA <- c(62.5, 72.5, 77.5, 57.5, 82.5, 50.0, 67.5, 70.0, 52.5, 82.5)

WebB <- c(82.5, 72.5, 87.5, 70.0, 80.0, 75.0, 97.5, 57.5, 70.0, 85.0)

MobB <- c(100.0, 80.0, 90.0, 80.0, 85.0, 80.0, 92.5, 75.0, 100.0, 77.5)

t.test(WebA,MobA,var.equal = TRUE)

t.test(WebB,MobB,var.equal = TRUE)

t.test(WebA,WebB,var.equal = TRUE)

t.test(MobA,MobB,var.equal = TRUE)

compute.mcadjustments(4, .05)

The first four commands put the data into the four survey variables (WebA, MobA, WebB, and MobB). The next four commands perform four pairwise t-tests with those four variables (using the standard R command for independent t-tests and, to match the values in *Quantifying the User Experience*, assuming equal variance). These four t-tests were selected because they are the four that best explore the interaction. The last command produces the adjusted p-values for the Bonferroni

and Benjamini-Hochberg methods. The results (for comparison withe the results
table above) are:

```
> t.test(WebA,MobA,var.equal = TRUE)

        Two Sample t-test

data:  WebA and MobA
t = 1.7011, df = 18, p-value = 0.1061
alternative hypothesis: true difference in means is not equal to 0
95 percent confidence interval:
 -1.821757 17.321757
sample estimates:
mean of x mean of y
    75.25     67.50

> t.test(WebB,MobB,var.equal = TRUE)

        Two Sample t-test

data:  WebB and MobB
t = -1.8036, df = 18, p-value = 0.08806
alternative hypothesis: true difference in means is not equal to 0
95 percent confidence interval:
 -17.860108   1.360108
sample estimates:
mean of x mean of y
    77.75     86.00

> t.test(WebA,WebB,var.equal = TRUE)

        Two Sample t-test

data:  WebA and WebB
t = -0.5651, df = 18, p-value = 0.579
alternative hypothesis: true difference in means is not equal to 0
95 percent confidence interval:
 -11.793925   6.793925
sample estimates:
mean of x mean of y
    75.25     77.75

> t.test(MobA,MobB,var.equal = TRUE)

        Two Sample t-test

data:  MobA and MobB
t = -3.9343, df = 18, p-value = 0.0009722
alternative hypothesis: true difference in means is not equal to 0
95 percent confidence interval:
 -28.379051  -8.620949
sample estimates:
mean of x mean of y
    67.5      86.0
```

```
> compute.mcadjustments(4, .05)

RESULTS

Bonferroni adjustment for critical value of p: 0.0125

Benjamini-Hochberg adjustments for critical values of p
Rank 1: 0.0125
Rank 2: 0.025
Rank 3: 0.0375
Rank 4: 0.05
```

Chapter 11: Final Words

In this book we've shown **how** to use Excel and R to solve the over 100 quantitative examples and exercises from *Quantifying the User Experience: Practical Statistics for User Research* (2nd ed.). We provided only minimal guidance for **why** we used the methods we did. For detailed information about methods and interpreting results, see *Quantifying the User Experience: Practical Statistics for User Research* (2nd ed).

We used the tools in the preparation of *Quantifying the User Experience: Practical Statistics for User Research* (2nd ed.) to verify the examples and exercises, and found them useful for that. We hope you also find this book and the tools useful. If you do, please let us know. If you encounter any problems using the book or the tools, definitely let us know.

We plan to continue investigating and publishing our findings on statistical methods for user research. Probably the best source for updates on our research is the website www.measuringu.com. The easiest way to stay informed is to subscribe to the newsletter by clicking the Email Updates link in the upper right corner of the home page. The website also contains online tutorials and courses that cover many of the concepts in this book using visualizations and interactive demonstrations.

We wish you the best of luck as you collect and analyze user data in support of the goal of making products easier to use and, as a consequence, making life better for your users. As you do your research, keep in mind that statistics provides "the world's most specific way of saying maybe" (Searles, 1978). The use of statistical methods does not guarantee 100% correct decisions, but it doesn't have to be perfect to be effective. It is important, however, to understand its strengths, limitations, and leading practices when applied to user research to ensure its most effective use.

James R. (Jim) Lewis: drjimnfl@comcast.net

Jeff Sauro: jeff@measuringu.com

References

Campbell, I. (2007). Chi-squared and Fisher-Irwin tests of two-by-two tables with small sample recommendations. *Statistics in Medicine, 26*, 3661-3675.

Sauro, J. (2011). *A practical guide to the System Usability Scale (SUS): Background, benchmarks & best practices*. Denver, CO: Measuring Usability LLC.

Sauro, J., & Lewis, J. R. (2010). Average task times in usability tests: What to report? In *Proceedings of CHI 2010* (pp. 2347-2350). Atlanta, GA: ACM.

Sauro. J., & Lewis, J. R. (2016). *Quantifying the user experience: Practical statistics for user research* (2nd ed.). Cambridge, MA: Morgan-Kaufmann.

Searles, D. (1978). PSI burn: A study of physiological deterioration in parapsychological experimentation. *Omni Magazine, 1(3)*, 108-110. <Satire with amusing definitions of statistical terms>

Appendix: The R Functions

This appendix contains the R code for the custom R functions used in this book, in alphabetical order by function name.

```
# Analyze 0/1 matrix from R-Files directory
# This path just works on Jim's computer -- tailor to your computer by changing intro path
# This is for a data file in which rows are cases of within-case data
# The input file should have row and column labels and be a tab delimited text file
# There should be no missing data
# The R syntax for getting a file on a PC uses a path like this:
# "C:\\Documents and Settings\\jimlewis\\My Documents\\R-Files\\table501.txt"
#
analyze.01matrix.fromfile <- function(filename) {
f <- filename
data <- read.table(f,header=TRUE,row.names=1)
rows <- nrow(data)
cols <- ncol(data)
cells <- rows * cols
cellsum <- 0
colsum <- 0
Nonce <- 0
N <- cols
n <- rows
x <- 1
y <- 1
while (y <= cols) {
  while (x <= rows) {
  cellsum <- cellsum + data[x,y]
  colsum <- colsum + data[x,y]
  x <- x+1
  }
y <- y+1
x <- 1
if (colsum == 1) Nonce = Nonce + 1
colsum <- 0
}
pest <- cellsum/cells
GTadj <- Nonce/N
pGT <- pest/(1+GTadj)
pdef <- (pest - 1/n)*(1 - 1/n)
padj <- (pGT + pdef)/2
discoverysofar <- 1 - (1-padj)^n
problemsavailablefordiscovery <- N/discoverysofar
estimatedremaining <- problemsavailablefordiscovery - N
cat("\nRESULTS\n\n")
cat("Number of participants:",n,"\n")
cat("Number of known problems:",N,"\n")
cat("Number of known problems that occurred just once:",Nonce,"\n")
```

```
cat("Observed p:",pest,"\n")
cat("pdef:",pdef,"\n")
cat("pGT:",pGT,"\n")
cat("Adjusted p:",padj,"\n")
cat("Estimated proportion of discovery (so far):",discoverysofar,"\n")
cat("Estimated number of problems available for discovery:",ceiling(problemsavailablefordiscovery),"\n")
cat("Estimated number of undiscovered problems:",ceiling(estimatedremaining),"\n")
cat("\n")
}


# Analyze 0/1 matrix from Jim's Web directory
# Get data from a stored matrix of data from Jim's website
# This is for a data file in which rows are cases of within-case data
# The input file should have row and column labels and be a tab delimited text file
# There should be no missing data
#
analyze.01matrix.fromweb <- function(filename) {
intro <- "http://drjim.0catch.com/PracStatPackV2/"
f <- paste(intro,filename,sep="")
data <- read.table(f,header=TRUE,row.names=1)
rows <- nrow(data)
cols <- ncol(data)
cells <- rows * cols
cellsum <- 0
colsum <- 0
Nonce <- 0
N <- cols
n <- rows
x <- 1
y <- 1
while (y <= cols) {
  while (x <= rows) {
  cellsum <- cellsum + data[x,y]
  colsum <- colsum + data[x,y]
  x <- x+1
  }
y <- y+1
x <- 1
if (colsum == 1) Nonce = Nonce + 1
colsum <- 0
}
pest <- cellsum/cells
GTadj <- Nonce/N
pGT <- pest/(1+GTadj)
pdef <- (pest - 1/n)*(1 - 1/n)
padj <- (pGT + pdef)/2
discoverysofar <- 1 - (1-padj)^n
problemsavailablefordiscovery <- N/discoverysofar
estimatedremaining <- problemsavailablefordiscovery - N
cat("\nRESULTS\n\n")
cat("Number of participants:",n,"\n")
cat("Number of known problems:",N,"\n")
cat("Number of known problems that occurred just once:",Nonce,"\n")
```

```
cat("Observed p:",pest,"\n")
cat("pdef:",pdef,"\n")
cat("pGT:",pGT,"\n")
cat("Adjusted p:",padj,"\n")
cat("Estimated proportion of discovery (so far):",discoverysofar,"\n")
cat("Estimated number of problems available for discovery:",ceiling(problemsavailablefordiscovery),"\n")
cat("Estimated number of undiscovered problems:",ceiling(estimatedremaining),"\n")
cat("\n")
}


# Analyze PSSUQ matrix from R-Files directory (only for Version 3, with 16 items)
# This path just works on Jim's computer -- tailor to your computer by changing intro path
# This is for a data file in which rows are cases of within-case data
# Also need to provide desired level for confidence intervals (e.g., .95 or 95 for 95% confidence)
# The input file should have row and column labels and be a tab delimited text file
# Any missing data should be denoted NA and will be ignored when computing means
# Sysuse is Items 1-6; InfoQual is Items 7-12; IntQual is Items 13-15
# If an entire scale is missing, delete the case from the input file before running this function
# The R syntax for getting a file on a PC uses a path like this:
# "C:\\Documents and Settings\\jimlewis\\My Documents\\R-Files\\table501.txt"
#
analyze.pssuq.fromfile <- function(filename,conf) {
if (conf > 1) conf <- conf/100
confper <- paste(conf*100,"%",sep="")
f <- filename
origdata <- read.table(f,header=TRUE,row.names=1)
data <- origdata
attach(data)
rows <- nrow(data)
cols <- ncol(data)
n <- rows
x <- 1
y <- 1
# PSSUQ Version 3 Norms from Lewis (2002, 2012), Sauro & Lewis (2012)
# Values for norms are 99% lower limit, mean, 99% uppper limit for each item 1-16;
# 17-20 are for scales, respectively, SysUse, InfoQual, IntQual, Overall
pssuqnorms <- array(0,c(3,20))
pssuqnorms[,1] <- c(2.6,2.85,3.09)
pssuqnorms[,2] <- c(2.45,2.69,2.93)
pssuqnorms[,3] <- c(2.86,3.16,3.45)
pssuqnorms[,4] <- c(2.40,2.66,2.91)
pssuqnorms[,5] <- c(2.07,2.27,2.48)
pssuqnorms[,6] <- c(2.54,2.86,3.17)
pssuqnorms[,7] <- c(3.36,3.70,4.05)
pssuqnorms[,8] <- c(2.93,3.21,3.49)
pssuqnorms[,9] <- c(2.65,2.96,3.27)
pssuqnorms[,10] <- c(2.79,3.09,3.38)
pssuqnorms[,11] <- c(2.46,2.74,3.01)
pssuqnorms[,12] <- c(2.41,2.66,2.92)
pssuqnorms[,13] <- c(2.06,2.28,2.49)
pssuqnorms[,14] <- c(2.18,2.42,2.66)
pssuqnorms[,15] <- c(2.51,2.79,3.07)
pssuqnorms[,16] <- c(2.55,2.80,3.02)
```

```
pssuqnorms[,17] <- c(2.57,2.80,3.02)
pssuqnorms[,18] <- c(2.79,3.02,3.24)
pssuqnorms[,19] <- c(2.28,2.49,2.71)
pssuqnorms[,20] <- c(2.62,2.82,3.02)
# Building item/scale arrays
itemarray <- array(0,c(n,20))
while (y <= cols) {
  while (x <= rows) {
  itemarray[x,y] <- data[x,y]
  x <- x+1
  }
y <- y+1
x <- 1
}
while (x <= rows) {
  itemarray[x,17] <- mean(itemarray[x,1:6], na.rm=TRUE)
  itemarray[x,18] <- mean(itemarray[x,7:12], na.rm=TRUE)
  itemarray[x,19] <- mean(itemarray[x,13:15], na.rm=TRUE)
  itemarray[x,20] <- mean(itemarray[x,1:16], na.rm=TRUE)
  x <- x+1
}
# Confidence intervals for items/scales
y <- 1
x <- 1
itemconf <- array(0,c(3,20))
itemsderr <- array(0,c(20))
d <- array(0,c(20))
u <- array(0,c(20))
upper <- array(0,c(20))
lower <- array(0,c(20))
df = n-1
t <- abs(qt((1-conf)/2,df))
while (y <= 20) {
  itemsderr[y] <- sd(itemarray[,y], na.rm=TRUE)/n^.5
  d[y] <- t*itemsderr[y]
  u[y] <- mean(itemarray[,y], na.rm=TRUE)
  lower[y] <- u[y]-d[y]
  upper[y] <- u[y]+d[y]
  itemconf[1,y] <- lower[y]
  itemconf[2,y] <- u[y]
  itemconf[3,y] <- upper[y]
  y <- y+1
  }
# Comparison of observed confidence intervals with norms
y <- 1
x <- 1
compci <- array("",c(20))
while (y <= 20) {
  if (itemconf[3,y] < pssuqnorms[1,y]) compci[y] <- "interval lower than norm"
  if (itemconf[1,y] > pssuqnorms[3,y]) compci[y] <- "interval higher than norm"
  if (itemconf[3,y] >= pssuqnorms[1,y] && itemconf[1,y] <= pssuqnorms[3,y]) compci[y] <- "interval consistent with
norm"
  y <- y+1
```

```
 }
# Comparison of observed means with norms
y <- 1
x <- 1
compmean <- array("",c(20))
while (y <= 20) {
  if (itemconf[2,y] < pssuqnorms[1,y]) compmean[y] <- "Mean lower than norm;"
  if (itemconf[2,y] > pssuqnorms[3,y]) compmean[y] <- "Mean higher than norm;"
  if (itemconf[2,y] >= pssuqnorms[1,y] && itemconf[1,y] <= pssuqnorms[3,y]) compmean[y] <- "Mean consistent with
norm;"
  y <- y+1
  }
# Print the results
cat("RESULTS OF PSSUQ ANALYSIS \n\n")
cat("Scales \n\n")
cat("Overall mean:",format(itemconf[2,20],digits=3),"\t ",confper,"confidence
interval:",format(itemconf[1,20],digits=3),"-",format(itemconf[3,20],digits=3),"\t
Comparisons:",compmean[20],compci[20],"\n")
cat("SysUse  mean:",format(itemconf[2,17],digits=3),"\t ",confper,"confidence
interval:",format(itemconf[1,17],digits=3),"-",format(itemconf[3,17],digits=3),"\t
Comparisons:",compmean[17],compci[17],"\n")
cat("InfoQual mean:",format(itemconf[2,18],digits=3),"\t ",confper,"confidence
interval:",format(itemconf[1,18],digits=3),"-",format(itemconf[3,18],digits=3),"\t
Comparisons:",compmean[18],compci[18],"\n")
cat("IntQual mean:",format(itemconf[2,19],digits=3),"\t ",confper,"confidence
interval:",format(itemconf[1,19],digits=3),"-",format(itemconf[3,19],digits=3),"\t
Comparisons:",compmean[19],compci[19],"\n\n")
cat("Items \n\n")
cat("Item 01 mean:",format(itemconf[2,1],digits=3),"\t ",confper,"confidence
interval:",format(itemconf[1,1],digits=3),"-",format(itemconf[3,1],digits=3),"\t
Comparisons:",compmean[1],compci[1],"\n")
cat("Item 02 mean:",format(itemconf[2,2],digits=3),"\t ",confper,"confidence
interval:",format(itemconf[1,2],digits=3),"-",format(itemconf[3,2],digits=3),"\t
Comparisons:",compmean[2],compci[2],"\n")
cat("Item 03 mean:",format(itemconf[2,3],digits=3),"\t ",confper,"confidence
interval:",format(itemconf[1,3],digits=3),"-",format(itemconf[3,3],digits=3),"\t
Comparisons:",compmean[3],compci[3],"\n")
cat("Item 04 mean:",format(itemconf[2,4],digits=3),"\t ",confper,"confidence
interval:",format(itemconf[1,4],digits=3),"-",format(itemconf[3,4],digits=3),"\t
Comparisons:",compmean[4],compci[4],"\n")
cat("Item 05 mean:",format(itemconf[2,5],digits=3),"\t ",confper,"confidence
interval:",format(itemconf[1,5],digits=3),"-",format(itemconf[3,5],digits=3),"\t
Comparisons:",compmean[5],compci[5],"\n")
cat("Item 06 mean:",format(itemconf[2,6],digits=3),"\t ",confper,"confidence
interval:",format(itemconf[1,6],digits=3),"-",format(itemconf[3,6],digits=3),"\t
Comparisons:",compmean[6],compci[6],"\n")
cat("Item 07 mean:",format(itemconf[2,7],digits=3),"\t ",confper,"confidence
interval:",format(itemconf[1,7],digits=3),"-",format(itemconf[3,7],digits=3),"\t
Comparisons:",compmean[7],compci[7],"\n")
cat("Item 08 mean:",format(itemconf[2,8],digits=3),"\t ",confper,"confidence
interval:",format(itemconf[1,8],digits=3),"-",format(itemconf[3,8],digits=3),"\t
Comparisons:",compmean[8],compci[8],"\n")
```

```
cat("Item 09 mean:",format(itemconf[2,9],digits=3),"\t  ",confper,"confidence
interval:",format(itemconf[1,9],digits=3),"-",format(itemconf[3,9],digits=3),"\t
Comparisons:",compmean[9],compci[9],"\n")
cat("Item 10 mean:",format(itemconf[2,10],digits=3),"\t  ",confper,"confidence
interval:",format(itemconf[1,10],digits=3),"-",format(itemconf[3,10],digits=3),"\t
Comparisons:",compmean[10],compci[10],"\n")
cat("Item 11 mean:",format(itemconf[2,11],digits=3),"\t  ",confper,"confidence
interval:",format(itemconf[1,11],digits=3),"-",format(itemconf[3,11],digits=3),"\t
Comparisons:",compmean[11],compci[11],"\n")
cat("Item 12 mean:",format(itemconf[2,12],digits=3),"\t  ",confper,"confidence
interval:",format(itemconf[1,12],digits=3),"-",format(itemconf[3,12],digits=3),"\t
Comparisons:",compmean[12],compci[12],"\n")
cat("Item 13 mean:",format(itemconf[2,13],digits=3),"\t  ",confper,"confidence
interval:",format(itemconf[1,13],digits=3),"-",format(itemconf[3,13],digits=3),"\t
Comparisons:",compmean[13],compci[13],"\n")
cat("Item 14 mean:",format(itemconf[2,14],digits=3),"\t  ",confper,"confidence
interval:",format(itemconf[1,14],digits=3),"-",format(itemconf[3,14],digits=3),"\t
Comparisons:",compmean[14],compci[14],"\n")
cat("Item 15 mean:",format(itemconf[2,15],digits=3),"\t  ",confper,"confidence
interval:",format(itemconf[1,15],digits=3),"-",format(itemconf[3,15],digits=3),"\t
Comparisons:",compmean[15],compci[15],"\n")
cat("Item 16 mean:",format(itemconf[2,16],digits=3),"\t  ",confper,"confidence
interval:",format(itemconf[1,16],digits=3),"-",format(itemconf[3,16],digits=3),"\t
Comparisons:",compmean[16],compci[16],"\n\n")
}


# Analyze PSSUQ matrix from Jim's Web directory (only for Version 3, with 16 items)
# This is for a data file in which rows are cases of within-case data
# Also need to provide desired level for confidence intervals (e.g., .95 or 95 for 95% confidence)
# The input file should have row and column labels and be a tab delimited text file
# Any missing data should be denoted NA and will be ignored when computing means
# Sysuse is Items 1-6; InfoQual is Items 7-12; IntQual is Items 13-15
# If an entire scale is missing, delete the case from the input file before running this function
#
analyze.pssuq.fromweb <- function(filename,conf) {
if (conf > 1) conf <- conf/100
confper <- paste(conf*100,"%",sep="")
intro <- "http://drjim.0catch.com/PracStatPackV2/"
f <- paste(intro,filename,sep="")
origdata <- read.table(f,header=TRUE,row.names=1)
data <- origdata
attach(data)
rows <- nrow(data)
cols <- ncol(data)
n <- rows
x <- 1
y <- 1
# PSSUQ Version 3 Norms from Lewis (2002, 2012), Sauro & Lewis (2012)
# Values for norms are 99% lower limit, mean, 99% uppper limit for each item 1-16;
# 17-20 are for scales, respectively, SysUse, InfoQual, IntQual, Overall
pssuqnorms <- array(0,c(3,20))
pssuqnorms[,1] <- c(2.6,2.85,3.09)
pssuqnorms[,2] <- c(2.45,2.69,2.93)
```

```
pssuqnorms[,3] <- c(2.86,3.16,3.45)
pssuqnorms[,4] <- c(2.40,2.66,2.91)
pssuqnorms[,5] <- c(2.07,2.27,2.48)
pssuqnorms[,6] <- c(2.54,2.86,3.17)
pssuqnorms[,7] <- c(3.36,3.70,4.05)
pssuqnorms[,8] <- c(2.93,3.21,3.49)
pssuqnorms[,9] <- c(2.65,2.96,3.27)
pssuqnorms[,10] <- c(2.79,3.09,3.38)
pssuqnorms[,11] <- c(2.46,2.74,3.01)
pssuqnorms[,12] <- c(2.41,2.66,2.92)
pssuqnorms[,13] <- c(2.06,2.28,2.49)
pssuqnorms[,14] <- c(2.18,2.42,2.66)
pssuqnorms[,15] <- c(2.51,2.79,3.07)
pssuqnorms[,16] <- c(2.55,2.80,3.02)
pssuqnorms[,17] <- c(2.57,2.80,3.02)
pssuqnorms[,18] <- c(2.79,3.02,3.24)
pssuqnorms[,19] <- c(2.28,2.49,2.71)
pssuqnorms[,20] <- c(2.62,2.82,3.02)
# Building item/scale arrays
itemarray <- array(0,c(n,20))
while (y <= cols) {
  while (x <= rows) {
  itemarray[x,y] <- data[x,y]
  x <- x+1
  }
y <- y+1
x <- 1
}
while (x <= rows) {
  itemarray[x,17] <- mean(itemarray[x,1:6], na.rm=TRUE)
  itemarray[x,18] <- mean(itemarray[x,7:12], na.rm=TRUE)
  itemarray[x,19] <- mean(itemarray[x,13:15], na.rm=TRUE)
  itemarray[x,20] <- mean(itemarray[x,1:16], na.rm=TRUE)
  x <- x+1
}
# Confidence intervals for items/scales
y <- 1
x <- 1
itemconf <- array(0,c(3,20))
itemsderr <- array(0,c(20))
d <- array(0,c(20))
u <- array(0,c(20))
upper <- array(0,c(20))
lower <- array(0,c(20))
df = n-1
t <- abs(qt((1-conf)/2,df))
while (y <= 20) {
  itemsderr[y] <- sd(itemarray[,y], na.rm=TRUE)/n^.5
  d[y] <- t*itemsderr[y]
  u[y] <- mean(itemarray[,y], na.rm=TRUE)
  lower[y] <- u[y]-d[y]
  upper[y] <- u[y]+d[y]
  itemconf[1,y] <- lower[y]
```

```
  itemconf[2,y] <- u[y]
  itemconf[3,y] <- upper[y]
  y <- y+1
  }
# Comparison of observed confidence intervals with norms
y <- 1
x <- 1
compci <- array("",c(20))
while (y <= 20) {
  if (itemconf[3,y] < pssuqnorms[1,y]) compci[y] <- "interval lower than norm"
  if (itemconf[1,y] > pssuqnorms[3,y]) compci[y] <- "interval higher than norm"
  if (itemconf[3,y] >= pssuqnorms[1,y] && itemconf[1,y] <= pssuqnorms[3,y]) compci[y] <- "interval consistent with
norm"
  y <- y+1
  }
# Comparison of observed means with norms
y <- 1
x <- 1
compmean <- array("",c(20))
while (y <= 20) {
  if (itemconf[2,y] < pssuqnorms[1,y]) compmean[y] <- "Mean lower than norm;"
  if (itemconf[2,y] > pssuqnorms[3,y]) compmean[y] <- "Mean higher than norm;"
  if (itemconf[2,y] >= pssuqnorms[1,y] && itemconf[1,y] <= pssuqnorms[3,y]) compmean[y] <- "Mean consistent with
norm;"
  y <- y+1
  }
# Print the results
cat("RESULTS OF PSSUQ ANALYSIS \n\n")
cat("Scales \n\n")
cat("Overall mean:",format(itemconf[2,20],digits=3),"\t  ",confper,"confidence
interval:",format(itemconf[1,20],digits=3),"-",format(itemconf[3,20],digits=3),"\t
Comparisons:",compmean[20],compci[20],"\n")
cat("SysUse  mean:",format(itemconf[2,17],digits=3),"\t  ",confper,"confidence
interval:",format(itemconf[1,17],digits=3),"-",format(itemconf[3,17],digits=3),"\t
Comparisons:",compmean[17],compci[17],"\n")
cat("InfoQual mean:",format(itemconf[2,18],digits=3),"\t  ",confper,"confidence
interval:",format(itemconf[1,18],digits=3),"-",format(itemconf[3,18],digits=3),"\t
Comparisons:",compmean[18],compci[18],"\n")
cat("IntQual mean:",format(itemconf[2,19],digits=3),"\t  ",confper,"confidence
interval:",format(itemconf[1,19],digits=3),"-",format(itemconf[3,19],digits=3),"\t
Comparisons:",compmean[19],compci[19],"\n\n")
cat("Items \n\n")
cat("Item 01 mean:",format(itemconf[2,1],digits=3),"\t  ",confper,"confidence
interval:",format(itemconf[1,1],digits=3),"-",format(itemconf[3,1],digits=3),"\t
Comparisons:",compmean[1],compci[1],"\n")
cat("Item 02 mean:",format(itemconf[2,2],digits=3),"\t  ",confper,"confidence
interval:",format(itemconf[1,2],digits=3),"-",format(itemconf[3,2],digits=3),"\t
Comparisons:",compmean[2],compci[2],"\n")
cat("Item 03 mean:",format(itemconf[2,3],digits=3),"\t  ",confper,"confidence
interval:",format(itemconf[1,3],digits=3),"-",format(itemconf[3,3],digits=3),"\t
Comparisons:",compmean[3],compci[3],"\n")
```

```
cat("Item 04 mean:",format(itemconf[2,4],digits=3),"\t ",confper,"confidence
interval:",format(itemconf[1,4],digits=3),"-",format(itemconf[3,4],digits=3),"\t
Comparisons:",compmean[4],compci[4],"\n")
cat("Item 05 mean:",format(itemconf[2,5],digits=3),"\t ",confper,"confidence
interval:",format(itemconf[1,5],digits=3),"-",format(itemconf[3,5],digits=3),"\t
Comparisons:",compmean[5],compci[5],"\n")
cat("Item 06 mean:",format(itemconf[2,6],digits=3),"\t ",confper,"confidence
interval:",format(itemconf[1,6],digits=3),"-",format(itemconf[3,6],digits=3),"\t
Comparisons:",compmean[6],compci[6],"\n")
cat("Item 07 mean:",format(itemconf[2,7],digits=3),"\t ",confper,"confidence
interval:",format(itemconf[1,7],digits=3),"-",format(itemconf[3,7],digits=3),"\t
Comparisons:",compmean[7],compci[7],"\n")
cat("Item 08 mean:",format(itemconf[2,8],digits=3),"\t ",confper,"confidence
interval:",format(itemconf[1,8],digits=3),"-",format(itemconf[3,8],digits=3),"\t
Comparisons:",compmean[8],compci[8],"\n")
cat("Item 09 mean:",format(itemconf[2,9],digits=3),"\t ",confper,"confidence
interval:",format(itemconf[1,9],digits=3),"-",format(itemconf[3,9],digits=3),"\t
Comparisons:",compmean[9],compci[9],"\n")
cat("Item 10 mean:",format(itemconf[2,10],digits=3),"\t ",confper,"confidence
interval:",format(itemconf[1,10],digits=3),"-",format(itemconf[3,10],digits=3),"\t
Comparisons:",compmean[10],compci[10],"\n")
cat("Item 11 mean:",format(itemconf[2,11],digits=3),"\t ",confper,"confidence
interval:",format(itemconf[1,11],digits=3),"-",format(itemconf[3,11],digits=3),"\t
Comparisons:",compmean[11],compci[11],"\n")
cat("Item 12 mean:",format(itemconf[2,12],digits=3),"\t ",confper,"confidence
interval:",format(itemconf[1,12],digits=3),"-",format(itemconf[3,12],digits=3),"\t
Comparisons:",compmean[12],compci[12],"\n")
cat("Item 13 mean:",format(itemconf[2,13],digits=3),"\t ",confper,"confidence
interval:",format(itemconf[1,13],digits=3),"-",format(itemconf[3,13],digits=3),"\t
Comparisons:",compmean[13],compci[13],"\n")
cat("Item 14 mean:",format(itemconf[2,14],digits=3),"\t ",confper,"confidence
interval:",format(itemconf[1,14],digits=3),"-",format(itemconf[3,14],digits=3),"\t
Comparisons:",compmean[14],compci[14],"\n")
cat("Item 15 mean:",format(itemconf[2,15],digits=3),"\t ",confper,"confidence
interval:",format(itemconf[1,15],digits=3),"-",format(itemconf[3,15],digits=3),"\t
Comparisons:",compmean[15],compci[15],"\n")
cat("Item 16 mean:",format(itemconf[2,16],digits=3),"\t ",confper,"confidence
interval:",format(itemconf[1,16],digits=3),"-",format(itemconf[3,16],digits=3),"\t
Comparisons:",compmean[16],compci[16],"\n\n")
}

# Simple Linear Regression with Confidence Intervals
#
# data1 and data1 are arrays of matched scores and must be of equal length
# data1 are the y data -- the variable to be predicted; data2 are the x (predictor) data
# conf is the desired level of confidence for the confidence intervals
# predfor is a specific value of x to enter in the regression equation to get an estimate of y
# If not interested in predicting a value for y from x, use 0 (the x-intercept) as a placeholder
analyze.regression <- function(data1,data2,conf,predfor) {
if (conf > 1) conf <- conf/100
confper <- paste(conf*100,"%",sep="")
correl <- cor(data1, data2)
n <- length(data1)
```

```
r2t <- correl/((1-correl^2)/(n-2))^.5
df <- n - 2
p <- 2*(1-pt(r2t,df))
zprime <- 0.5*log((1+correl)/(1-correl))
z <- abs(qnorm((1-conf)/2))
critd <- z/(n-3)^.5
upperzprime <- zprime + critd
lowerzprime <- zprime - critd
upper <- (exp(2*upperzprime)-1)/(exp(2*upperzprime)+1)
lower <- (exp(2*lowerzprime)-1)/(exp(2*lowerzprime)+1)
rsquared <- paste(round((correl^2)*100,digits=2),"%",sep="")
rsquaredupper <- paste(round((upper^2)*100,digits=2),"%",sep="")
rsquaredlower <- paste(round((lower^2)*100,digits=2),"%",sep="")
sy <- sd(data1)
sx <- sd(data2)
slope <- correl*sy/sx
bary <- mean(data1)
barx <- mean(data2)
intercept <- bary - slope*barx
deviations <- (data1 - (slope*data2+intercept))^2
sumdev <- sum(deviations)
xdev <- (data2 - barx)^2
sumxdev <- sum(xdev)
seslope <- (((sumdev)/df)^.5)/(sumxdev^.5)
tcrit <- abs(qt((1-conf)/2,df))
critdslope <- seslope*tcrit
slopeupper <- slope + critdslope
slopelower <- slope - critdslope
seintercept <- ((sumdev/df)^.5)*((1/n)+(barx^2/sumxdev))^.5
critdintercept <- seintercept*tcrit
interceptupper <- intercept + critdintercept
interceptlower <- intercept - critdintercept
predicted <- slope*predfor+intercept
sepredicted <- ((sumdev/df)^.5)*((1/n)+((predfor-barx)^2/sumxdev))^.5
critdpredicted <- sepredicted*tcrit
predictedupper <- predicted + critdpredicted
predictedlower <- predicted - critdpredicted
cat("\nRESULTS\n\n")
cat ("Slope and Intercept","\n")
cat ("Slope:",slope,"\n")
cat ("Intercept:",intercept,"\n","\n")
cat (confper,"Confidence Interval for Slope","\n")
cat ("Standard error:",seslope,"\n")
cat ("Upper limit:", slopeupper, "\n")
cat ("Slope:", slope, "\n")
cat ("Lower limit:", slopelower, "\n\n")
cat (confper,"Confidence Interval for Intercept","\n")
cat ("Standard error:",seintercept,"\n")
cat ("Upper limit:", interceptupper, "\n")
cat ("Intercept:", intercept, "\n")
cat ("Lower limit:", interceptlower, "\n\n")
cat ("Overall Significance of Model","\n")
cat ("r:",correl,"\n")
```

```
cat ("df:",df,"\n")
cat ("p:",p,"\n\n")
cat (confper,"Confidence Interval for Correlation","\n")
cat ("Upper limit:", upper, "\n")
cat ("r:", correl, "\n")
cat ("Lower limit:", lower, "\n\n")
cat (confper,"Confidence Interval for R-squared","\n")
cat ("Upper limit:", rsquaredupper, "\n")
cat ("R-squared:", rsquared, "\n")
cat ("Lower limit:", rsquaredlower, "\n\n")
cat (confper,"Confidence Interval for Predicted Value","\n")
cat ("Standard error:",sepredicted,"\n")
cat ("Upper limit:", predictedupper, "\n")
cat ("Predicted value of y given x =",predfor,":", predicted, "\n")
cat ("Lower limit:", predictedlower, "\n\n")
cat ("Values for Sample Size Estimation","\n")
cat ("Mean of x:",barx,"\n")
cat ("Population variability of x:",sumxdev/n,"\n")
cat ("Population variability of error:",sumdev/n,"\n","\n")
cat ("\n")
}


# Analyze SUS matrix from R-Files directory (standard version of SUS with varied tone, raw untransformed data)
# This path just works on Jim's computer -- tailor to your computer by changing intro path
# This is for a data file in which rows are cases of within-case data
# Also need to provide desired level for confidence intervals as proportion or percentage (e.g., .95 or 95 for 95% confidence)
# The input file should have row and column labels and be a tab delimited text file
# Missing data should be denoted NA and the entire case will be deleted
# The R syntax for getting a file on a PC uses a path like this:
# "C:\\Documents and Settings\\jimlewis\\My Documents\\R-Files\\table501.txt"
#
analyze.sus.fromfile <- function(filename,conf) {
f <- filename
origdata <- read.table(f,header=TRUE,row.names=1)
data <- na.omit(origdata)
norig <- nrow(origdata)
nleft <- nrow(data)
nmissing <- norig - nleft
attach(data)
if (conf > 1) conf <- conf/100
confper <- paste(conf*100,"%",sep="")
rows <- nrow(data)
cols <- ncol(data)
n <- rows
x <- 1
y <- 1
# Defining odd and even items
oddeven <- array("",c(10))
oddeven[1] <- "odd"
oddeven[2] <- "even"
oddeven[3] <- "odd"
oddeven[4] <- "even"
```

```
oddeven[5] <- "odd"
oddeven[6] <- "even"
oddeven[7] <- "odd"
oddeven[8] <- "even"
oddeven[9] <- "odd"
oddeven[10] <- "even"
# Building item/scale arrays and recoding scores
itemarray <- array(0,c(n,13))
while (y <= cols) {
  while (x <= rows) {
  if (oddeven[y] == "odd") itemarray[x,y] <- data[x,y] - 1
  if (oddeven[y] == "even") itemarray[x,y] <- 5 - data[x,y]
  x <- x+1
  }
y <- y+1
x <- 1
}
while (x <= rows) {
  itemarray[x,11] <- (sum(itemarray[x,1:3]) + sum(itemarray[x,5:9]))*3.125
  itemarray[x,12] <- (sum(itemarray[x,4]) + sum(itemarray[x,10]))*12.5
  itemarray[x,13] <- sum(itemarray[x,1:10])*2.5
  x <- x+1
}
# Confidence intervals for items/scales
y <- 1
x <- 1
itemconf <- array(0,c(3,13))
itemsderr <- array(0,c(13))
d <- array(0,c(13))
u <- array(0,c(13))
upper <- array(0,c(13))
lower <- array(0,c(13))
df = n-1
t <- abs(qt((1-conf)/2,df))
while (y <= 13) {
  itemsderr[y] <- sd(itemarray[,y])/n^.5
  d[y] <- t*itemsderr[y]
  u[y] <- mean(itemarray[,y])
  lower[y] <- u[y]-d[y]
  upper[y] <- u[y]+d[y]
  itemconf[1,y] <- lower[y]
  itemconf[2,y] <- u[y]
  itemconf[3,y] <- upper[y]
  y <- y+1
  }
# SUS Percentiles and from Sauro 2011
suspercentiles <- array(0,c(1,100))
suspercentiles[1] <- c(0.2)
suspercentiles[2] <- c(0.2)
suspercentiles[3] <- c(0.3)
suspercentiles[4] <- c(0.3)
suspercentiles[5] <- c(0.3)
suspercentiles[6] <- c(0.3)
```

```
suspercentiles[7] <- c(0.4)
suspercentiles[8] <- c(0.4)
suspercentiles[9] <- c(0.4)
suspercentiles[10] <- c(0.5)
suspercentiles[11] <- c(0.5)
suspercentiles[12] <- c(0.6)
suspercentiles[13] <- c(0.6)
suspercentiles[14] <- c(0.7)
suspercentiles[15] <- c(0.7)
suspercentiles[16] <- c(0.8)
suspercentiles[17] <- c(0.8)
suspercentiles[18] <- c(0.9)
suspercentiles[19] <- c(1.0)
suspercentiles[20] <- c(1.1)
suspercentiles[21] <- c(1.2)
suspercentiles[22] <- c(1.3)
suspercentiles[23] <- c(1.4)
suspercentiles[24] <- c(1.5)
suspercentiles[25] <- c(1.6)
suspercentiles[26] <- c(1.8)
suspercentiles[27] <- c(1.9)
suspercentiles[28] <- c(2.1)
suspercentiles[29] <- c(2.3)
suspercentiles[30] <- c(2.5)
suspercentiles[31] <- c(2.7)
suspercentiles[32] <- c(2.9)
suspercentiles[33] <- c(3.2)
suspercentiles[34] <- c(3.4)
suspercentiles[35] <- c(3.8)
suspercentiles[36] <- c(4.1)
suspercentiles[37] <- c(4.4)
suspercentiles[38] <- c(4.8)
suspercentiles[39] <- c(5.3)
suspercentiles[40] <- c(5.7)
suspercentiles[41] <- c(6.2)
suspercentiles[42] <- c(6.8)
suspercentiles[43] <- c(7.3)
suspercentiles[44] <- c(8.0)
suspercentiles[45] <- c(8.7)
suspercentiles[46] <- c(9.4)
suspercentiles[47] <- c(10.2)
suspercentiles[48] <- c(11.1)
suspercentiles[49] <- c(12.1)
suspercentiles[50] <- c(13.1)
suspercentiles[51] <- c(14.2)
suspercentiles[52] <- c(15.4)
suspercentiles[53] <- c(16.7)
suspercentiles[54] <- c(18.1)
suspercentiles[55] <- c(19.6)
suspercentiles[56] <- c(21.2)
suspercentiles[57] <- c(22.9)
suspercentiles[58] <- c(24.7)
suspercentiles[59] <- c(26.7)
```

```
suspercentiles[60] <- c(28.8)
suspercentiles[61] <- c(31.0)
suspercentiles[62] <- c(33.3)
suspercentiles[63] <- c(35.8)
suspercentiles[64] <- c(38.4)
suspercentiles[65] <- c(41.1)
suspercentiles[66] <- c(43.9)
suspercentiles[67] <- c(46.9)
suspercentiles[68] <- c(50.0)
suspercentiles[69] <- c(53.2)
suspercentiles[70] <- c(56.4)
suspercentiles[71] <- c(59.8)
suspercentiles[72] <- c(63.1)
suspercentiles[73] <- c(66.5)
suspercentiles[74] <- c(69.9)
suspercentiles[75] <- c(73.2)
suspercentiles[76] <- c(76.5)
suspercentiles[77] <- c(79.7)
suspercentiles[78] <- c(82.7)
suspercentiles[79] <- c(85.5)
suspercentiles[80] <- c(88.1)
suspercentiles[81] <- c(90.5)
suspercentiles[82] <- c(92.6)
suspercentiles[83] <- c(94.4)
suspercentiles[84] <- c(95.9)
suspercentiles[85] <- c(97.2)
suspercentiles[86] <- c(98.1)
suspercentiles[87] <- c(98.8)
suspercentiles[88] <- c(99.3)
suspercentiles[89] <- c(99.6)
suspercentiles[90] <- c(99.8)
suspercentiles[91] <- c(99.9)
suspercentiles[92] <- c(100.0)
suspercentiles[93] <- c(100.0)
suspercentiles[94] <- c(100.0)
suspercentiles[95] <- c(100.0)
suspercentiles[96] <- c(100.0)
suspercentiles[97] <- c(100.0)
suspercentiles[98] <- c(100.0)
suspercentiles[99] <- c(100.0)
suspercentiles[100] <- c(100.0)
# Curved grades from Sauro 2011
suslow <- itemconf[1,13]
susave <- itemconf[2,13]
sushigh <- itemconf[3,13]
while (x <= 3) {
  if (x == 1) susval <- suslow
  if (x == 2) susval <- susave
  if (x == 3) susval <- sushigh
  if (susval >= 84.1) curvedgrade <- "A+"
  if (susval >= 80.8 && susval < 84.1) curvedgrade <- "A"
  if (susval >= 78.9 && susval < 80.8) curvedgrade <- "A-"
  if (susval >= 77.2 && susval < 78.9) curvedgrade <- "B+"
```

```
  if (susval >= 74.1 && susval < 77.2) curvedgrade <- "B"
  if (susval >= 72.6 && susval < 74.1) curvedgrade <- "B-"
  if (susval >= 71.1 && susval < 72.6) curvedgrade <- "C+"
  if (susval >= 65.0 && susval < 71.1) curvedgrade <- "C"
  if (susval >= 62.7 && susval < 65.0) curvedgrade <- "C-"
  if (susval >= 51.7 && susval < 62.7) curvedgrade <- "D"
  if (susval < 51.7) curvedgrade <- "F"
  if (x == 1) susgradelow <- curvedgrade
  if (x == 2) susgradeave <- curvedgrade
  if (x == 3) susgradehigh <- curvedgrade
  x <- x+1
  }
# Converting observed results to percentiles (based on Sauro 2011)
y <- 1
x <- 1
susindexlow <- round(suslow)
susindexave <- round(susave)
susindexhigh <- round(sushigh)
susperclow <- suspercentiles[susindexlow]
suspercave <- suspercentiles[susindexave]
susperchigh <- suspercentiles[susindexhigh]
# Predicting likelihood to recommend and associated Net Promoter Score
promoters <- array(0,c(n))
detractors <- array(0,c(n))
passives <- array(0,c(n))
while (x <= n) {
  ltr <- round(0.1*itemarray[x,13])
  if (ltr >= 9) promoters[x] <- promoters[x]+1
  if (ltr <= 6) detractors[x] <- detractors[x]+1
  if (ltr >6 && ltr < 9) passives[x] <- passives[x]+1
  x <- x+1
  }
x <-1
promosum <- sum(promoters)
detractsum <- sum(detractors)
nps <- (promosum/n - detractsum/n)*100
npsper <- paste(nps,"%",sep="")
# Print the results
cat("\n")
cat("RESULTS OF SUS ANALYSIS \n\n")
cat("Overall \n\n")
cat("Overall SUS mean:",format(susave,digits=3),"\t ",confper,"confidence interval:",format(suslow,digits=3),"-
",format(sushigh,digits=3),"\n")
cat("Percentiles:",format(suspercave,digits=3),"\t ",confper,"confidence interval:",format(susperclow,digits=3),"-
",format(susperchigh,digits=3),"\n")
cat("Curve grades:",susgradeave,"\t ",confper,"confidence interval:",susgradelow,"-",susgradehigh,"\n")
cat("Estimated NPS:",npsper,"\n\n")
cat("Subscales \n\n")
cat("Usable scale:",format(itemconf[2,11],digits=3),"\t ",confper,"confidence
interval:",format(itemconf[1,11],digits=3),"-",format(itemconf[3,11],digits=3),"\n")
cat("Learnable scale:",format(itemconf[2,12],digits=3),"\t ",confper,"confidence
interval:",format(itemconf[1,12],digits=3),"-",format(itemconf[3,12],digits=3),"\n\n")
if (nmissing > 0) cat("Number of deleted cases due to missing data:",nmissing,"\n\n")
```

```
}

# Analyze SUS matrix from Jim's Web directory (standard version of SUS with varied tone, raw untransformed data)
# This is for a data file in which rows are cases of within-case data
# Also need to provide desired level for confidence intervals as proportion or percentage (e.g., .95 or 95 for 95%
confidence)
# The input file should have row and column labels and be a tab delimited text file
# Missing data should be denoted NA and the entire case will be deleted
#
analyze.sus.fromweb <- function(filename,conf) {
intro <- "http://drjim.0catch.com/PracStatPackV2/"
f <- paste(intro,filename,sep="")
origdata <- read.table(f,header=TRUE,row.names=1)
data <- na.omit(origdata)
norig <- nrow(origdata)
nleft <- nrow(data)
nmissing <- norig - nleft
attach(data)
if (conf > 1) conf <- conf/100
confper <- paste(conf*100,"%",sep="")
rows <- nrow(data)
cols <- ncol(data)
n <- rows
x <- 1
y <- 1
# Defining odd and even items
oddeven <- array("",c(10))
oddeven[1] <- "odd"
oddeven[2] <- "even"
oddeven[3] <- "odd"
oddeven[4] <- "even"
oddeven[5] <- "odd"
oddeven[6] <- "even"
oddeven[7] <- "odd"
oddeven[8] <- "even"
oddeven[9] <- "odd"
oddeven[10] <- "even"
# Building item/scale arrays and recoding scores
itemarray <- array(0,c(n,13))
while (y <= cols) {
  while (x <= rows) {
  if (oddeven[y] == "odd") itemarray[x,y] <- data[x,y] - 1
  if (oddeven[y] == "even") itemarray[x,y] <- 5 - data[x,y]
  x <- x+1
  }
y <- y+1
x <- 1
}
while (x <= rows) {
  itemarray[x,11] <- (sum(itemarray[x,1:3]) + sum(itemarray[x,5:9]))*3.125
  itemarray[x,12] <- (sum(itemarray[x,4]) + sum(itemarray[x,10]))*12.5
  itemarray[x,13] <- sum(itemarray[x,1:10])*2.5
  x <- x+1
```

```
}
# Confidence intervals for items/scales
y <- 1
x <- 1
itemconf <- array(0,c(3,13))
itemsderr <- array(0,c(13))
d <- array(0,c(13))
u <- array(0,c(13))
upper <- array(0,c(13))
lower <- array(0,c(13))
df = n-1
t <- abs(qt((1-conf)/2,df))
while (y <= 13) {
  itemsderr[y] <- sd(itemarray[,y])/n^.5
  d[y] <- t*itemsderr[y]
  u[y] <- mean(itemarray[,y])
  lower[y] <- u[y]-d[y]
  upper[y] <- u[y]+d[y]
  itemconf[1,y] <- lower[y]
  itemconf[2,y] <- u[y]
  itemconf[3,y] <- upper[y]
  y <- y+1
  }
# SUS Percentiles and from Sauro 2011
suspercentiles <- array(0,c(1,100))
suspercentiles[1] <- c(0.2)
suspercentiles[2] <- c(0.2)
suspercentiles[3] <- c(0.3)
suspercentiles[4] <- c(0.3)
suspercentiles[5] <- c(0.3)
suspercentiles[6] <- c(0.3)
suspercentiles[7] <- c(0.4)
suspercentiles[8] <- c(0.4)
suspercentiles[9] <- c(0.4)
suspercentiles[10] <- c(0.5)
suspercentiles[11] <- c(0.5)
suspercentiles[12] <- c(0.6)
suspercentiles[13] <- c(0.6)
suspercentiles[14] <- c(0.7)
suspercentiles[15] <- c(0.7)
suspercentiles[16] <- c(0.8)
suspercentiles[17] <- c(0.8)
suspercentiles[18] <- c(0.9)
suspercentiles[19] <- c(1.0)
suspercentiles[20] <- c(1.1)
suspercentiles[21] <- c(1.2)
suspercentiles[22] <- c(1.3)
suspercentiles[23] <- c(1.4)
suspercentiles[24] <- c(1.5)
suspercentiles[25] <- c(1.6)
suspercentiles[26] <- c(1.8)
suspercentiles[27] <- c(1.9)
suspercentiles[28] <- c(2.1)
```

```
suspercentiles[29] <- c(2.3)
suspercentiles[30] <- c(2.5)
suspercentiles[31] <- c(2.7)
suspercentiles[32] <- c(2.9)
suspercentiles[33] <- c(3.2)
suspercentiles[34] <- c(3.4)
suspercentiles[35] <- c(3.8)
suspercentiles[36] <- c(4.1)
suspercentiles[37] <- c(4.4)
suspercentiles[38] <- c(4.8)
suspercentiles[39] <- c(5.3)
suspercentiles[40] <- c(5.7)
suspercentiles[41] <- c(6.2)
suspercentiles[42] <- c(6.8)
suspercentiles[43] <- c(7.3)
suspercentiles[44] <- c(8.0)
suspercentiles[45] <- c(8.7)
suspercentiles[46] <- c(9.4)
suspercentiles[47] <- c(10.2)
suspercentiles[48] <- c(11.1)
suspercentiles[49] <- c(12.1)
suspercentiles[50] <- c(13.1)
suspercentiles[51] <- c(14.2)
suspercentiles[52] <- c(15.4)
suspercentiles[53] <- c(16.7)
suspercentiles[54] <- c(18.1)
suspercentiles[55] <- c(19.6)
suspercentiles[56] <- c(21.2)
suspercentiles[57] <- c(22.9)
suspercentiles[58] <- c(24.7)
suspercentiles[59] <- c(26.7)
suspercentiles[60] <- c(28.8)
suspercentiles[61] <- c(31.0)
suspercentiles[62] <- c(33.3)
suspercentiles[63] <- c(35.8)
suspercentiles[64] <- c(38.4)
suspercentiles[65] <- c(41.1)
suspercentiles[66] <- c(43.9)
suspercentiles[67] <- c(46.9)
suspercentiles[68] <- c(50.0)
suspercentiles[69] <- c(53.2)
suspercentiles[70] <- c(56.4)
suspercentiles[71] <- c(59.8)
suspercentiles[72] <- c(63.1)
suspercentiles[73] <- c(66.5)
suspercentiles[74] <- c(69.9)
suspercentiles[75] <- c(73.2)
suspercentiles[76] <- c(76.5)
suspercentiles[77] <- c(79.7)
suspercentiles[78] <- c(82.7)
suspercentiles[79] <- c(85.5)
suspercentiles[80] <- c(88.1)
suspercentiles[81] <- c(90.5)
```

```
suspercentiles[82] <- c(92.6)
suspercentiles[83] <- c(94.4)
suspercentiles[84] <- c(95.9)
suspercentiles[85] <- c(97.2)
suspercentiles[86] <- c(98.1)
suspercentiles[87] <- c(98.8)
suspercentiles[88] <- c(99.3)
suspercentiles[89] <- c(99.6)
suspercentiles[90] <- c(99.8)
suspercentiles[91] <- c(99.9)
suspercentiles[92] <- c(100.0)
suspercentiles[93] <- c(100.0)
suspercentiles[94] <- c(100.0)
suspercentiles[95] <- c(100.0)
suspercentiles[96] <- c(100.0)
suspercentiles[97] <- c(100.0)
suspercentiles[98] <- c(100.0)
suspercentiles[99] <- c(100.0)
suspercentiles[100] <- c(100.0)
# Curved grades from Sauro 2011
suslow <- itemconf[1,13]
susave <- itemconf[2,13]
sushigh <- itemconf[3,13]
while (x <= 3) {
  if (x == 1) susval <- suslow
  if (x == 2) susval <- susave
  if (x == 3) susval <- sushigh
  if (susval >= 84.1) curvedgrade <- "A+"
  if (susval >= 80.8 && susval < 84.1) curvedgrade <- "A"
  if (susval >= 78.9 && susval < 80.8) curvedgrade <- "A-"
  if (susval >= 77.2 && susval < 78.9) curvedgrade <- "B+"
  if (susval >= 74.1 && susval < 77.2) curvedgrade <- "B"
  if (susval >= 72.6 && susval < 74.1) curvedgrade <- "B-"
  if (susval >= 71.1 && susval < 72.6) curvedgrade <- "C+"
  if (susval >= 65.0 && susval < 71.1) curvedgrade <- "C"
  if (susval >= 62.7 && susval < 65.0) curvedgrade <- "C-"
  if (susval >= 51.7 && susval < 62.7) curvedgrade <- "D"
  if (susval < 51.7) curvedgrade <- "F"
  if (x == 1) susgradelow <- curvedgrade
  if (x == 2) susgradeave <- curvedgrade
  if (x == 3) susgradehigh <- curvedgrade
  x <- x+1
  }
# Converting observed results to percentiles (based on Sauro 2011)
y <- 1
x <- 1
susindexlow <- round(suslow)
susindexave <- round(susave)
susindexhigh <- round(sushigh)
susperclow <- suspercentiles[susindexlow]
suspercave <- suspercentiles[susindexave]
susperchigh <- suspercentiles[susindexhigh]
# Predicting likelihood to recommend and associated Net Promoter Score
```

```
promoters <- array(0,c(n))
detractors <- array(0,c(n))
passives <- array(0,c(n))
while (x <= n) {
  ltr <- round(.1*itemarray[x,13])
  if (ltr >= 9) promoters[x] <- promoters[x]+1
  if (ltr <= 6) detractors[x] <- detractors[x]+1
  if (ltr >6 && ltr < 9) passives[x] <- passives[x]+1
  x <- x+1
  }
x <-1
promosum <- sum(promoters)
detractsum <- sum(detractors)
nps <- (promosum/n - detractsum/n)*100
npsper <- paste(nps,"%",sep="")
# Print the results
cat("\n")
cat("RESULTS OF SUS ANALYSIS \n\n")
cat("Overall \n\n")
cat("Overall SUS mean:",format(susave,digits=3),"\t ",confper,"confidence interval:",format(suslow,digits=3),"-
",format(sushigh,digits=3),"\n")
cat("Percentiles:",format(suspercave,digits=3),"\t ",confper,"confidence interval:",format(susperclow,digits=3),"-
",format(susperchigh,digits=3),"\n")
cat("Curve grades:",susgradeave,"\t ",confper,"confidence interval:",susgradelow,"-",susgradehigh,"\n")
cat("Estimated NPS:",npsper,"\n\n")
cat("Subscales \n\n")
cat("Usable scale:",format(itemconf[2,11],digits=3),"\t ",confper,"confidence
interval:",format(itemconf[1,11],digits=3),"-",format(itemconf[3,11],digits=3),"\n")
cat("Learnable scale:",format(itemconf[2,12],digits=3),"\t ",confper,"confidence
interval:",format(itemconf[1,12],digits=3),"-",format(itemconf[3,12],digits=3),"\n\n")
if (nmissing > 0) cat("Number of deleted cases due to missing data:",nmissing,"\n\n")
}


# bench.rate.largesample: Comparing completion rate to benchmark one-tailed binomial test for large samples (np <
15)
# x is the number of targeted events (e.g., successes), n is the sample size,
# bench is the targeted benchmark expressed as a number between 0 and 1
# (e.g., a target of 90% successes would be .90)
#
bench.rate.largesample <- function(x,n,bench) {
mle <- x/n
d <- mle - bench
np <- n*bench
se <- ((bench * (1-bench))/n)^.5
z <- d/se
appgreaterthanp <- pnorm(z)
applessthanp <- 1-pnorm(z)
cat("\nRESULTS\n\n")
cat("Observed proportion:",mle,"\n")
cat("z:",z,"\n")
cat("Probability of exceeding benchmark:",appgreaterthanp,"(p <",1- appgreaterthanp,")\n")
cat("Probability of being below benchmark:",applessthanp,"(p <",1- applessthanp,")\n")
if (np < 15) cat("Warning: sample size too small -- np < 15 \n")
```

```
cat("\n")
}


# Comparing completion rate to benchmark one-tailed binomial test for small samples (np < 15)
# x is the number of targeted events (e.g., successes), n is the sample size,
# bench is the targeted benchmark expressed as a number between 0 and 1
# (e.g., a target of 90% successes would be .90)
#
bench.rate.smallsample <- function(x,n,bench) {
mle <- x/n
np <- n*bench
exactexceedsp <- pbinom(x-1,n,bench)
midpexceedsp <- pbinom(x-1,n,bench) + .5*dbinom(x,n,bench)
exactislessthanp <- 1 - pbinom(x,n,bench)
midpislessthanp <- 1 - midpexceedsp
cat("\nRESULTS (mid-p recommended)\n\n")
cat("Observed proportion:",mle,"\n")
cat("Exact probability of exceeding benchmark:",exactexceedsp,"(p <",1- exactexceedsp,")\n")
cat("Mid probability of exceeding benchmark:",midpexceedsp,"(p <",1- midpexceedsp,")\n")
cat("Exact probability of being below benchmark:",exactislessthanp,"(p <",1- exactislessthanp,")\n")
cat("Mid probability of being below benchmark:",midpislessthanp,"(p <",1-midpislessthanp,")\n\n")
}


# Comparing mean to criterion with t with array as input (one-tailed test)
# x is an array of scores, bench is the targeted benchmark
#
bench.t.fromarray <- function(x,bench) {
mean <- mean(x)
n <- length(x)
df <- n - 1
sd <- sd(x)
t <- (mean - bench)/(sd/(n^.5))
p <- pt(t,df)
cat("\nRESULTS\n\n")
cat("Observed mean:",mean,"\n")
cat("t:",t,"  df:",df,"\n")
cat("Probability of exceeding benchmark:",p,"(p <",1 - p,")\n")
cat("Probability of being below benchmark:",1 - p,"(p <",p,")\n\n")
}

# Comparing mean of logs to log criterion with t with array as input (one-tailed test)
# x is an array of time scores, or any other type of data on which
# to perform a log transformation; bench is the specified benchmark value
#
bench.t.fromarray.withlogconversion <- function(x,bench) {
logx <- log(x)
logmean <- mean(logx)
geomean <- exp(logmean)
logbench <- log(bench)
regmean <- mean(x)
regmedian <- median(x)
n <- length(logx)
df <- n - 1
```

```
sd <- sd(logx)
t <- (logmean - logbench)/(sd/(n^.5))
p <- pt(t,df)
cat("\nRESULTS\n\n")
cat ("Arithmetic mean:",regmean,"\n")
cat ("Median:",regmedian, "\n")
cat("Geometric mean:",geomean,"\n")
cat("t:",t,"  df:",df,"\n")
cat("Probability of exceeding benchmark:",p,"(p <",1 - p,")\n")
cat("Probability of being below benchmark:",1 - p,"(p <",p,")\n\n")
}


# Comparing mean to criterion with t with array as input (one-tailed test)
# mean is the observed mean, bench is the targeted benchmark value,
# sd is the standard deviation, n is the sample size
#
bench.t.fromsummary <- function(mean,bench,sd,n) {
df <- n - 1
t <- (mean - bench)/(sd/(n^.5))
p <- pt(t,df)
cat("\nRESULTS\n\n")
cat("t:",t,"\n")
cat("df:",df,"\n")
cat("Probability of exceeding benchmark:",p,"(p <",1 - p,")\n")
cat("Probability of being below benchmark:",1 - p,"(p <",p,")\n\n")
}


# Adjusted-Wald binomial confidence interval given array of 0s and 1s
# Scores is an array made up of 0s and 1s; conf is the desired level of confidence
# expressed as a number between 0 and 1 or between 1 and 100 (e.g., 95% confidence would be .95 or 95)
# z adjusted to one-sided interval if all x's are 0 or 1
#
ci.adjwald.fromarray <- function(scores,conf) {
if (conf > 1) conf <- conf/100
confper <- paste(conf*100,"%",sep="")
n <- length(scores)
x <- sum(scores)
p <- x/n
z <- abs(qnorm((1-conf)/2))
if (mean(scores) == 0) z <- abs(qnorm(1-conf))
if (mean(scores) == 1) z <- abs(qnorm(1-conf))
xadj <- x + (z^2)/2
nadj <- n + z^2
padj <- xadj/nadj
se <- ((padj*(1-padj))/nadj)^.5
d <- se*z
lower <- padj - d
upper <- padj + d
cat ("\nRESULTS \n\n")
cat ("Adjusted p (Wilson):\t",padj, "\n")
cat ("Margin of error:\t",d, "\n")
if (upper <= 1) cat(confper,"upper limit:\t", upper, "\n") else cat(confper,"upper limit:\t>.999999 \n")
cat ("p (maximum likelihood):\t", p, "\n")
```

```
if (lower >= 0) cat(confper,"lower limit:\t", lower, "\n") else cat(confper,"lower limit:\t<.000001 \n")
cat ("","\n")
}


# Adjusted-Wald binomial confidence interval given x and n
# x is the number of targeted events (e.g., successes), n is the sample size,
# conf is the desired level of confidence expressed as a number between 0 and 1 or between 1 and 100
# (e.g., 95% confidence would be .95 or 95)
# z adjusted to one-sided interval if all x's are 0 or 1
#
ci.adjwald.fromsummary <- function(x,n,conf) {
if (conf > 1) conf <- conf/100
confper <- paste(conf*100,"%",sep="")
z <- abs(qnorm((1-conf)/2))
if (x == 0) z <- abs(qnorm(1-conf))
if (x == n) z <- abs(qnorm(1-conf))
p <- x/n
xadj <- x + (z^2)/2
nadj <- n + z^2
padj <- xadj/nadj
se <- ((padj*(1-padj))/nadj)^.5
d <- se*z
lower <- padj - d
upper <- padj + d
cat ("\nRESULTS \n\n")
cat ("Adjusted p (Wilson):\t",padj, "\n")
cat ("Margin of error:\t",d, "\n")
if (upper <= 1) cat(confper,"upper limit:\t", upper, "\n") else cat(confper,"upper limit:\t>.999999 \n")
cat ("p (maximum likelihood):\t", p, "\n")
if (lower >= 0) cat(confper,"lower limit:\t", lower, "\n") else cat(confper,"lower limit:\t<.000001 \n")
cat ("","\n")
}


# Confidence interval (with test of significance) for N-1 Two-Proportion Test given p and n
# Inputs are p1, n1, p2, n2, and conf
# conf is the level for the confidence interval
# expressed as a number between 0 and 1 or between 1 and 100 (e.g., 95% confidence would be .95 or 95)
#
ci.independentproportions.difference <- function(p1,n1,p2,n2,conf) {
if (conf > 1) conf <- conf/100
confper <- paste(conf*100,"%",sep="")
x1 <- p1 * n1
x2 <- p2 * n2
N <- n1 + n2
a <- round(x1)
b <- round(n1 - x1)
c <- round(x2)
d <- round(n2 - x2)
m <- a + b
n <- c + d
r <- a + c
s <- b + d
P <- (x1 + x2)/(n1 + n2)
```

```
Q <- 1 - P
testznum <- (p1 - p2)*((N-1)/N)^.5
testzden <- (P * Q * (1/n1 + 1/n2))^.5
testz <- testznum/testzden
ptestz <- 2*pnorm(-abs(testz))
z <- abs(qnorm((1-conf)/2))
p1adj <- (a + z^2/4)/(m + z^2/2)
p2adj <- (c + z^2/4)/(n + z^2/2)
n1adj <- m + z^2/2
n2adj <- n + z^2/2
diff <- p1 - p2
diffadj <- p1adj - p2adj
se <- ((p1adj*(1 - p1adj)/n1adj) + (p2adj*(1 - p2adj)/n2adj))^.5
critdiff <- z*se
upper <- diffadj + critdiff
lower <- diffadj - critdiff
cat("\nRESULTS\n\n")
cat (confper,"confidence interval of difference between proportions","\n\n")
cat ("p1:",p1,"\n")
cat ("p2:",p2,"\n")
cat ("Adjusted value of p1:",p1adj,"\n")
cat ("Adjusted value of p2:",p2adj,"\n")
cat ("Adjusted difference:",diffadj,"\n")
cat ("Margin of error:",critdiff,"\n\n")
cat("Upper limit:", upper, "\n")
cat ("Maximum likelihood estimate (observed difference):", diff, "\n")
cat("Lower limit:", lower, "\n\n")
cat ("N-1 Two-Proportion z:",testz,"   p:",ptestz,"\n\n")
}


# Confidence interval for difference in matched proportions (with McNemar test)
# Focuses on McNemar Test (two-tailed) with confidence interval on difference in proportions
# Inputs are p1, p2, p12, p21, n and conf
# p1 and p2 are the overall proportions for the study (e.g., success rates)
# p12 and p21 are the discordance rates (p12: passed A, failed B; p21: passed B, failed A)
# n is the sample size (number of people who experienced both test conditions)
# conf is the level for the confidence interval
# expressed as a number between 0 and 1 or between 1 and 100 (e.g., 95% confidence would be .95 or 95)
#
ci.matchedproportions.difference <- function(p1,p2,p12,p21,n,conf) {
if (conf > 1) conf <- conf/100
confper <- paste(conf*100,"%",sep="")
N <- n
z <- abs(qnorm((1-conf)/2))
p11 <- p2 - p21
p22 <- (1 - p2) - p12
a <- round(p11 * N)
b <- round(p12 * N)
c <- round(p21 * N)
d <- round(p22 * N)
m <- a + b
n <- c + d
r <- a + c
```

```
s <- b + d
adj = z^2/8
aadj <- a + adj
badj <- b + adj
cadj <- c + adj
dadj <- d + adj
madj <- aadj + badj
nadj <- cadj + dadj
radj <- aadj + cadj
sadj <- badj + dadj
Nadj <- aadj + badj + cadj + dadj
p1adj <- madj/Nadj
p2adj <- radj/Nadj
p12adj <- badj/Nadj
p21adj <- cadj/Nadj
diffadj <- p2adj - p1adj
se <- (((p12adj + p21adj) - (p21adj - p12adj)^2)/Nadj)^.5
critdiff <- se*z
upper <- diffadj + critdiff
lower <- diffadj - critdiff
ndiscord <- b + c
smaller <- min(b,c)
bench <- .5
mle <- smaller/ndiscord
exactexceedsp <- pbinom(smaller-1,ndiscord,bench)
midpexceedsp <- pbinom(smaller-1,ndiscord,bench) + .5*dbinom(smaller,ndiscord,bench)
exactislessthanp <- 1 - pbinom(smaller,ndiscord,bench)
midpislessthanp <- 1 - midpexceedsp
mcnemarmidp <- 2*(1-midpislessthanp)
mcnemarexactp <- 2*(1- exactislessthanp)
cat("\nRESULTS\n\n")
cat(confper,"CONFIDENCE INTERVAL \n\n")
cat("p1:",p1,"\n")
cat("p2:",p2,"\n")
cat ("Adjusted value of p1:",p1adj,"\n")
cat ("Adjusted value of p2:",p2adj,"\n")
cat("Adjusted difference:",diffadj,"\n")
cat("Margin of error:",critdiff,"\n")
cat("Upper limit:",upper,"\n")
cat("Observed difference:",p2-p1,"\n")
cat("Lower limit:",lower,"\n\n")
cat("TESTS OF SIGNIFICANCE \n\n")
if (mcnemarmidp <= 1) cat("McNemar Mid Probability (recommended):", mcnemarmidp, "\n\n") else cat("McNemar
Mid Probability (recommended): 1 \n\n")
cat("Alternate analyses (not recommended) \n")
if (mcnemarexactp <= 1) cat("McNemar Exact Probability:", mcnemarexactp, "\n") else cat("McNemar Exact
Probability: 1 \n")
mcnemarchisquared <- ((c - b)^2)/(c + b)
df <- 1
pmcnemarchisquared <- 1-pchisq(mcnemarchisquared,df)
cat("McNemar Chi-Squared:",mcnemarchisquared,"   df:",df,"   p:",pmcnemarchisquared,"\n")
mcnemaryates <- ((abs(c - b)-1)^2)/(c + b)
pmcnemaryates <- 1-pchisq(mcnemaryates,df)
```

```
cat("McNemar Chi-Squared with Yates Correction:",mcnemaryates,"  df:",df,"  p:",pmcnemaryates,"\n\n")
}


# Confidence interval around the median (use for n > 25 scores)
# x is an array of scores; conf is the desired level of confidence
# expressed as a number between 0 and 1 or between 1 and 100
# (e.g., 95% confidence would be .95 or 95)
#
ci.median.fromarray <- function(x,conf) {
if (conf > 1) conf <- conf/100
confper <- paste(conf*100,"%",sep="")
n <- length(x)
m <- median(x)
p <- .5
np <- n*p
z <- abs(qnorm((1-conf)/2))
se <- (np*(1-p))^.5
d <- z*se
sortx <- sort(x)
lowerdatapoint <- ceiling(np-d) #ceiling is roundup function
upperdatapoint <- ceiling(np+d)
lower <- sortx[lowerdatapoint]
upper <- sortx[upperdatapoint]
cat ("\nRESULTS:",confper,"CONFIDENCE INTERVAL \n\n")
cat("Upper limit:", upper, "\n")
cat("Median:", m, "\n")
cat("Lower limit:", lower, "\n")
if (n < 25) cat("Warning: sample size too small -- n < 25")
cat("\n")
}


# Confidence interval around a percentile (use for large samples -- np > 15 -- smaller p needs larger n)
# x is an array of scores, p is the specified percentile,
# conf is the level of confidence expressed as a number between 0 and 1 or between 1 and 100
# (e.g., 95% confidence would be .95 or 95)
#
ci.percentile.fromarray <- function(x,p,conf) {
if (conf > 1) conf <- conf/100
confper <- paste(conf*100,"%",sep="")
n <- length(x)
np <- n*p
z <- abs(qnorm((1-conf)/2))
se <- (np*(1-p))^.5
d <- z*se
sortx <- sort(x)
lowerdatapoint <- ceiling(np-d)
upperdatapoint <- ceiling(np+d)
lower <- sortx[lowerdatapoint]
upper <- sortx[upperdatapoint]
percentile <- quantile(x,p)
cat ("\nRESULTS:",confper,"CONFIDENCE INTERVAL \n\n")
cat("Upper limit:", upper, "\n")
cat("Percentile (",p,"):",percentile, "\n")
```

```
cat("Lower limit:", lower, "\n")
if (np < 15) cat("Warning: sample size too small -- np < 15 \n")
cat("\n")
}
```

```
# Confidence interval using t-score given an array of scores
# x is an array of scores; conf is the desired level of confidence
# expressed as a number between 0 and 1 or between 1 and 100 (e.g., 95% confidence would be .95 or 95)
#
ci.t.fromarray <- function(x,conf) {
if (conf > 1) conf <- conf/100
confper <- paste(conf*100,"%",sep="")
n <- length(x)
df = n-1
t <- abs(qt((1-conf)/2,df))
se <- sd(x)/n^.5
d <- t*se
u <- mean(x)
lower <- u-d
upper <- u+d
cat ("\nRESULTS:",confper,"CONFIDENCE INTERVAL \n\n")
cat ("Upper limit:", upper, "\n")
cat ("Mean:", u, "\n")
cat ("Lower limit:", lower, "\n")
cat ("Margin of error:",d, "\n\n")
}
```

```
# Confidence interval using t-Score given an array of time scores (use for n < 25 scores)
# x is an array of time scores, or any other type of data on which
# to perform a log transformation;
# conf is the level of confidence expressed as a number between 0 and 1 or between 1 and 100
# (e.g., 95% confidence would be .95 or 95)
#
ci.t.fromarray.withlogconversion <- function(x,conf) {
if (conf > 1) conf <- conf/100
confper <- paste(conf*100,"%",sep="")
n <- length(x)
regmean <- mean(x)
regmedian <- median(x)
df = n-1
xlog <- log(x)
t <- abs(qt((1-conf)/2,df))
se <- sd(xlog)/n^.5
d <- t*se
ulog <- mean(xlog)
lowerlog <- ulog-d
upperlog <- ulog+d
u <- exp(ulog)
lower <- exp(lowerlog)
upper <- exp(upperlog)
cat ("\nRESULTS:",confper,"CONFIDENCE INTERVAL \n\n")
cat ("Arithmetic mean:",regmean,"\n")
cat ("Median:",regmedian, "\n")
```

```
cat ("Upper limit:", upper, "\n")
cat ("Geometric Mean:", u, "\n")
cat ("Lower limit:", lower, "\n")
cat ("Critical value of t:",t,"\n")
cat ("\n")
}


# Confidence interval using t-Score given summary data
# u is the mean, sd the standard deviation, n the sample size
# conf is the level of confidence expressed as a number between 0 and 1 or between 1 and 100
# (e.g., 95% confidence would be .95 or 95)
#
ci.t.fromsummary <- function(u,sd,n,conf) {
if (conf > 1) conf <- conf/100
confper <- paste(conf*100,"%",sep="")
df = n-1
t <- abs(qt((1-conf)/2,df))
d <- t*sd/n^.5
lower <- u-d
upper <- u+d
cat ("\nRESULTS:",confper,"CONFIDENCE INTERVAL \n\n")
cat ("Upper limit:", upper, "\n")
cat ("Mean:", u, "\n")
cat ("Lower limit:", lower, "\n")
cat ("Margin of error:",d, "\n")
cat ("Standard error:",sd/n^.5,"\n")
cat ("Critical value of t:",t,"\n\n")
}


# Compute equivalent confidence given nominal confidence and power and number of tails
#
compute.equivalentconfidence <- function(conf,power,tails) {
if (conf > 1) conf <- conf/100
if (power > 1) power <- power/100
if (tails != 1) zconf <- abs(qnorm((1-conf)/2))
if (tails == 1) zconf <- abs(qnorm((1-conf)))
zpower <- abs(qnorm((1-power)))
z <- zconf + zpower
if (tails != 1) equivconf <- 1 - 2*(1-pnorm(z))
if (tails == 1) equivconf <- pnorm(z)
cat("\nRESULTS\n\n")
cat("z(confidence):",zconf,"\n")
cat("z(power):",zpower,"\n")
cat("z(combined):",z,"\n\n")
cat("Equivalent confidence:",equivconf,"\n\n")
}


# Value of critical difference for log data given the arithmetic (non-logged) mean and the critical difference
#
compute.logcritdiff <- function(u,d) {
sum <- u + d
dlog <- log(sum) - log(u)
cat("\nRESULT\n\n")
```

```
cat("Value to use for log critical difference:",dlog,"\n\n")
}


# Preprocessing for time data to use as input for sample size estimation
# Input is an array of times (or any other data to undergo log transformation) and a planned critical difference (x and d)
# Output are the arithmetic mean, the median, the geometric mean, the variance and standard deviations of the log data,
# and the value to use for the critical difference
compute.logsummary.fromarray <- function (x,d) {
n <- length(x)
regmean <- mean(x)
regmedian <- median(x)
xlog <- log(x)
meanlog <- mean(xlog)
geomean <- exp(meanlog)
sdlog <- sd(xlog)
varlog <- sd(xlog)^2
selog <- sdlog/n^.5
sum <- regmean + d
dlog <- log(sum) - log(regmean)
cat("\nRESULTS\n\n")
cat("Arithmetic mean:",regmean,"\n")
cat("Median:",regmedian,"\n")
cat("Geometric Mean:", geomean,"\n")
cat("Mean of log data:",meanlog,"\n")
cat("Standard deviation of log data:", sdlog,"\n")
cat("Variance of log data:", varlog, "\n")
cat("Standard error of the mean of the log data:",selog,"\n")
cat("Sample size:",n,"\n")
cat("Value to use for log critical difference:",dlog,"\n")
cat("\n")
}


# Bonferroni and Benjamini-Hochberg adjustment
#
# n is the planned number of comparisons
# alpha is the overall desired level of of significance
# The value for Bonferroni is alpha divided by the number of comparisons
# The values for Benjamini-Hochberg use their rank-based approach
#
compute.mcadjustments <- function(n,alpha) {
bonferroni <- alpha/n
cat("\nRESULTS\n\n")
cat("Bonferroni adjustment for critical value of p:",bonferroni,"\n\n")
cat("Benjamini-Hochberg adjustments for critical values of p","\n")
iteration <- 1
while (iteration < n+1) {
  bh <- iteration*alpha/n
  rank <- paste("Rank ",iteration,":",sep="")
  cat(rank,bh,"\n")
  iteration <- iteration + 1
  }
cat("\n")
```

```
}

# Compute Net Promoter Score from array of raw NPS data
# Raw NPS data are Likelihood to Recommend (LTR) scores -- integers ranging from 0 to 10
#
compute.nps.fromarray <- function(scores) {
n <- length(scores)
promoters <- array(0,c(n))
detractors <- array(0,c(n))
passives <- array(0,c(n))
x <- 1
while (x <= n) {
  if (scores[x] >= 9) promoters[x] <- promoters[x]+1
  if (scores[x] <= 6) detractors[x] <- detractors[x]+1
  if (scores[x] >6 && scores[x] < 9) passives[x] <- passives[x]+1
  x <- x+1
  }
promosum <- sum(promoters)
detractsum <- sum(detractors)
passivesum <- sum(passives)
nps <- (promosum/n - detractsum/n)*100
npsper <- paste(format(nps, digits=4),"%",sep="")
cat("\nRESULTS \n\n")
cat("Number of promoters:",promosum,"\n")
cat("Number of passives:",passivesum,"\n")
cat("Number of detractors:",detractsum,"\n")
cat("Net Promoter Score (NPS):",npsper,"\n\n")
}


# Estimating padj from p (from Jeff's regression equation)
#
compute.padjfromp <- function(p) {
padj <- .9*p - .046
cat("\nRESULT\n\n")
cat("Estimate of adjusted p:",padj,"\n")
cat("\n")
}


# Get case-style data from a stored matrix of data
# This is for a data file in which rows are cases of within-case data
# The names of the dependent variables come from the column headers
# Missing data needs to be represented by NA in file
# This function deletes cases with missing data
# The R syntax for getting a file on a PC uses a path like this:
# "C:\\Documents and Settings\\jimlewis\\My Documents\\R-Files\\table501.txt"
#
getdata.fromfile <- function(filename) {
f <- filename
origdata <- read.table(f,header=TRUE)
data <- na.omit(origdata)
norig <- nrow(origdata)
nleft <- nrow(data)
nmissing <- norig - nleft
```

```
attach(data)
if (nmissing > 0) cat("Number of deleted cases due to missing data:",nmissing,"\n")
}


# Get case-style data from a stored matrix of data from Jim's website
# This is for a data file in which rows are cases of within-case data
# The names of the dependent variables come from the column headers
# Missing data needs to be represented by NA before input
# This function deletes cases with missing data
#
getdata.fromweb <- function(filename) {
intro <- "http://drjim.0catch.com/PracStatPackV2/"
f <- paste(intro,filename,sep="")
origdata <- read.table(f,header=TRUE)
data <- na.omit(origdata)
norig <- nrow(origdata)
nleft <- nrow(data)
nmissing <- norig - nleft
attach(data)
if (nmissing > 0) cat("Number of deleted cases due to missing data:",nmissing,"\n")
}


# Sample size estimation for "at least once" problem discovery
# Inputs are the problem discovery goal expressed as a proportion between 0 and 1 (e.g., .80 for 80% discovery),
# and the lowest probability of problem occurrence for which you want to achieve the problem discovery goal,
# also expressed as a number between 0 and 1 (e.g., .15)
#
n.atleastonce <- function(discoverygoal,problemprob) {
n <- ceiling(log(1 - discoverygoal)/log(1 - problemprob))
cat("\nRESULT\n\n")
cat("Recommended sample size:",n,"\n")
cat("\n")
}


# Sample size estimation for comparing rate with upper benchmark (iterative method based on adjusted-Wald)
# bench is the target proportion; critd is the minimum (critical) difference to be able to detect
# Desired levels of confidence and power expressed as a number between 0 and 1 or between 1 and 100
# (e.g., 95% confidence would be .95 or 95; 80% power would be .8 or 80)
# Because is test against benchmark, uses one-tailed confidence
#
n.bench.rate <- function(bench,critd,conf,power) {
# Initialize values
tails <- 1
if (conf > 1) conf <- conf/100
if (power > 1) power <- power/100
zconf <- abs(qnorm((1-conf)))
zpower <- abs(qnorm((1-power)))
z <- zconf + zpower
if (tails != 1) equivconf <- 1 - 2*(1-pnorm(z))
if (tails == 1) equivconf <- pnorm(z)
if (tails != 1) equivconfper <- paste(format(equivconf*100,digits=7),"% (two-sided)",sep="")
if (tails == 1) equivconfper <- paste(format(equivconf*100,digits=7),"% (two-sided)",sep="")
ncurr <- 2
```

```
ninit <- 1
iteration <- 0
p = bench + critd
q = 1 - p
# Standard (Cohen, 1988) estimate of n (nstd)
es1 <- 2*asin(sqrt(p))
es2 <- 2*asin(sqrt(bench))
h <- abs(es1-es2)*sqrt(2)
nstd <- ceiling(((z/h)^2)*2)
# Get initial estimate of n and compute first adjusted-Wald lower bound
ninit <- ceiling((z^2*p*q)/critd^2)
x <- round(ninit*p)
xadj <- x + (z^2)/2
nadj <- ninit + z^2
padj <- xadj/nadj
se <- ((padj*(1-padj))/nadj)^.5
d <- se*z
lower <- padj - d
upper <- padj + d
cat ("\nRESULTS \n\n")
cat("z(confidence):",zconf,"\n")
cat("z(power):",zpower,"\n")
cat("z(combined):",z,"\n")
cat("Equivalent confidence:",equivconf,"\n\n")
cat("Standard estimate of n:",nstd,"\n\n")
cat ("Initial estimate of n:",ninit,"\n")
cat ("Initial adjusted p (Wilson):",padj, "\n")
cat ("Initial margin of error:",d, "\n")
cat ("p (maximum likelihood):", p, "\n")
if (lower >= 0) cat("Initial lower limit:", lower, "\n") else cat("Initial lower limit:<.000001 \n")
cat("\n")
# Search for lowest sample size that has lower bound above criterion for given p (which is sum of bench and critd)
n <- ninit
while ((lower < bench) && (iteration < 10001)) {
  iteration <- iteration + 1
  n <- n +1
  x <- round(n * p)
  mle <- x/n
  xadj <- x + (z^2)/2
  nadj <- n + z^2
  padj <- xadj/nadj
  se <- ((padj*(1-padj))/nadj)^.5
  dadj <- se*z
  lower <- padj - dadj
  upper <- padj + dadj

cat("Iteration:",iteration,"\tn:",n,"\tx:",x,"\tp:",format(mle,digits=5),"\txadj:",format(xadj,digits=5),"\tnadj:",format(nadj,digits=5))
  cat("\tpadj:",format(padj,digits=5),"\tdadj:",format(dadj,digits=5),"\tlower:",format(lower,digits=5))
  cat("\n")
  }
cat("\n")
```

```
if (iteration < 10000) cat("Recommended sample size:",n,"\n") else cat("WARNING: Over 10000 iterations -- problem
finding adequate sample size \n")
cat("\n")
# Determine maximum number of errors that can occur and still accomplish test goals
midpexceedsp <- 1
while ((x > 0) && ((1-midpexceedsp) < (1-conf))) {
  midpexceedsp <- pbinom(x-1,n,bench) + .5*dbinom(x,n,bench)
  x <- x - 1
  }
x <- x + 2
midpexceedsp <- pbinom(x-1,n,bench) + .5*dbinom(x,n,bench)
cat("Maximum tolerable number of failures given alpha =",1-conf,"with an observed mid-p significance level of",1-
midpexceedsp,"is:",n-x,"\n\n")
}


# Binomial sample size estimation for large samples given confidence, power, p, the critical difference, and number
of tails
# conf is the desired level of confidence expressed as a number between 0 and 1 or 1 and 100
# e.g., 95% confidence would be .95 or 95
# power is also a number between 0 and 1 or 1 and 100, always one-sided,
# e.g., 50% confidence would be .50 or 50 (with z = 0)
#
n.binomial.largesample <- function(conf,power,p,d,tails) {
if (conf > 1) conf <- conf/100
if (power > 1) power <- power/100
if (tails != 1) zconf <- abs(qnorm((1-conf)/2))
if (tails == 1) zconf <- abs(qnorm((1-conf)))
zpower <- abs(qnorm((1-power)))
z <- zconf + zpower
q <- 1 - p
n <- ceiling((z^2)*p*q/(d^2))
cat("\nRESULT\n\n")
cat("Recommended sample size:",n,"\n")
cat("\n")
}


# Binomial sample size estimation for small samples given confidence, power, p, the critical difference, and number
of tails
# conf is the desired level of confidence expressed as a number between 0 and 1 or 1 and 100
# e.g., 95% confidence would be .95 or 95
# power is also a number between 0 and 1 or 1 and 100, always one-sided,
# e.g., 50% confidence would be .50 or 50 (with z = 0)
#
n.binomial.smallsample <- function(conf,power,p,d,tails) {
if (conf > 1) conf <- conf/100
if (power > 1) power <- power/100
if (tails != 1) zconf <- abs(qnorm((1-conf)/2))
if (tails == 1) zconf <- abs(qnorm((1-conf)))
zpower <- abs(qnorm((1-power)))
z <- zconf + zpower
q <- 1 - p
ninit <- ceiling((z^2)*p*q/(d^2))
padj <- (ninit*p + (z^2)/2)/(ninit + z^2)
```

```
qadj <- 1 - padj
n <- ceiling(((z^2)*padj*qadj/(d^2)) - (z^2))
cat("\nRESULT\n\n")
cat("Recommended sample size:",n,"\n")
cat("\n")
}


# Sample size estimation for correlation
#
# r is the expected correlation -- if unknown, set to 0
# conf is the desired level of confidence
# critd is the desired width of the resulting confidence interval
n.correlation <- function(r,d,conf) {
if (conf > 1) conf <- conf/100
confper <- paste(conf*100,"%",sep="")
z <- abs(qnorm((1-conf)/2))
n <- ceiling(((z^2*(1-r^2)^2)/d^2)+1+6*r^2)
cat("\nRESULTS\n\n")
cat ("n:",n,"\n")
cat ("\n")
}


# Sample size estimation for a McNemar (difference in dependent proportions) test
# p12 is the expected proportion of discordant pairs in which participants succeed with A but fail with B
# p21 is the expected proportion of discordant pairs in which participants succeed with B but fail with A
# d is the difference between p12 and p21
# conf is the desired level of confidence expressed as a number between 0 and 1 or 1 and 100
# e.g., 95% confidence would be .95 or 95
# power is also a number between 0 and 1 or 1 and 100, always one-sided,
# e.g., 50% confidence would be .50 or 50 (with z = 0)
#
n.mcnemar <- function(conf,power,p12,p21) {
d <- abs(p12 - p21)
if (conf > 1) conf <- conf/100
if (power > 1) power <- power/100
zconf <- abs(qnorm((1-conf)/2))
zpower <- abs(qnorm((1-power)))
z <- zconf + zpower
Ninit <- ceiling(((z^2)*(p12 + p21)/(d^2)) - (z^2))
padj12 <- ((p12*Ninit) + (z^2)/8)/(Ninit + (z^2)/2)
padj21 <- ((p21*Ninit) + (z^2)/8)/(Ninit + (z^2)/2)
dadj <- padj21 - padj12
N <- ((z^2)*(padj12 + padj21)/(dadj^2)) - 1.5*(z^2)
n <- ceiling(N)
cat("\nRESULT\n\n")
cat("Recommended sample size:",n,"\n")
cat("\n")
}


# Sample size estimation for two-by-two N-1 Chi-Squared (difference in independent proportions) test
# conf is the desired level of confidence expressed as a number between 0 and 1 or 1 and 100
# e.g., 95% confidence would be .95 or 95
# power is also a number between 0 and 1 or 1 and 100, always one-sided,
```

```
# e.g., 50% confidence would be .50 or 50 (with z = 0)
#
n.nminusonechisquared <- function(conf,power,p1,p2) {
if (conf > 1) conf <- conf/100
if (power > 1) power <- power/100
d <- abs(p1 - p2)
zconf <- abs(qnorm((1-conf)/2))
zpower <- abs(qnorm((1-power)))
z <- zconf + zpower
p <- (p1 + p2)/2
q <- 1 - p
n <- ceiling((2*(z^2)*p*q/(d^2)) + .5)
cat("\nRESULTS\n\n")
cat("Recommended sample size per group:",n,"\n")
cat("Recommended total sample size:",2*n,"\n")
cat("\n")
}


# Sample size estimation for focus on intercept (or any other prediction)
#
# s2x and s2e are the estimated population variances
# conf is the desired level of confidence (e.g., 95% confidence would be .95 or 95)
# d is the desired magnitude of the resulting margin of error
# predictor is the value of x for the targeted prediction of y
# barx is the mean of the
# When focusing on the y-intercept, use 0 for the value of "prediction" in the function
# Uses iteration to estimate required sample size, max of 1000 iterations
#
n.prediction <- function(s2x,s2e,d,conf,predictor, barx) {
if (conf > 1) conf <- conf/100
ncurr <- -1
nprev1 <- -2
nprev2 <- -3
iteration <- 0
z <- abs(qnorm((1-conf)/2))
nprev1 <- ceiling((z^2*s2e*(1+(predictor-barx)^2/s2x))/(d^2)+2)
df <- nprev1 - 2
while ((ncurr != nprev1 ) && (ncurr != nprev2) && (iteration < 1001)) {
  iteration <- iteration + 1
  nprev2 <- nprev1
  nprev1 <- ncurr
  t <- abs(qt((1-conf)/2,df))
  ncurr <- ceiling((t^2*s2e*(1+(predictor-barx)^2/s2x))/(d^2)+2)
  df <- ncurr - 2
  }
cat("\nRESULTS\n\n")
if (ncurr == nprev2 && ncurr < nprev1) cat("No convergence, fluctuating between:",ncurr,"and",nprev1,"\n")
if (ncurr == nprev2 && ncurr < nprev1) ncurr <- nprev1
cat("Recommended sample size:",ncurr,"\n")
cat("Number of iterations:",iteration,"\n")
if (iteration > 999) cat("WARNING: Over 1000 iterations -- problem converging \n")
cat("\n")
}
```

```
# Sample size estimation for focus on slope given x and e population variances, conf, and d
#
# s2x and s2e are the estimated population variances
# conf is the desired level of confidence (e.g., 95% confidence would be .95 or 95)
# d is the desired magnitude of the resulting margin of error
# Uses iteration to estimate required sample size, max of 1000 iterations
#
n.slope <- function(s2x,s2e,d,conf) {
if (conf > 1) conf <- conf/100
ncurr <- -1
nprev1 <- -2
nprev2 <- -3
iteration <- 0
z <- abs(qnorm((1-conf)/2))
nprev1 <- ceiling((z^2*s2e)/(d^2*s2x)+2)
df <- nprev1 - 2
while ((ncurr != nprev1 ) && (ncurr != nprev2) && (iteration < 1001)) {
  iteration <- iteration + 1
  nprev2 <- nprev1
  nprev1 <- ncurr
  t <- abs(qt((1-conf)/2,df))
  ncurr <- ceiling((t^2*s2e)/(d^2*s2x)+2)
  df <- ncurr - 2
  }
cat("\nRESULTS\n\n")
if (ncurr == nprev2 && ncurr < nprev1) cat("No convergence, fluctuating between:",ncurr,"and",nprev1,"\n")
if (ncurr == nprev2 && ncurr < nprev1) ncurr <- nprev1
cat("Recommended sample size:",ncurr,"\n")
cat("Number of iterations:",iteration,"\n")
if (iteration > 999) cat("WARNING: Over 1000 iterations -- problem converging \n")
cat("\n")
}


# Sample size estimation for one-sample t-test given confidence, power, sd, critical difference, and 1 vs 2 tailed
# conf is the desired level of confidence expressed as a number between 0 and 1 or between 1 and 100
# e.g., 95% confidence would be .95 or 95
# power is also a number between 0 and 1 or 1 and 100, always one-sided,
# e.g., 50% confidence would be .50 or 50 (with z = 0)
# Uses iteration to estimate required sample size, max of 1000 iterations
#
n.t.onesample.givensd <- function(conf,power,sd,d,tails) {
if (conf > 1) conf <- conf/100
if (power > 1) power <- power/100
var <- sd^2
ncurr <- -1
nprev1 <- -2
nprev2 <- -3
iteration <- 0
if (tails != 1) zconf <- abs(qnorm((1-conf)/2))
if (tails == 1) zconf <- abs(qnorm((1-conf)))
zpower <- abs(qnorm((1-power)))
z <- zconf + zpower
```

```
nprev1 <- ceiling((z^2)*var/(d^2))
df <- nprev1 - 1
while ((ncurr != nprev1 ) && (ncurr != nprev2) && (iteration < 1001)) {
  iteration <- iteration + 1
  nprev2 <- nprev1
  nprev1 <- ncurr
  if (tails != 1) tconf <- abs(qt((1-conf)/2,df))
  if (tails == 1) tconf <- abs(qt((1-conf),df))
  tpower <- abs(qt((1-power),df))
  t <- tconf + tpower
  ncurr <- ceiling((t^2)*var/(d^2))
  df <- ncurr -1
  }
cat("\nRESULTS\n\n")
if (ncurr == nprev2 && ncurr < nprev1) cat("No convergence, fluctuating between:",ncurr,"and",nprev1,"\n")
if (ncurr == nprev2 && ncurr < nprev1) ncurr <- nprev1
cat("Recommended sample size:",ncurr,"\n")
cat("Number of iterations:",iteration,"\n")
if (iteration > 999) cat("WARNING: Over 1000 iterations -- problem converging \n")
cat("\n")
}


# Sample size estimation for one-sample t-test given confidence, power, variance, critical difference, and 1 vs 2 tailed
# conf is the desired level of confidence expressed as a number between 0 and 1 or between 1 and 100
# e.g., 95% confidence would be .95 or 95
# power is also a number between 0 and 1 or 1 and 100, always one-sided,
# e.g., 50% confidence would be .50 or 50 (with z = 0)
# Uses iteration to estimate required sample size, max of 1000 iterations
#
n.t.onesample.givenvar <- function(conf,power,var,d,tails) {
if (conf > 1) conf <- conf/100
if (power > 1) power <- power/100
ncurr <- -1
nprev1 <- -2
nprev2 <- -3
iteration <- 0
if (tails != 1) zconf <- abs(qnorm((1-conf)/2))
if (tails == 1) zconf <- abs(qnorm((1-conf)))
zpower <- abs(qnorm((1-power)))
z <- zconf + zpower
nprev1 <- ceiling((z^2)*var/(d^2))
df <- nprev1 - 1
while ((ncurr != nprev1 ) && (ncurr != nprev2) && (iteration < 1001)) {
  iteration <- iteration + 1
  nprev2 <- nprev1
  nprev1 <- ncurr
  if (tails != 1) tconf <- abs(qt((1-conf)/2,df))
  if (tails == 1) tconf <- abs(qt((1-conf),df))
  tpower <- abs(qt((1-power),df))
  t <- tconf + tpower
  ncurr <- ceiling((t^2)*var/(d^2))
  df <- ncurr -1
  }
```

```
cat("\nRESULTS\n\n")
if (ncurr == nprev2 && ncurr < nprev1) cat("No convergence, fluctuating between:",ncurr,"and",nprev1,"\n")
if (ncurr == nprev2 && ncurr < nprev1) ncurr <- nprev1
cat("Recommended sample size:",ncurr,"\n")
cat("Number of iterations:",iteration,"\n")
if (iteration > 999) cat("WARNING: Over 1000 iterations -- problem converging \n")
cat("\n")
}


# Sample size estimation for two-sample t-test given confidence, power, sd, critical difference, and 1 vs 2 tailed
# conf is the desired level of confidence expressed as a number between 0 and 1 or between 1 and 100
# e.g., 95% confidence would be .95 or 95
# power is also a number between 0 and 1 or 1 and 100, always one-sided,
# e.g., 50% confidence would be .50 or 50 (with z = 0)
# Uses iteration to estimate required sample size, max of 1000 iterations
#
n.t.twosample.givenequalsd <- function(conf,power,sd,d,tails) {
if (conf > 1) conf <- conf/100
if (power > 1) power <- power/100
var <- sd^2
ncurr <- -1
nprev1 <- -2
nprev2 <- -3
iteration <- 0
if (tails != 1) zconf <- abs(qnorm((1-conf)/2))
if (tails == 1) zconf <- abs(qnorm((1-conf)))
zpower <- abs(qnorm((1-power)))
z <- zconf + zpower
nprev1 <- ceiling(2*(z^2)*var/(d^2))
df <- 2*(nprev1 - 1)
while ((ncurr != nprev1 ) && (ncurr != nprev2) && (iteration < 1001)) {
  iteration <- iteration + 1
  nprev2 <- nprev1
  nprev1 <- ncurr
  if (tails != 1) tconf <- abs(qt((1-conf)/2,df))
  if (tails == 1) tconf <- abs(qt((1-conf),df))
  tpower <- abs(qt((1-power),df))
  t <- tconf + tpower
  ncurr <- ceiling(2*(t^2)*var/(d^2))
  df <- 2*(ncurr - 1)
  }
cat("\nRESULTS\n\n")
if (ncurr == nprev2 && ncurr < nprev1) cat("No convergence, fluctuating between:",ncurr,"and",nprev1,"\n")
if (ncurr == nprev2 && ncurr < nprev1) ncurr <- nprev1
cat("Recommended sample size per group:",ncurr,"\n")
cat("Recommended total sample size:",2*ncurr,"\n")
cat("Number of iterations:",iteration,"\n")
if (iteration > 999) cat("WARNING: Over 1000 iterations -- problem converging \n")
cat("\n")
}


# Sample size estimation for two-sample t-test given confidence, power, variance, critical difference, and 1 vs 2
tailed
```

```
# conf is the desired level of confidence expressed as a number between 0 and 1 or between 1 and 100
# e.g., 95% confidence would be .95 or 95
# power is also a number between 0 and 1 or 1 and 100, always one-sided,
# e.g., 50% confidence would be .50 or 50 (with z = 0)
# Uses iteration to estimate required sample size, max of 1000 iterations
#
n.t.twosample.givenequalvar <- function(conf,power,var,d,tails) {
if (conf > 1) conf <- conf/100
if (power > 1) power <- power/100
ncurr <- -1
nprev1 <- -2
nprev2 <- -3
iteration <- 0
if (tails != 1) zconf <- abs(qnorm((1-conf)/2))
if (tails == 1) zconf <- abs(qnorm((1-conf)))
zpower <- abs(qnorm((1-power)))
z <- zconf + zpower
nprev1 <- ceiling(2*(z^2)*var/(d^2))
df <- 2*(nprev1 - 1)
while ((ncurr != nprev1 ) && (ncurr != nprev2) && (iteration < 1001)) {
  iteration <- iteration + 1
  nprev2 <- nprev1
  nprev1 <- ncurr
  if (tails != 1) tconf <- abs(qt((1-conf)/2,df))
  if (tails == 1) tconf <- abs(qt((1-conf),df))
  tpower <- abs(qt((1-power),df))
  t <- tconf + tpower
  ncurr <- ceiling(2*(t^2)*var/(d^2))
  df <- 2*(ncurr - 1)
  }
cat("\nRESULTS\n\n")
if (ncurr == nprev2 && ncurr < nprev1) cat("No convergence, fluctuating between:",ncurr,"and",nprev1,"\n")
if (ncurr == nprev2 && ncurr < nprev1) ncurr <- nprev1
cat("Recommended sample size per group:",ncurr,"\n")
cat("Recommended total sample size:",2*ncurr,"\n")
cat("Number of iterations:",iteration,"\n")
if (iteration > 999) cat("WARNING: Over 1000 iterations -- problem converging \n")
cat("\n")
}


# Probability of an event happening at least once
#
p.atleastonce <- function(p,n) {
prob <- 1 - (1 - p)^n
cat("\nRESULT\n\n")
cat("Probability of an event of p =",p,"happening at least once in",n,"trials:",prob,"\n")
cat("\n")
}


# Probability of x or more events
# The application is to assess the number of significant outcomes for multiple tests
# The inputs are the number of significant results given alpha, the number of tests run, alpha,
```

```
# and a criterion for determining the critical value of x -- the value of x at which the likelihood of x or more events is
less than the criterion
# For example, in Table 9.5 of Practical Statistics for User Research, the criterion was .10
#
p.xormore <- function(numsig,numtests,alpha,criterion) {
# Build array of binomial probabilities
binomprobs <- array(0,c(numtests+1,2))
x <- 0
prob <- 0
while (x <= numtests) {
  binomprobs[x+1,1] <- x
  binomprobs[x+1,2] <- dbinom(x,numtests,alpha)
  if (x >= numsig) prob <- prob + dbinom(x,numtests,alpha)
  x <- x+1
  }
x <- 0
stopsearching <- 0
while (x <= numtests) {
  if (sum(binomprobs[x:numtests+1,2]) <= criterion && stopsearching == 0) {
    critx <- x
    stopsearching <- 1
    }
  x <- x+1
  }
cat("\nRESULTS\n\n")
cat("Probability of",numsig,"or more significant outcomes given",numtests,"tests with alpha of",alpha,"is:",prob,"\n")
cat("For the criterion of",criterion,"the critical value of x is:",critx,"\n")
cat("\n")
}


# Standard error of the mean given an array of scores (x)
#
se.fromarray <- function(x) {
n <- length(x)
stder <- sd(x)/(n^.5)
cat ("\nRESULTS \n\n")
cat ("Std deviation:\t",sd(x),"\n")
cat ("Sample size:\t",n,"\n")
cat ("Standard error:\t",stder,"\n")
cat ("","\n")
}


# Correlation magnitude, significance, and confidence interval
#
# data1 and data1 are arrays of matched scores and must be of equal length
# conf is the desired level of confidence
test.correlation <- function(data1,data2,conf) {
if (conf > 1) conf <- conf/100
confper <- paste(conf*100,"%",sep="")
correl <- cor(data1, data2)
n <- length(data1)
r2t <- correl/((1-correl^2)/(n-2))^.5
df <- n - 2
```

```
p <- 2*(1-pt(r2t,df))
zprime <- 0.5*log((1+correl)/(1-correl))
z <- abs(qnorm((1-conf)/2))
critd <- z/(n-3)^.5
upperzprime <- zprime + critd
lowerzprime <- zprime - critd
upper <- (exp(2*upperzprime)-1)/(exp(2*upperzprime)+1)
lower <- (exp(2*lowerzprime)-1)/(exp(2*lowerzprime)+1)
rsquared <- paste(round((correl^2)*100,digits=2),"%",sep="")
cat("\nRESULTS\n\n")
cat ("r:",correl,"\n")
cat ("df:",df,"\n")
cat ("p:",p,"\n\n")
cat (confper,"Confidence Interval","\n")
cat ("Upper limit:", upper, "\n")
cat ("r:", correl, "\n")
cat ("Lower limit:", lower, "\n\n")
cat ("R-squared:",rsquared,"\n")
cat ("\n")
}


# N-1 Two-Proportion Test with confidence interval given p and n
# Inputs are p1, n1, p2, n2, and conf
# conf is the level for the confidence interval
# expressed as a number between 0 and 1 or between 1 and 100 (e.g., 95% confidence would be .95 or 95)
#
test.nminusonetwoproportion.givenpandn <- function(p1,n1,p2,n2,conf) {
if (conf > 1) conf <- conf/100
confper <- paste(conf*100,"%",sep="")
x1 <- p1 * n1
x2 <- p2 * n2
N <- n1 + n2
a <- x1
b <- n1 - x1
c <- x2
d <- n2 - x2
m <- a + b
n <- c + d
r <- a + c
s <- b + d
P <- (x1 + x2)/(n1 + n2)
Q <- 1 - P
testznum <- (p1 - p2)*((N-1)/N)^.5
testzden <- (P * Q * (1/n1 + 1/n2))^.5
testz <- testznum/testzden
ptestz <- 2*pnorm(-abs(testz))
z <- abs(qnorm((1-conf)/2))
p1adj <- (a + z^2/4)/(m + z^2/2)
p2adj <- (c + z^2/4)/(n + z^2/2)
n1adj <- m + z^2/2
n2adj <- n + z^2/2
diff <- p1 - p2
diffadj <- p1adj - p2adj
```

```
se <- ((p1adj*(1 - p1adj)/n1adj) + (p2adj*(1 - p2adj)/n2adj))^.5
critdiff <- z*se
upper <- diffadj + critdiff
lower <- diffadj - critdiff
cat("\nRESULTS\n\n")
cat ("N-1 Two-Proportion z:",testz,"\n")
cat ("p:",ptestz,"\n\n")
cat (confper,"confidence interval of difference between proportions","\n")
cat ("p1:",p1,"\n")
cat ("p2:",p2,"\n")
cat ("P:",P,"\n")
cat ("Adjusted value of p1:",p1adj,"\n")
cat ("Adjusted value of p2:",p2adj,"\n")
cat ("Adjusted difference:",diffadj,"\n")
cat ("Margin of error:",critdiff,"\n")
cat ("Upper limit:", upper, "\n")
cat ("Maximum likelihood estimate (observed difference):", diff, "\n")
cat ("Lower limit:", lower, "\n")
cat ("\n")
}


# Phi correlation magnitude, significance, and confidence interval
#
# data1 and data1 are arrays of matched scores and must be of equal length
# conf is the desired level of confidence
test.phi <- function(a,b,c,d,conf) {
if (conf > 1) conf <- conf/100
confper <- paste(conf*100,"%",sep="")
phi <- (a*d-b*c)/((a+b)*(c+d)*(a+c)*(b+d))^.5
n <- a+b+c+d
chi <- n*phi^2
df <- 1
p <- 1-(pchisq(chi,df))
zprime <- 0.5*log((1+phi)/(1-phi))
z <- abs(qnorm((1-conf)/2))
critd <- z/(n-3)^.5
upperzprime <- zprime + critd
lowerzprime <- zprime - critd
upper <- (exp(2*upperzprime)-1)/(exp(2*upperzprime)+1)
lower <- (exp(2*lowerzprime)-1)/(exp(2*lowerzprime)+1)
cat("\nRESULTS\n\n")
cat ("phi:",phi,"\n")
cat ("chi-squared:",chi,"\n")
cat ("df:",df,"\n")
cat ("p:",p,"\n\n")
cat (confper,"Confidence Interval","\n")
cat ("Upper limit:", upper, "\n")
cat ("r:", phi, "\n")
cat ("Lower limit:", lower, "\n\n")
cat ("\n")
}


# N-1 Two-Proportion Test with confidence interval given x and n
```

```
# Inputs are x1, n1, x2, n2, and conf
# conf is the level for the confidence interval
# expressed as a number between 0 and 1 or between 1 and 100 (e.g., 95% confidence would be .95 or 95)
#
test.nminusonetwoproportion.givenxandn <- function(x1,n1,x2,n2,conf) {
if (conf > 1) conf <- conf/100
confper <- paste(conf*100,"%",sep="")
a <- x1
b <- n1 - x1
c <- x2
d <- n2 - x2
m <- a + b
n <- c + d
r <- a + c
s <- b + d
N <- a + b + c + d
p1 <- a/m
p2 <- c/n
P <- (x1 + x2)/(n1 + n2)
Q <- 1 - P
testznum <- (p1 - p2)*((N-1)/N)^.5
testzden <- (P * Q * (1/n1 + 1/n2))^.5
testz <- testznum/testzden
ptestz <- 2*pnorm(-abs(testz))
z <- abs(qnorm((1-conf)/2))
p1adj <- (a + z^2/4)/(m + z^2/2)
p2adj <- (c + z^2/4)/(n + z^2/2)
n1adj <- m + z^2/2
n2adj <- n + z^2/2
diff <- p1 - p2
diffadj <- p1adj - p2adj
se <- ((p1adj*(1 - p1adj)/n1adj) + (p2adj*(1 - p2adj)/n2adj))^.5
critdiff <- z*se
upper <- diffadj + critdiff
lower <- diffadj - critdiff
cat("\nRESULTS\n\n")
cat ("N-1 Two-Proportion z:",testz,"\n")
cat ("p:",ptestz,"\n\n")
cat (confper,"confidence interval of difference between proportions","\n")
cat ("p1:",p1,"\n")
cat ("p2:",p2,"\n")
cat ("P:",P,"\n")
cat ("Adjusted value of p1:",p1adj,"\n")
cat ("Adjusted value of p2:",p2adj,"\n")
cat ("Adjusted difference:",diffadj,"\n")
cat ("Margin of error:",critdiff,"\n")
cat ("Upper limit:", upper, "\n")
cat ("Maximum likelihood estimate (observed difference):", diff, "\n")
cat ("Lower limit:", lower, "\n")
cat ("\n")
}


# Two-tailed between-subjects (independent) t-test with confidence interval given two arrays
```

```
# x and y are the two arrays; conf is the level for the confidence interval
# expressed as a number between 0 and 1 or between 1 and 100 (e.g., 95% confidence would be .95 or 95)
#
test.t.independent.fromarrays <- function(x1,x2,conf) {
if (conf > 1) conf <- conf/100
confper <- paste(conf*100,"%",sep="")
u1 <- mean(x1)
u2 <- mean(x2)
d <- u1 - u2
sd1 <- sd(x1)
sd2 <- sd(x2)
n1 <- length(x1)
n2 <- length(x2)
var1 <- sd1^2
var2 <- sd2^2
se <- ((var1/n1) + (var2/n2))^.5
t <- d/se
swdfnum <- ((var1/n1) + (var2/n2))^2
swdfden <- ((var1/n1)^2/(n1-1)) + ((var2/n2)^2/(n2-1))
df <- floor(swdfnum/swdfden)
p <- 2*pt(-abs(t),df)
cat("\nRESULTS\n\n")
cat("t:",t,"\n")
cat("df:",df,"\n")
cat("p:",p,"\n\n")
critt <- abs(qt((1-conf)/2,df))
critd <- critt*se
lower <- d-critd
upper <- d+critd
cat (confper,"confidence interval \n")
cat ("Upper limit:", upper, "\n")
cat ("Mean difference:", d, "\n")
cat ("Lower limit:", lower, "\n")
cat ("Margin of error:",critd, "\n")
cat ("\n")
}


# Two-tailed between-subjects (independent) t-test with confidence interval given summary data
# u1, sd1, and n1 are the mean, standard deviation, and sample size of the first group,
# u2, sd2, and n2 are the mean, standard deviation, and sample size of the second group,
# conf is the level for the confidence interval
# expressed as a number between 0 and 1 or between 1 and 100 (e.g., 95% confidence would be .95 or 95),
# df computation uses the Welch-Satterthwaite procedure
# (appropriate for unequal group variances -- slightly conservative if variances equal)
#
test.t.independent.fromsummary <- function(u1,sd1,n1,u2,sd2,n2,conf) {
if (conf > 1) conf <- conf/100
confper <- paste(conf*100,"%",sep="")
d <- u1 - u2
var1 <- sd1^2
var2 <- sd2^2
se <- ((var1/n1) + (var2/n2))^.5
t <- d/se
```

```
swdfnum <- ((var1/n1) + (var2/n2))^2
swdfden <- ((var1/n1)^2/(n1-1)) + ((var2/n2)^2/(n2-1))
df <- floor(swdfnum/swdfden)
p <- 2*pt(-abs(t),df)
cat("\nRESULTS\n\n")
cat("t:",t,"\n")
cat("df:",df,"\n")
cat("p:",p,"\n\n")
critt <- abs(qt((1-conf)/2,df))
critd <- critt*se
lower <- d-critd
upper <- d+critd
cat (confper,"confidence interval \n")
cat ("Upper limit:", upper, "\n")
cat ("Mean difference:", d, "\n")
cat ("Lower limit:", lower, "\n")
cat ("Margin of error:",critd, "\n")
cat ("\n")
}


# Two-tailed within-subjects (paired) t-test with confidence interval on difference scores
# d is a single array of difference scores; conf is the level for the confidence interval
# expressed as a number between 0 and 1 or between 1 and 100 (e.g., 95% confidence would be .95 or 95)
#
test.t.paired.fromarray.ofdifferences <- function(d,conf) {
if (conf > 1) conf <- conf/100
confper <- paste(conf*100,"%",sep="")
n <- length(d)
mean <- mean(d)
sd <- sd(d)
se <- sd/(n^.5)
df <- n - 1
t <- mean/se
p <- 2*pt(-abs(t),df)
cat("\nRESULTS\n\n")
cat("t:",t,"\n")
cat("df:",df,"\n")
cat("p:",p,"\n\n")
critt <- abs(qt((1-conf)/2,df))
critd <- critt*se
lower <- mean-critd
upper <- mean+critd
cat (confper,"confidence interval \n")
cat ("Upper limit:", upper, "\n")
cat ("Mean difference:", mean, "\n")
cat ("Lower limit:", lower, "\n")
cat ("Margin of error:",critd, "\n")
cat ("\n")
}


# Two-tailed within-subjects (paired) t-test with confidence interval on two sets of dependent raw scores
# x and y are paired sets of scores; conf is the level for the confidence interval
# expressed as a number between 0 and 1 (e.g., 95% confidence would be .95)
```

```
#
test.t.paired.fromarrays <- function(x,y,conf) {
if (conf > 1) conf <- conf/100
confper <- paste(conf*100,"%",sep="")
d <- x - y
n <- length(d)
mean <- mean(d)
sd <- sd(d)
se <- sd/(n^.5)
df <- n - 1
t <- mean/se
p <- 2*pt(-abs(t),df)
cat("\nRESULTS\n\n")
cat("t:",t,"\n")
cat("df:",df,"\n")
cat("p:",p,"\n\n")
critt <- abs(qt((1-conf)/2,df))
critd <- critt*se
lower <- mean-critd
upper <- mean+critd
cat (confper,"confidence interval \n")
cat ("Upper limit:", upper, "\n")
cat ("Mean difference:", mean, "\n")
cat ("Lower limit:", lower, "\n")
cat ("Margin of error:",critd, "\n")
cat ("\n")
}


# Two-tailed within-subjects (paired) t-test with confidence interval on difference score summary data
# difmean is the mean of the difference scores, difsd is their standard deviation,
# n is the sample size; conf is the level for the confidence interval
# expressed as a number between 0 and 1 or between 1 and 100 (e.g., 95% confidence would be .95 or 95)
#
test.t.paired.fromsummary <- function(difmean,difsd,n,conf) {
if (conf > 1) conf <- conf/100
confper <- paste(conf*100,"%",sep="")
se <- difsd/(n^.5)
df <- n - 1
t <- difmean/se
p <- 2*pt(-abs(t),df)
cat("\nRESULTS\n\n")
cat("t:",t,"\n")
cat("df:",df,"\n")
cat("p:",p,"\n\n")
critt <- abs(qt((1-conf)/2,df))
critd <- critt*se
lower <- difmean-critd
upper <- difmean+critd
cat (confper,"confidence interval \n")
cat ("Upper limit:", upper, "\n")
cat ("Mean difference:", difmean, "\n")
cat ("Lower limit:", lower, "\n")
cat ("Margin of error:",critd, "\n")
```

```
cat ("\n")
}


# Test of two-by-two contingency table (dependent data)
# Focuses on McNemar Test (two-tailed) with confidence interval on difference in proportions
# a, b, c, and d refer to counts in the table's cells
# (a: upper left, b: upper right, c: lower left, d: lower right)
# b and c are the two different discordance counts
# conf is the level for the confidence interval
# expressed as a number between 0 and 1 or between 1 and 100 (e.g., 95% confidence would be .95 or 95)
#
test.twobytwo.dependent <- function(a,b,c,d,conf) {
if (conf > 1) conf <- conf/100
confper <- paste(conf*100,"%",sep="")
m <- a + b
n <- c + d
r <- a + c
s <- b + d
N <- a + b + c + d
p1 <- m/N
p2 <- r/N
z <- abs(qnorm((1-conf)/2))
adj = z^2/8
aadj <- a + adj
badj <- b + adj
cadj <- c + adj
dadj <- d + adj
madj <- aadj + badj
nadj <- cadj + dadj
radj <- aadj + cadj
sadj <- badj + dadj
Nadj <- aadj + badj + cadj + dadj
p1adj <- madj/Nadj
p2adj <- radj/Nadj
p12adj <- badj/Nadj
p21adj <- cadj/Nadj
diffadj <- p2adj - p1adj
se <- (((p12adj + p21adj) - (p21adj - p12adj)^2)/Nadj)^.5
critdiff <- se*z
upper <- diffadj + critdiff
lower <- diffadj - critdiff
ndiscord <- b + c
smaller <- min(b,c)
bench <- .5
mle <- smaller/ndiscord
exactexceedsp <- pbinom(smaller-1,ndiscord,bench)
midpexceedsp <- pbinom(smaller-1,ndiscord,bench) + .5*dbinom(smaller,ndiscord,bench)
exactislessthanp <- 1 - pbinom(smaller,ndiscord,bench)
midpislessthanp <- 1 - midpexceedsp
mcnemarmidp <- 2*(1-midpislessthanp)
mcnemarexactp <- 2*(1- exactislessthanp)
mcnemarz <- (c - b)/(c + b)^.5
mcnemarzp <- 2*pnorm(-abs(mcnemarz))
```

```
cat("\nRESULTS\n\n")
if (mcnemarmidp <= 1) cat("McNemar Mid Probability (recommended):", mcnemarmidp, "\n\n") else cat("McNemar
Mid Probability (recommended): 1 \n\n")
cat("Alternate analyses (not recommended) \n")
if (mcnemarexactp <= 1) cat("McNemar Exact Probability:", mcnemarexactp, "\n") else cat("McNemar Exact
Probability: 1 \n")
mcnemarchisquared <- ((c - b)^2)/(c + b)
df <- 1
pmcnemarchisquared <- 1-pchisq(mcnemarchisquared,df)
cat("McNemar Chi-Squared:",mcnemarchisquared,"  df:",df,"  p:",pmcnemarchisquared,"\n")
cat("McNemar z:",mcnemarz,"  p:",mcnemarzp,"\n")
mcnemaryates <- ((abs(c - b)-1)^2)/(c + b)
pmcnemaryates <- 1-pchisq(mcnemaryates,df)
cat("McNemar Chi-Squared with Yates Correction:",mcnemaryates,"  df:",df,"  p:",pmcnemaryates,"\n\n")
cat(confper,"CONFIDENCE INTERVAL \n\n")
cat("p1:",p1,"\n")
cat("p2:",p2,"\n")
cat ("Adjusted value of p1:",p1adj,"\n")
cat ("Adjusted value of p2:",p2adj,"\n")
cat("Adjusted difference in p:",diffadj,"\n")
cat("Margin of error:",critdiff,"\n")
cat("Upper limit:",upper,"\n")
cat("Observed difference:",p2-p1,"\n")
cat("Lower limit:",lower,"\n")
cat("\n")
}


# Test of independence of two-by-two contingency table (independent data)
# a, b, c, and d refer to counts in the table's cells
# (a: upper left, b: upper right, c: lower left, d: lower right)
# conf is the level for the confidence interval
# expressed as a number between 0 and 1 or between 1 and 100 (e.g., 95% confidence would be .95 or 95),
# Function returns results for N-1 chi-squared (recommended in most cases),
# standard chi-squared, standard chi-squared with Yates continuity correction,
# Fisher's exact probability test, and a confidence interval around the
# difference in the proportions
#
test.twobytwo.independent <- function(a,b,c,d,conf) {
if (conf > 1) conf <- conf/100
confper <- paste(conf*100,"%",sep="")
m <- a + b
n <- c + d
r <- a + c
s <- b + d
N <- a + b + c + d
chisquared <- (((a*d - b*c)^2)*N)/(m*n*r*s)
df <- 1
pchisquared <- 1-pchisq(chisquared,df)
mat <- matrix(c(a,b,c,d), nr=2, dimnames=list(c("A1A1", "A1A2"), c("A1", "A2")))
chisquaredyates <- (((abs(a*d - b*c) - .5*N)^2)*N)/(m*n*r*s)
pchisquaredyates <- 1-pchisq(chisquaredyates,df)
nminusonechisquared <- (((a*d - b*c)^2)*(N-1))/(m*n*r*s)
pnminusonechisquared <- 1-pchisq(nminusonechisquared,df)
```

```
if (r*m/N > 1) ae <- 0 else ae <- 1
if (s*m/N > 1) be <- 0 else be <- 1
if (r*n/N > 1) ce <- 0 else ce <- 1
if (s*n/N > 1) de <- 0 else de <- 1
check <- ae + be + ce + de
if (check > 0) rec <- "Fisher Exact Test" else rec <- "N-1 Chi-Squared Test"
p1 <- a/m
p2 <- c/n
P <- (a + c)/(m + n)
Q <- 1 - P
testznum <- (p1 - p2)*((N-1)/N)^.5
testzden <- (P * Q * (1/m + 1/n))^.5
testz <- testznum/testzden
ptestz <- 2*pnorm(-abs(testz))
z <- abs(qnorm((1-conf)/2))
p1adj <- (a + z^2/4)/(m + z^2/2)
p2adj <- (c + z^2/4)/(n + z^2/2)
n1adj <- m + z^2/2
n2adj <- n + z^2/2
diff <- p1 - p2
diffadj <- p1adj - p2adj
se <- ((p1adj*(1 - p1adj)/n1adj) + (p2adj*(1 - p2adj)/n2adj))^.5
critdiff <- z*se
upper <- diffadj + critdiff
lower <- diffadj - critdiff
fish <- fisher.test(mat)
cat("\nRESULTS\n\n")
cat ("Recommended test:",rec,"\n\n")
cat ("N-1 chi-squared:",nminusonechisquared,"\n")
cat ("df:",df,"\n")
cat ("p:",pnminusonechisquared,"\n\n")
cat ("N-1 two-proportion z:",testz,"\n")
cat ("p:",ptestz,"\n\n")
cat (confper,"confidence interval of difference between proportions","\n")
cat ("p1:",p1,"\n")
cat ("p2:",p2,"\n")
cat ("Adjusted value of p1:",p1adj,"\n")
cat ("Adjusted value of p2:",p2adj,"\n")
cat ("Adjusted difference:",diffadj,"\n")
cat ("Margin of error:",critdiff,"\n")
cat ("Upper limit:", upper, "\n")
cat ("Maximum likelihood estimate (observed difference):", diff, "\n")
cat ("Lower limit:", lower, "\n\n")
cat ("Fisher Exact Probability:",fish$p.value,"\n\n")
cat ("Standard chi-squared:",chisquared,"\n")
cat ("df:",df,"\n")
cat ("p:",pchisquared,"\n\n")
cat ("Standard chi-squared with Yates correction:",chisquaredyates,"\n")
cat ("df:",df,"\n")
cat ("p:",pchisquaredyates,"\n")
cat ("\n")
}
```

About the Authors

James R. (Jim) Lewis

Dr. James R. (Jim) Lewis is a senior human factors engineer (at IBM since 1981) with a current focus on the measurement and evaluation of the user experience. He is a Certified Human Factors Professional with a PhD in Experimental Psychology (Psycholinguistics), an MA in Engineering Psychology, and an MM in Music Theory and Composition. Jim is an internationally recognized expert in usability testing and measurement, contributing (by invitation) the chapter on usability testing for the third and fourth editions of the Handbook of Human Factors and Ergonomics, presenting tutorials on usability testing and metrics at various professional conferences, and serving as the keynote speaker at HCII 2014. He was the lead interaction designer for the product now regarded as the first smart phone, the Simon, and is the author of Practical Speech User Interface Design.

Jim is an IBM Master Inventor Emeritus with 88 patents issued to date by the US Patent Office. He serves on the editorial board of the International Journal of Human-Computer Interaction, is co-editor in chief of the Journal of Usability Studies, and is on the scientific advisory board of the Center for Research and Education on Aging and Technology Enhancement (CREATE). He is a member of the Human Factors and Ergonomics Society (HFES), the ACM Special Interest Group in Computer-Human Interaction (SIGCHI), past-president of the Association for Voice Interaction Design (AVIxD), and is a fifth degree black belt and certified instructor with the American Taekwondo Association (ATA).

Jeff Sauro

Jeff Sauro PhD, is a six-sigma trained statistical analyst and founding principal of MeasuringU, a user experience research firm based in Denver. For over fifteen years he's been conducting usability and statistical analysis for companies such as Google, eBay, Walmart, Autodesk, Lenovo and Drobox. Prior to founding his firm, he worked for Oracle, PeopleSoft, Intuit and General Electric.

Jeff has published over twenty peer-reviewed research articles and five books, including Customer Analytics for Dummies. Jeff received his Ph.D. in Research Methods and Statistics from the University of Denver, Masters in Learning, Design and Technology from Stanford University, and B.S. in Information Management & Technology and B.S. in Television, Radio and Film from Syracuse University. He lives with his wife and three children in Denver, CO.

For more information on the statistical consulting services of MeasuringU, contact Jeff Sauro:

Email: jeff@measuringu.com

Phone (303) 578-2801

Twitter @MeasuringU

Made in the USA
Middletown, DE
08 November 2022